RAISING HAPPY CHILDREN

RAISING
HAPPY
CHILDREN

What Every Child Needs Their Parents
to Know – from 0 to 7 years

Jan Parker and Jan Stimpson

Hodder & Stoughton

British Library Cataloguing in Publication Data
ISBN 0 340 71249 X

Printed and bound in Great Britain by
Mackays of Chatham Plc
Chatham, Kent

HODDER AND STOUGHTON
A division of Hodder Headline Plc
338 Euston Road
London NW1 3BH

Thank you to our families and friends for their invaluable support, and to all the parents and contributors who made this book possible.

CONTENTS

FOREWORD

By Dr Dorothy Rowe

Being a parent takes up a great deal of time, effort and expense. Even if you only do the basics – keep your children fed, clothed, healthy and provide a good education – you put a great deal into the whole exercise. What is the reward for all this? A few parents might be able to boast later that their son kicked the winning goal in the World Cup or their daughter was Prime Minister, but is all that most parents can expect a few hugs and kisses and a Christmas present?

No, it isn't. The reward can be the best prize of all – a close, loving relationship with another adult. When all the business of being a parent or a child is left behind what remains is two adults who see one another as equals, who share a history, who know and accept one another. They keep in touch with one another, not out of guilt or a fear of what other people might think if they don't, but because they love one another and are always interested in what the other is doing and thinking.

Such a relationship does not occur automatically when the child reaches a certain age. Many parents and children never achieve it because the basis of the relationship has not been laid down in the early years.

Babies are born wanting to love their parents. They are primed to love those one or two people who are with them often and who smile at them and talk to them with kindness.

In fact, parents have to work very hard to stop their children loving them. Babies always try to make the most of what's on offer, and older children will try again and again to win their parents' love and approval. Nevertheless, many parents do succeed in withering their children's love. They do this by controlling their children through fear, and fear drives out love. Love is open and fearless, and thus you cannot love someone whom you fear. Many children grow up telling themselves that they love the parent whom they fear, but what they feel is guilt, which they think is proof of love, and a sad, painful longing for the parent they never had.

I like to think that such tragedies will be fewer in the future because so many young parents see their role very differently from the way my parents' generation saw theirs. In my family my father was under constant criticism from my mother and other relatives because he was pleasant to his two daughters. He never hit us or even yelled at us.

Meanwhile my mother slapped me, sometimes hitting with great force when she was very angry, not so much with me but with herself and her life, and she was constantly criticising me and denigrating me. My big sister joined in this criticism and denigration, and was not corrected by my mother. (In my work in later years I found that this was a very common family style of communication.) Yet there was nothing my mother did which other adults found strange or reprehensible. At school, I and others were hit by the teachers using their hand or a cane. It would not cross a teacher's mind to be concerned about how a child might feel. The attitude of adults was that children should think what they were told to think and do what they were told to do.

Thankfully, views are changing. Hitting children was never an effective way of teaching them and is now increasingly recognised as such. Treating children as human beings, deserving respect, dignity and being listened to, is the best way to bring up children. As *Raising Happy Children* illustrates so clearly, it is possible to provide the discipline and guidance all children need without resorting to physical punishment.

Bringing up children in this way is not easy, but the rewards are huge. It does not require you to be the perfect parent, but a considerate, loving and respectful one. If parents were perfect, children would never need to grow up. If you were able to read correctly every need and wish of your tiny baby and were able to fulfil that every need and wish, your child would have no desire to become independent.

Children will forgive their parents' fallibility if they are certain that their parents accept them as they are. If they believe that their parents never wanted them, or they had them only to make use of them, or that they can never be the kind of person their parents really want, they will always have cause for grievance. However, they can accept that their parents sometimes lose their temper, or get tired, or don't pay attention, or get involved in other things, or get things wrong if they know with the certainty that night follows day that their parents love them simply because they exist.

If this is the basis on which you operate as a parent then all you need to help you on your way is guidance about what to expect as children develop, and constructive, informed ideas and approaches about how to tackle the issues which arise. *Raising Happy Children* is not about spoiling children, but about how to help children to grow up feeling comfortable with themselves and with other people, and having the courage to face the inherent difficulties of life. Such children are indeed happy children.

Dr Dorothy Rowe

CHAPTER ONE
MAKING A DIFFERENCE

Raising Happy Children breaks the mould of 'one expert, one dogma' childcare books. Its range of contributors is extraordinary and draws on all walks of life – from parents of children with everyday difficulties to those facing extreme problems, from childcare professionals and organisations to academics at the forefront of research into how children develop and flourish. The issues it covers range from the prosaic to the profound, from sleep solutions to building children's social confidence, from food wars to understanding children's feelings.

The first seven years are key to your child's future – how they feel about themselves, how they feel about others, how they communicate, behave, learn, cope and enjoy life. *Raising Happy Children* offers the information, skills and insight you will need to raise a child equipped for love and life, to help you avoid common problems and also to tackle them head-on if they arise.

This is a book to help you *both* make the very best of *real* life – and in real life happy children do not smile benignly at every dropped toy, parental request or poke in the ribs in the playground. They are sometimes sad, unreasonable, angry, needy and damned hard work as well as often loving, exuberant, hilarious and joyful.

Happy children are not the ones allowed to do exactly as they please whatever the consequences, or those trained to display only impeccable behaviour and the 'acceptable' face of childhood. Happy children are loved and loving, allowed to be children and given the guidance they need to flourish. They are children:

— who are loved for who they are
— who appreciate their worth and the worth of others
— whose feelings, needs and development are understood
— who are shown how to be caring and considerate

5

— who develop the confidence and understanding to make the best of themselves

— who have the resilience to deal with problems and the capacity to delight in life.

Raising Happy Children is not an instruction manual. It will not tell you how to live your life or impose a child-rearing regime. Instead, it provides you with a set of craftsmen's tools, of knowledge, skills, experience and expertise — the information you need to build on skills you already have and the confidence and understanding to try new ones.

For clarity, issues relating to a parent's relationship with their baby are dealt with first (see Baby's needs, yours needs, opposite). Other issues are then considered subject by subject. Parents themselves suggested this structure would be helpful.

The skills each chapter contains are not difficult to learn but are not obvious if you have not been brought up with them. Almost all are relevant and astonishingly effective for most people, in most circumstances, most of the time and nothing has been included that has not been tried, tested and proven to work by parents themselves. Yet you will choose which feel right for you and your child.

So, the power of these skills lies in your hands. Whether you have a baby or a school-age child, every single positive step you take now will have an enormous impact on your child and your relationship. This book provides the tools — which you use, when you use them and what you create with them is something uniquely yours.

This is one of the joys of *Raising Happy Children*. It will draw out strengths and abilities you never knew you had and help you forge new ones. It is positive, exciting and empowering in what is almost certainly the most important and most rewarding task you will ever undertake. It will help you through today and tomorrow and could benefit you and your child for the rest of your lives.

CHAPTER TWO

BABY'S NEEDS, YOUR NEEDS

How is life with your baby? Here are a few words other parents have used to describe their first weeks and months: 'magical', 'beautiful', 'terrifying', 'numb', 'warm', 'sublime', 'scary'. It can be all these things, and usually is, in varying degrees and at various times.

It's heady stuff, so it helps to get straight down to essentials. At the moment and for a very long time to come, you are the most important person in your baby's life.

What your baby needs – and what you need once you've had your baby – will change over time and sometimes take you by surprise. Responding to those needs is key to your relationship together, now and for the rest of your lives.

Getting to know each other

Bonding

I think the reality is shocking. So much time in the pregnancy is spent preparing for labour. Even if all the baby bits are bought, unpacked and washed, actually putting the baby into them is overwhelming. Babies don't come pre-packed and they do all sorts of odd things. Most parents, when they take baby home, feel they don't know what to do. It can take them a few days, a few weeks, even a few months to settle down to having a real live baby as opposed to a romantically imagined child.

Ann Herreboudt, midwife and family therapist

In the hospital after my first was born I even called the midwife to ask if
I could pick him up. I literally didn't know what to do with him.
Christine Chittick, NCT ante-natal teacher

The highs are higher and the lows are lower than I ever imagined.
But my limits are also more flexible than I thought, sometimes out of
necessity, sometimes out of love.
Clare H

You have all been on an incredible journey, you to parenthood and your child from the womb to the world. You all need time to recover and to build a relationship.

So many factors influence this bonding process, from the birth itself to your new baby's temperament and the support you receive, that there can be no 'average' experience. Certain things may help you get to know each other better, however, including skin-to-skin contact so you can touch, smell, hear and respond to each other more easily. Setting aside time for a little mutual adoration is also important.

Allowing yourself this time may seem difficult, especially when life intervenes to disrupt the best of intentions. In the first weeks, it can take all your wits and resources to look after your baby, drink that cup of cold tea and think about getting out of your pyjamas. But try to make it a priority.

You may already be astonished at the intensity of emotion you feel for your new child. If not, remember this is the beginning. If you have responded to your baby, held him, comforted him and helped him feel safe and loved, the relationship between you is already unfolding. Hold on to the knowledge that this is something vital and precious to you both – and to hell with the ironing.

We so often just expect these things to happen and if they don't we tend to get
more frantic and do more. So the key to this process is the 'undoing', the slowing
down, quietening down and waiting. It is about giving time. You may be feeling
quite damaged, and there does have to be time for the mother to heal. Sometimes
mother and baby need quiet warmth to 'undo' all that before they can move on.
Barbara Dale, Parent Network co-ordinator

For the first two to three months it is best for the baby to stay with the
mother as much as possible. Once their senses become a little more developed,

a baby can feel their way into the world, but initially their world is their mother and they are set up to see her and get to know her first.

Peter Walker, author, yoga teacher and physical therapist specialising in mothers and babies

Communicating with your baby

There is now a huge body of evidence to show that babies are born ready to communicate and interact with adults – which finally lays to rest the old myth about babies not communicating positively until their

Beginnings

Some love affairs begin at first sight, but not many. None can be forced, most take time to grow and a parent's love for their child is no different.

He was hauled out by a doctor called Martin and placed into my arms. And I wasn't hit by that overwhelming feeling of love I'd been led to expect. He was flesh and bone and blood and slime. His skin was scarlet and he had a pointy head. His feet were still blue. He had dark hair and enormous wrinkled hands that reminded me of my grandfather's. He was real. It was extraordinary. But it wasn't love.

David F

When Matthew was born my husband told me his foot was twisted and his ear was flat on his face. They were just the effects of the birth and soon righted themselves. But at that moment, what he was saying just did not register. I really did not care. This feeling went away once I'd slept, but at first I was too exhausted to feel anything like love.

Mary C

With my first child I had a long and difficult labour, but the moment I saw my little baby and held him I felt a rush of love so powerful I knew instantly I would never, ever be the same again.

Jane R

Your first 'conversations'

The ability of very young babies to communicate with the important adults in their life was highlighted in scientific studies as long ago as the late 1960s and early 1970s.

'We noticed immediately that babies were showing many skills for communication by one month,' explains Professor Colwyn Trevarthen, a specialist in child communication. 'These special abilities for communicating with people were quite different from the ones babies used for tracking objects with their eyes or reaching, and they included the use of emotional and other kinds of expression that only other people can understand.'

There is now astonishing evidence that even very premature babies can interact with their parents, exchanging sounds in a gentle, poignant vocal dance that displays what Professor Trevarthen calls the 'innate musicality of infant communication'.

'We have recordings[1] of a father while he is cuddling his two-month-premature baby on his chest. There evolves a sort of dance, in which the pattern of the baby's sounds changes and the baby pauses for the father to echo them. In effect, baby and father are involved in a conversation, an expressive, emotional narrative.

'How can parents engage in these "conversations"? They will be doing so already, by affectionately responding to their baby. It is very difficult to be conscious of all that goes on because it is so intricate and registers with the parents at such a deep level. So have enjoyment and faith in the process, and don't over-analyse, don't distance yourself from your intuition.'

I talk to my third baby in a way I just didn't to my first two, not for any other reason than that I simply didn't know they could be so responsive so early. He is now ten weeks, but we started from when he was born, talking to him and noticing and responding when he 'talks' back. Now, if I stick my tongue out at him, he will copy me. It's very funny.

There's no great technique, it's almost as simple as recognising that babies are people from day one. It's about listening to him and allowing him time to respond to you — just as you would pause to let an adult respond in a conversation. It's also about letting the baby sometimes take the initiative and take the lead. He gets so much out of it and so do we.

Careen H

first 'proper' smile and that anything before that is wind. Your baby is sending out signals all the time and, if you cuddle, listen, watch, play and enjoy, you'll begin to pick up and respond to them without even realising the process is happening. Your responsiveness – echoing back your baby's sounds, mimicking his movements and expressions – will help your confidence in each other to grow.

> *Even very young babies can engage in 'conversations'.*
> *All it takes is another person who can respond to the baby's facial*
> *expressions, gestures and vocalisations with imitations,*
> *comments and warm interest.*
> John Oates, developmental psychologist in The Centre for Human
> Development and Learning, Open University

Your child will already be communicating feelings and needs through gestures, noises and expressions. As you spend time together and observe his actions and reactions, you will become skilled at interpreting and responding to these signs and the relationship between you will deepen and develop.

The Pleasure Principle

> *The purely social interactions, sometimes called 'free play', between*
> *mother and infant are among the most crucial experiences in the infant's*
> *first phase of learning and participating in human events.*
> Daniel Stern, Professor of Psychology, University of Geneva[2]

Playing with your young baby is a crucial part of this communication and interaction process. It is a precursor to the fun and games you can play with older children (see Play and learning, p.275) but works on a simpler, gentler, quieter level – smiling at your baby, stroking and cuddling him in ways he likes, laughing when you find something funny.

If you can help your child experience delight in himself and his world, you're one hell of a parent. It is not only vital to his self-esteem and therefore crucial to his healthy emotional and behavioural development (see Dealing with feelings, p.94), there is now evidence that it is good for his brain, too.

There is good evidence that the kind of joy which comes from having a lot of fun with somebody is very good for the brain. Chemical changes in the brain during positive emotions have beneficial effects on brain growth.

Colwyn Trevarthen, Emeritus Professor of Child Psychology and Psychobiology, University of Edinburgh

Baby massage

Peter Walker, author, yoga teacher and physical therapist specialising in mothers and babies

Baby massage provides a whole range of benefits for you and your baby:
— It fosters mutual trust and understanding, and develops your confidence in your ability to handle your baby.
— It can stimulate your baby's immune system and circulation, both of which are immature at birth.
— It aids your baby's digestion. It can relieve colic and constipation.
— It is the perfect preparation for co-ordinated movement and mobility and is a natural response to your baby's inherent need for tactile stimulation.

When can you begin?
Your baby can be massaged soon after birth. Touch is the most developed of the senses at birth, and your newborn baby's prime means of communication.

Do not worry too much about how you stroke the baby – massage at this stage involves doing what feels relaxing, comfortable and right for you both. It has no set technique.

If babies are warm enough they rarely mind if they are clothed or not; however, they often dislike the process of being dressed and undressed in these early weeks. Touch and massage for a newborn can take place at any time, within natural activities and with clothes on. You can also clean and massage your baby with oils every 24-48 hours if it feels comfortable.

Ensure that:
— Your hands are warm and clean.
— You keep the oil away from the baby's face as it can blur vision if it gets into eyes.
— Your baby is lying on a soft, clean, cotton surface (the combination of wool and oil may irritate the skin).
— Your baby is not too full and certainly not hungry. Baby massage is best done between feeds.
— Remember you are doing this*with* your baby, not *to* him. Move the baby in ways he wants to go.
— You stop if your baby becomes upset. Return to the massage when he is ready and willing.

If your baby is unwell or has a skin disorder, seek professional advice before massaging. Wait 48 hours after immunisation to see how

You can set up opportunities for pleasure (see Baby Massage, below), but fun and pleasure in each other can also be a part of what goes on in your daily routine. There will be times when you'll feel as much like having fun as flying to the moon. No person is happy and responsive all the time and the combination of little sleep and little

---

he is affected before massaging, avoiding the injection site until it is no longer sensitive.

Massaging Oils

Organic grapeseed and organic sweet almond oil are best. (Many of the mineral-based so-called baby oils are made from petro-chemicals. I do not recommend their use for newborns or babies.)

Introducing a Light Massage

This can be introduced once your baby is happy to be undressed and enjoys being naked (often from about six to eight weeks).

Ensure you are comfortable. Keep your hands well oiled and shake out your hands from time to time to keep them relaxed.

1: Pull your baby's leg through your palms and fingers, hand over hand, from the thigh to foot. Give your baby's leg a gentle shake. Do the same with the other leg.

2: Now do both legs together. Place your well-oiled hands on the inside thighs and pull downwards around the back of the thighs, down the back of the knees and calves and feet.

3: Lay the weight of your open, relaxed hand on your baby's tummy and, without pressing downwards, massage in a clockwise direction – your left to your right. This is in the same direction as the baby's digestive system. (Only introduce tummy massage once the cord has healed and the baby has straightened from the foetal position.)

4: Place your hands on the centre of your baby's chest and massage upwards and outwards, over the shoulders. Draw both arms down vertically through the centre of your palms.

5: Rest your hands on the front of your baby's shoulders and draw them downwards over the chest, hips, legs and feet.

6: Lay your baby on his tummy and stroke down the back, hand over hand.

7: With a relaxed open hand, stroke clockwise around the base of the spine and buttocks.

8: Now lay your hands on the back of your baby's shoulders and stroke downwards over the back, down the back of the legs to the feet.

baby makes no one feel like a party animal. There is little point faking pleasure if you are not in the mood because children have an uncanny ability to spot inconsistencies between how you feel and what you do. Simply try to show your baby that you think he's splendid, loveable or funny, whenever you genuinely feel like it, whatever you're doing.

The early routines and patterns of young babies – of feeding, changing, bathing and so on – can become enjoyable rituals which can be made special and fun. There will be recognisable stages or moments in each of them to which the parent and baby can be primed; eye contact is important as an infant can feel 'held' and recognised in this moment. Sounds and tongue responses, movements of legs and arms all express the baby's vigour and pleasure at being together. These experiences contribute to how a baby begins to discover relationships.

Judith Philo, psychotherapist, social worker and parent adviceline consultant

Your baby's needs

Infant urgency

Babies feel and express a range of emotions, and tuning in to your baby's feelings by responding appropriately helps your baby gain a sense of closeness and being understood. Showing your love and acceptance of them – when they are feeling bad as well as when they are feeling good – helps them know the mutual pleasures of sharing happy times and that comfort can be found in others. This is an important part of building what psychologists call a 'secure attachment', which research is showing has many advantages for children's later development.

John Oates, developmental psychologist in The Centre for Human Development and Learning, Open University

My mother was always on at me to let him 'cry it out'. She would tell me to leave him even if he got distressed.

Angela C

Ignore anyone who bleats about making a rod for your own back. Young babies are not 'naughty' or 'manipulative', 'wilful' or 'trying to wrap you around their little finger' – they simply get hungry, hot, cold, windy, wet, frightened, tired, uncomfortable, lonely and need you to do something about it.

Responding to those needs sensitively and promptly is an investment:

1: In the short-term, because young babies who are comforted quickly when they are distressed tend to cry less than those who are not. So respond when your baby tells you he needs something and you up the chances of you both having a happier time (see Crying, p.16).
2: In the long-term, because by caring and responding you are showing your baby he is safe, secure and valued. This is the foundation of a child's self-esteem (see Dealing with feelings, p.94).

This is a relatively short, though intense, phase of your baby's life and the urgency of his needs will gradually diminish over his first few months as he begins to adjust to life outside the womb, you become familiar with his preferences and foibles and he learns to trust in your care.

Security

How you respond to your baby when you can't settle him easily is just as important as your best days together – it is a first lesson in the constancy of your love, that your care and regard are not conditional and that you are there for him even when the going gets tough.

This will support his budding confidence to explore the world around him – to touch, feel, look, listen, reach. Think of it in terms of his voyage into the unknown. It is bound to make him anxious at times, and he will need to keep coming back to you to 'refuel' on comfort and reassurance.

Imagining life from your baby's emotional and physical perspective may help you understand his emotional needs. How would it feel to be him at any particular moment – cuddling up to his mother? Crying alone in the night? Having a bath? Lying in his cot?

Crying

*I think our experience is very dependent on our expectations.
We may expect a baby to sleep, eat and be happy, but all babies
cry and it is a rare baby that doesn't cry a lot and rightly so,
it is their only way of expressing themselves and having their
needs met. We tend to view it as a problem, and crying can do dreadful
things to us as mothers, but they all need to do it.*

Ann Herreboudt, midwife and family therapist

Babies communicate their needs by crying. Until your baby's needs are met he will cry as if his life depends on it, because it does.

Some babies cry a little, some a great deal. They may be expressing a physical need, an emotional one, or both. The cause is not always clear or even under their parents' control, and learning the meaning of a child's different cries takes time. Comfort and reassure your baby while you try to work out what he needs and reassure yourself that most mothers depend on nothing more than intuition, trial and error and increasing familiarity with their child's ways.

The causes of crying

Babies can cry for the following reasons:
— hunger
— thirst
— discomfort or pain (too hot, too cold, nappy wet, nappy rash, etc)
— tiredness
— wind
— colic (see Excessive crying, p.18)
— boredom/frustration
— fear
— after-effects of the birth (foetal distress, drugs and anaesthesia etc)
— allergy
— sudden stimulation
— overstimulation

Important: *Crying can be a sign of illness. Trust your instincts – if your baby's cry is noticeably different from normal, or if you are concerned about your baby's health, contact your doctor or health practitioner*

Soothing your child

1: Is your baby's distress related to sleeping and/or feeding problems (see Sleep solutions, p.36 and Feeding, p.52)
2: Most young babies cry less when in

*Everything changes over time, and it can change very quickly.
Babies can change their habits and routines virtually overnight and,
because it changes, even bad times do not last long.*

Ann Herreboudt, midwife and family therapist

It is clear that some children do seem to like being babies more than others. Those who do not may seem frustrated and generally unhappy with their lot, despite their parents' best efforts to comfort and cheer them. The turning point may be when they become more mobile or when they are able to communicate verbally, and the root of their frustration ceases to be.

Dr Elizabeth Bryan, Honorary Consultant Paediatrician at Queen Charlotte's and Chelsea Hospital, London and Director of the Multiple Births Foundation

body contact with their mother[3] so simply holding a baby will often calm him. Rocking, rhythmic and gentle patting and singing may also help (see Settling for sleep, p.38). Baby massage can be particularly effective in calming 'jumpy' babies who startle easily or who are quickly distressed.

3: If your baby becomes more distressed the more you do to soothe him, he may need less stimulation. Some very sensitive babies need as much peace and quiet as you can provide.

4: Be pragmatic. If you hit on something that helps you through a particularly bad crying phase, use it. Feed your baby, carry your baby, snuggle down with your baby, consider that dummy you vowed would never enter your home, do whatever it takes to help you both get through the day – you can always return to your 'normal' routines once you and your baby are less stressed and less needy.

5: No young baby should be left in distress (see Sleep training, p.44). A baby whose mother is slow to respond to his cries is likely to cry more than a baby whose mother responds promptly.[4] Yet some babies do cry a little before they fall asleep, often more in protest than upset. If this happens, picking up your baby the instant he cries might overstimulate rather than soothe him. It may also prevent him from learning how to fall asleep on his own (see Sleep clues, p.39). Listen to your instincts and respond in the way you think is right and appropriate to your baby's needs at that moment.

6: If all else fails, put your baby in a pram or sling and go for a walk. The rhythmic movement may help settle him and the change of environment may help you both.

No little baby should be put away in a room and left to cry, but a mother doesn't have to jump to attention immediately the baby cries either.

Ann Herreboudt, midwife and family therapist

Excessive crying

*I get just as many calls from parents of second, third,
fourth babies, who thought they had cracked it but then
have a child who cries and cries. Anybody can have a crying baby.
This is a great comfort to many first-time mothers who think
it is something they are doing wrong, or that they haven't
got the maternal instinct or the magic touch.*

Louise Walters, Chair of Serene, incorporating the Cry-sis helpline,
the support group for families with excessively crying, sleepless
and demanding babies and children (see Contacts, p.355).

*Nothing can prepare you for it. I felt battered and stretched to my limit.
I was scared by how angry it made me feel.*

Helen C

Around one in ten babies cry 'excessively' and studies have shown this is not due to parental incompetence.[5] In other words, despite their parents doing all the 'right' things, some babies still cry a great deal. If your baby is one of them, it may be best to try to accept the situation and focus your efforts on coping the best you can (see Your needs, p.23 and Coping in hard times, p.229).

There are two identifiable crying 'peaks' – periods when a lot of crying is very common among babies. One of these is at eight weeks[6] and may be due to 'colic' (see right). The second, around seven months to one year, is thought to be due to changing sleep patterns.

If you are experiencing combined problems – ie crying and sleeplessness or feeding difficulties – decide which you find the most difficult. Tackling problems one at a time may help you feel less overwhelmed. Keeping a diary may help you detect emerging patterns and possible causes.

If you find yourself becoming distressed and exhausted, let your partner, relative or trusted friend take over for a while so you can rest or have a break. If you don't, your stress signals will be picked up by the baby who may cry all the more.

If you feel at breaking point, put the baby down safely in the cot and pick up the phone. Call a friend, your partner, the Cry-sis helpline (see Contacts, p.355), anyone who will give you the understanding, help and support you need.

People would say to me 'Excuse me love,
your baby's crying', as if I didn't know.
I remember evenings when my husband would
come home to find the baby at one end of the sofa
crying and me at the other end doing the same. I felt out
of control and totally inadequate. Once she could crawl,
she was suddenly happy and our lives turned round.

Karen M

The notion that parents can and should know what to do, always,
is nonsense. We'd had two children, then our third was a totally new
experience. She screamed her way through the first twelve months.

Professor Hilton Davis, clinical child psychologist

Colic

Colic is a catch-all phrase for bouts of what appear to be tummy pains, causing the baby to go tense, pull up his legs and cry or scream uncontrollably. Symptoms often appear somewhere between three and 12 weeks, often start in the late afternoon or evening and can occur in babies who seem perfectly happy and healthy at other times of the day. Some 20% of babies are thought to be affected.

The jury is still out as to the causes and nature of the condition, but what is not in doubt is the distress caused to parents trying to comfort a baby in pain. Baby massage may help (see p.12). Many parents report success with complementary approaches such as homoeopathy and cranial osteopathy (see Sleep solutions, p.40), but colic will pass of its own accord eventually, usually at or before three months and often stopping as suddenly as it began.

It is important for parents to try to find a way through this period.
Don't feel guilty if you can't find anything that works, because sometimes
nothing does. If you have to put the baby down because the crying
is too awful to bear, of course you will feel wretched, but that
doesn't mean you are a bad parent. You are a parent going
through a very bad time. And it will pass.

Louise Walters, Chair of Serene, incorporating the Cry-sis helpline

Putting yourself in his shoes may also make it easier to understand why something that calmed him down yesterday may be a washout today. Is he tired? Feeling off colour? Uncertain? Frustrated? (See Crying, p.16.)

It is a question of recognising the interior, or emotional needs of the baby, as well as the physical needs. I think babies are sometimes given very short change. The exterior of the baby is very visible, but the interior is somehow invisible. We wipe the baby's face clean, but we don't really think, 'How do you feel little baby?'

Ann Herreboudt, midwife and family therapist

Moments alone

Caring for and responding to your baby does not require you to carry him and cuddle him in your every waking moment. As he grows in confidence and trust, you may find he is happy to spend brief periods in his own company, physically separate from you without anxiety.

This is important for his emotional development and will help you both cope better with those times when the phone rings or the pan boils and you have to put him down.

Infancy is very much about responding to the baby's needs but gradually there will be times when the baby is awake and doesn't need to have anything practical done for him; when enjoyment in a quiet time may occur. As the baby awakes, ask yourself whether you need to pick him up straight away. This also depends on the infant and whether and how you are summoned, but being awake and quiet, feeling secure about being alone and being able to take in the sensations around him plays a very important part in the child's development of relationships and his sense of his own individuality.

Judith Philo, psychotherapist and parent adviceline consultant

It is a gradual process that should not be forced. If your baby is happy in his cot, for example, you might leave him there for a short while. From around three months, as your baby becomes more aware of his environment, you could try mobiles and other safe cot toys that may amuse him when he first wakes in the morning.

Just as some parents find the extreme dependency of a newborn baby delicious and others find it difficult, so some find the first signs of their baby's fledgling independence a very bittersweet experience. Yet raising children is sometimes about 'letting go' and allowing your child to move on to the next stage when he is ready.

Some women do find this hard. You may have got some kind
of a routine sorted out, you know where you are, and then it's
time to go into something different again. But it is part
of the job of being a parent.
Paula Bell, health visitor

Needs v. wants

He wanted me for comfort, but I'd been comforting him
for ages and he wasn't settling. What he needed was sleep,
so I wheeled him around in his pram until he went off. When he
was older, we had a similar situation. He was a compulsive climber
and would get really angry when I stopped him climbing on to the
table. That's what he wanted. What he needed was me to make
sure he was safe, and to have the chance to climb and exercise.
So I'd take him off the table, put up with his screams of
frustration and take him to the playground
or for a walk up the road.
Alison Y

From around six months on, you may sometimes notice a difference between what your baby shows you he wants and what you know he needs. Usually these match (ie he demands what he needs) but not always. When they don't, meeting his demands will not help as much as meeting the underlying need that provoked it. A baby beside himself with tiredness, for example, may demand more cuddles, yet you may know what he needs most is sleep. An older child may demand a

Learning fast

The focus of your baby's interest widens as he grows. He is no longer fascinated solely by the important people in his life (see Communicating with your baby, p.9) but also in other people, places and objects around him. He will have picked up an astonishing amount of information about himself and his environment before his first birthday, and he will receive most of the information from you.

'By one year babies display a cultural awareness that is uniquely human,' says Professor Colwyn Trevarthen. 'They go systematically from interpersonal contact to showing interest in objects and meanings – they have a lot of favourite objects and are interested in joining in what others are attending to around them. So they are not only conscious of, say, the importance of vacuum cleaners or pencils, they also like to show off how they can use them. This shared interest is called joint attention, and is the prerequisite for learning language and much more.

'Children become very clever at their mannerisms by this age, too – they can show off, clap hands, wave goodbye and so on. They are learning etiquette, conventional behaviour. They are also learning about institutions and already know the difference between, say, a shop and a play field and the different things that happen there. They have accumulated a great deal of knowledge and cultural awareness, often before they can say their first word.'

Your baby will be registering your responses to people and objects around him. As infancy researcher John Oates explains: 'Older babies engage in what has been called "social referencing", which is when a baby makes use of the emotion their mother shows towards another person or object to decide what their own reaction should be. For example, if a mother shows positive reactions to one toy and negative reactions to another, their baby is much more likely to choose the first to play with.'

Consider this next time you grimace at the contents of a nappy or laugh with friends or flinch at the sight of a dog – your own positive and negative responses are some of your child's most effective lessons in how he feels about himself and his world.

biscuit, yet you may know that will only pacify him in the short-term and what he actually needs is a meal.

Even if you give the tired child cuddles and the hungry child biscuits, they will keep demanding more because their real need (for sleep or food) remains. Only when they get what they need will their demands cease.

*I think a child's need, as opposed to a want, is something essential
to the child and thus essential for us to understand. It is something that
won't go away if it's not provided. As parents it can take far less energy
to meet or acknowledge that need than for it to become internalised
or expressed in another way. And I do mean acknowledging. I can't
always meet the need right there and then, I'm not Superwoman.*

Stella Ward, nurse and Parent Network co-ordinator

Discovery

Your baby is taking in information about himself and his world at an
astonishing rate. At six months a baby will know the basics of social
interaction[7] and by one year he is a culturally sophisticated being, even
displaying rudimentary social etiquette, such as waving goodbye.

He is as sensitive as ever to your own reactions and responses, and
these will have a profound influence on how he feels about himself and
the people, places and objects around him (see Learning fast, opposite).

Your needs

*At first the parents' needs may be met by attending 100% to the newborn,
but soon their own needs must arise – simply having a bath or preparing a
meal – so the balancing act begins. If we listen to ourselves and to our
babies, we can usually mediate successfully between the two.*

Barbara Dale, Parent Network co-ordinator

*I had to shake myself up, remember to do some things for me.
Looking after yourself is a habit, I think, and one that's pretty hard to
establish but I knew I must start so I could keep us all going.*

Anne-Marie I

Recognising your own needs is important throughout parenthood, but
never more so than during your child's first weeks and months. Look
after yourself a little more and your baby will benefit.

Be gentle on yourself

I didn't expect it, but from the moment he was born it felt like he'd always been here. There were times when I hoped I was doing the right thing, but I never panicked. It all seemed to unfold.

Lisa F

For me, the birth was the first thing I hadn't been able to sort out, control or otherwise fix in my entire adult life. The baby was the second.

Nicola B

I was breastfeeding him in bed at night. I'm still not sure how it happened but he slipped off the pillow and landed in the wastepaper bin.

Alison Y

New parenthood is full of clashes between expectation and reality. It may be much better or much harder than you predicted, or both. Whatever your experience, it may help to remember that:

1: Babies in advertisements do not cry, scream, throw up down your back or wake at horrible times. Mothers in advertisements are always smiling and have had time to brush their hair. Real life is not like this.
2: As a human being you are entitled to emotions, needs, strengths, weaknesses and the right to sometimes get things wrong.

You will never be the perfect mother, your child will never be the perfect child and that is as it should be. Burden yourself with unnecessary guilt or unrealistically high expectations of your achievements or your baby's behaviour and you risk focusing on what isn't happening rather than what is – an evolving relationship between two unique human beings.

There will be times when you misread the signs or when you don't have a clue why your child isn't settling. This doesn't mean there is anything 'wrong' with him as a baby or you as a parent, simply that life sometimes goes in ways parents cannot control or predict.

The fact also remains that some babies are temperamentally more demanding and less easy to comfort than others. We recognise the importance of individuality in older children and adults but, bizarrely, often expect babies to conform to predictable patterns of behaviour and response.

Who mothers new mothers?

Your experience of new motherhood depends hugely on the amount of support you receive. Many women are cosseted and given the time and help they need to adjust, recover and enjoy. Many more are not . . .

Chinese, Japanese, many cultures insist on the new mother resting for the first month. It is often called 'doing the month', when the mother is looked after by their families. Here, the focus after birth goes straight to the baby and the mother is expected to just carry on as soon as she is on her feet. She needs to recover properly, over about nine months.

Peter Walker, yoga teacher and physical therapist

My aunt came to the hospital and dressed my baby in the shawl and other clothes my family had made and sent, so symbolically the child was wrapped in the family's love. She brought me and my husband and child home, where my favourite foods had already been prepared. Prayers were said with a lantern and flowers, and we ate. I then fed my baby and he slept. When the sun went down, she warmed her hands on the prayer lamp and gave me a very deep massage. I was then wrapped in warm towels and she ran me a bath with the petals plucked from the flowers. She washed me and dried my hair, and put me into bed where I slept wonderfully. As well as the care it was hugely important for me symbolically. It made me feel I was welcomed into motherhood. All the customs are done as a recognition of the gateway to change, to welcome and guide the woman as she has just become a mother.

Sangamithra C

I'm not good at staying in bed and I don't believe having a baby should be thought of as an affliction. But because I was up and about, my partner thought I must be OK. I was exhausted but I didn't ask for help. I somehow hoped he'd realise.

Claire T

Children are born with their own individual characters and needs.
Even among identical twins, the difference in their temperaments may be
evident very soon after birth and the mother may find that what soothes one
baby may not suit another, what may entertain one may annoy his or her sibling.
The mother must try not to blame herself if one technique or approach does
not seem to work – the technique may be a fine one, the way she
did it may be admirable, but it simply may not have been the
right one for that baby at that time.

Dr Elizabeth Bryan, Honorary Consultant Paediatrician at Queen Charlotte's and
Chelsea Hospital, London and Director of the Multiple Births Foundation

As if caring for your new baby isn't enough, the weeks following the
birth are a time of deep and powerful emotions (see Baby blues, below).
The birth experience leaves many women feeling shocked and battered.
Some feel profoundly disappointed if it was very different to their hopes
and plans.

Most women also have to cope with new and major life changes
beyond the birth of their child – stopping work, even if temporarily;
adjusting to a new and unfamiliar role; coping with cuts in household
income; isolation from former social networks. Add to these all those

---

Baby blues

The 'baby blues' are experienced by more than half of all western mothers during the first week to ten days following the birth of their baby.[8]

The most common symptom is tearfulness, usually some time between the second and seventh day. Other symptoms include mood swings, memory lapses, sleeplessness, tension, loss of appetite and a feeling of helplessness and confusion – all of which can be exacerbated if you are exhausted or experiencing problems feeding your baby.

The symptoms are common but usually relatively mild and, with rest and the support of family and friends, mothers suffering from them feel they can cope.

Many find it helps to talk through their experiences of the birth and new motherhood with someone they know and trust.

If you feel the symptoms are worsening and that you can't cope, you may be experiencing the onset of post-natal depression (see Understanding post-natal depression, p.30) and it is very important that you consult your GP or health visitor as soon as possible.

changes in role, identity, sex life, money and power that can cause seismic shifts in the relationship between the new parents (see Important relationships, p.203) and you have a highly potent mix. Understanding and recognising these pressures may help you be a little gentler on yourself (see Consider yourself, p.33).

I can't remember individual days or events very well from those first weeks. It's more of a blur. I do remember doing contortions in the kitchen, jiggling her up and down while I did the washing up, and those long nights and that sense of never, ever getting any time for myself. We had this unspoken fear that this was how life was going to be from then on.

Margaret S

Help and advice

You are very vulnerable at this time and there is no great gain in pretending otherwise. You and the baby are like sponges and you need to be careful who you have around you. Learn to say 'no' kindly. In my experience 'second and third timers' keep unhelpful visits to a minimum, having learned first-time round. I took tranquillisers when my mother-in-law came to visit following the birth of my first child. Second-time I only let her come on my terms.

Gill Wood, NCT ante-natal teacher

You will need to develop two skills – asking for and accepting help and advice when it's useful, plus a diplomatic method of getting rid of those who think they're helping but aren't. Don't underestimate the importance of either.

You may receive much advice. Too much. Most of it well-meant, outdated and contradicted completely by the advice you were given ten minutes earlier. Babies should be picked up, put down, carried, jiggled, stroked, sat up, laid down, across your knee, over your shoulder . . . Friends and relatives may try to extrapolate a theory from their own, very particular experiences and tell you all about what worked for them as if it should be carved in stone. They are only trying to help, but it would be most helpful if they remembered that different babies like different things and that you'll soon know what yours responds to best.

Babies' needs change, so be willing to change tack and try something new if your once-successful technique now fails. But don't be encouraged into trying every bit of advice at once or you and your baby will become completely bamboozled.

What you may need most after your baby is born is logistical support – cooking food, washing and ironing, all the boring but essential bits – and emotional support, someone whose company boosts your confidence rather than undermines it and who knows how to help without taking over.

> *It is important to realise that apparent support is only as*
> *supportive as the woman experiences it to be.*
> Sarah Darton, health visitor

Asking for practical help can be hard, but think of it as asking for the support you require to give your child what he needs. Asking for advice can be even harder, especially in the face of such potent myths as the omniscient maternal instinct and our ridiculously high expectations of our own capabilities and understanding.

Do not to struggle on alone If you want advice, seek it. Whatever you are going through, someone will have been through it before and information and support are available that will benefit both you and your baby (see Contacts, p.355).

Be realistic You will be lucky to get the right help or the right information on your first enquiry. Some relatives, friends and health professionals are great communicators, bursting with appropriate advice and full of understanding of your situation. Others are not, but try not to let their shortcomings put you off your search for constructive advice.

Support groups can provide invaluable support, while telephone lines have the advantage of total anonymity for those who still feel uncertain about seeking help. But remember that no parent can know how to deal with every eventuality. There should be no embarrassment in admitting this, and the more of us who do so the sooner the daft and damaging fiction of the perfect parent will crumble.

*I'd called a helpline about my baby's crying and the advisor obviously
realised I felt dreadful about doing it. She told me that it is not bad or
incompetent mothers who seek advice, but ones who care enough to want to solve
their problem and who are responsible and motivated enough to seek the
information they need on which to base their decisions. That really helped.
And the advice was invaluable, for the baby and for me.*

Jo W

Meeting others

*We lack groups in which parents can talk through the day-to-day situations
they face. It may seem boring to someone outside the situation, but that day-to-day
stuff is what people are scrabbling with, it's life and if it is a problem you
can feel dragged down. If you've got the support of others in a similar
situation it can help you take pitfalls in your stride.*

Paula Bell, health visitor

It is easy to feel isolated when you have a baby. Where and how you
meet up with other mothers depends on your circumstances and your
interests – it may be a mother and baby group, your local park or NCT
branch. What matters is that you go somewhere where you may find
other people with young babies, some of whom you may feel comfortable with.

If you find it hard to mix on your own behalf, bear in mind the
positive impact it can have on your child. Babies are astonishingly
receptive from a surprisingly early age, and the foundations of their
ability to socialise are laid by what they see their parents do and by the
opportunities they are given to be with other children.

*Where, once, people would have raised children within the extended family
and could go round the corner to their mum, their aunt, whoever, for that
all-important change of scene and the opportunity to diffuse a possibly fraught
situation by just being somewhere else, the chances are that network is not
available now. It is very important that parents try to create networks of
their own. Whatever the activity, it is a way of comparing notes, letting
off steam and getting ideas from others in a similar situation.*

Vivienne Gross, Clinical Director, The Institute of Family Therapy

Understanding post-natal depression

Within a few days of having my second child, I was feeling very stressed out. The feelings just grew worse. You think that if you say anything they'll take your children away, but I knew I had to do something. In the end my health visitor walked through the door and I just said, 'I hate my baby. What are we going to do about it?' By this stage I didn't even want to be in the same house as him, let alone hold him. I felt isolated and terrified. My health visitor made me see my GP, who was very good. I also decided to tell my family and friends, who have been so understanding and supportive. My son is coming up to a year and a half and I feel so differently towards him, it's incredible.

Belinda M, former PND sufferer and telephone counsellor
for The Association for Post-natal Illness

Contrary to popular belief, not all post-natally depressed women have trouble bonding with their child or reject them in some way and not all post-natal illness manifests itself soon after birth – it may not be noticeable until many months after the baby is born.

PND affects between 70,000 and 100,000 women and their babies in the UK every year and we owe it to ourselves and those around us to be more informed and understanding about the condition and its consequences.

The Association for Post-natal Illness is clear in its guidance: 'Do remember that this is a condition which always results in complete recovery'.[9] But the longer it remains untreated the longer it can last, and the longer both mother and baby can suffer. Three-quarters of PND sufferers will not seek any form of medical help.[10] This may be partly due to the pressures on mothers to pretend that all is rosy, and partly due to a general unawareness of the illness and its symptoms.

Most sufferers experience a combination of the symptoms listed below in varying degrees, from mild to incapacitating. All may also be symptoms of other conditions, so expert help and diagnosis is vital.

— **Depression** Mother feels depressed, despondent and hopeless. May cry a lot, feel rejected by family and baby.
— **Tiredness** Feelings of constant tiredness, lethargy. Mother may also feel unable to cope with household chores or baby's care.
— **Anxiety** Mother may feel worried about her own health and experience severe but inexplicable pain (often in head, neck, back or chest). May also have unjustified worries about the health and well-being of other family members, especially the baby. May feel too anxious to go out, meet friends or even answer the telephone.
— **Fear** A fear of being left alone is a common but passing phase of the illness. Someone close to the mother should always be with her during this time.

— **Panic** Unpredictable feelings of confusion and panic about everyday situations.

— **Tension** An inability to relax, sometimes feeling on the point of explosion.

— **Obsession and inappropriate thoughts** A common but frightening symptom, often focused on a particular person (perhaps the baby), a situation or activity. A mother may fear she may harm her child. Such fears are almost entirely unjustified, but she should tell her family and doctor so she can receive treatment to recover from this distressing phase of the illness.

— **Lack of concentration** Inability to concentrate on television, books, even conversation.

— **Sleeping difficulties** Often, even when the baby is asleep.

— **Sex** Complete loss of interest in sex. A return of sexual desire is often the last sign that a depression has lifted, and great patience and sensitivity is required if a relationship is to be kept intact whilst the mother recovers.

List adapted, with kind persmission, from 'Post-natal Depression', produced by the Association for Post-natal Illness (see Contacts, p.355)

My son was 18 months old when I was finally persuaded to go to the doctor. I hadn't felt angry towards him, or rejected him, but I was very over-protective. All my emotions were for him and I had nothing for anybody else, including myself. I had this overwhelming fear of losing him, I thought he was going to die. If he didn't finish off all his food, every mouthful, I'd worry. I hated every minute of our holiday because I hated being so far away from our GP in case something went wrong. I was having panic attacks. I thought I was going mad.
I was so shocked when I was told I had post-natal depression. I feel it is behind me now, but if anyone feels they may be suffering from it, my advice is, for God's sake talk to someone. You are not going mad, nobody will take your baby away, and you will get better.

Alison H, former PND sufferer and telephone counsellor for
The Association for Post-natal Illness

Tiredness and eating irregularly seems to make post-natal depression worse, so try to eat regularly and rest. There is also growing evidence that 'listening therapy' – at least half an hour a week listening to the mother's account of her problems in a supportive, non-judgemental way – is helpful for at least a third of mothers with depression.[11]

If you feel you are experiencing the onset of PND (see also Baby blues, p.26), it is important to consult your GP or health visitor as soon as possible. The Association for Post-natal Illness has a register of phone volunteers, all previous PND sufferers themselves, who can offer support (see Contacts, p.355). Drug treatments are also available and usually involve the use of anti-depressants.

Avoiding competitive parents

*Part of this competitive parenting stems from the feeling that we should
consider ourselves so lucky to have a baby that no one will admit to having had
an awful day, to say, 'He has cried all day, and I have got nothing done.'
But honest friends will understand because they've experienced it too.
Without this honesty it all gets terribly confusing as to what is normal.*

Christine Chittick, NCT ante-natal teacher

Be warned – competitive parents are out there, smiling radiantly at
child clinics, beaming smugly at baby groups, offering unsolicited tips to
soothe your screaming baby in the Sainsbury's queue. These are not the
parents who are so happy at their lot that they can't help but show it,
but those whose happiness is bolstered by the fact that their baby is fat-
ter, longer, quieter, louder, sleepier, more alert, in fact anything more
than yours. They are to be avoided where possible because they are bad
for your soul and your sanity.

New parents, especially, have a habit of comparing the progress of
their child with others. Eventually you will learn to laugh, understand
exaggeration as an extension of pride, and ignore it. When your baby
is young, however, you are easy prey.

*My daughter was premature and seemed to do most things long after
the other babies at my post-natal group. When they were laughing and smiling,
she failed to perform apart from the occasional fart. By about six months
she'd caught up, and some mothers found it hard to contain their disappointment.
But I do understand that urge to compare – I've had three children and
even now find myself thinking 'Oh God, mine's got the smallest head
here' or quietly swelling with pride when he claps on cue.*

Clare T

Your baby is an individual who, like any other, will do some things fast
and some things slower and most things in between. It is remarkably
easy to start pouring over developmental charts, but the routine developmental checks with your health visitor will pick up the rare instances
when a child's progress is cause for concern. The vast majority of
children fall within the very wide band of what is considered 'normal',
and attempting to speed a child to the next developmental stage can
often do more harm than good.

*There is still a friendly battle between mothers as to which child will
walk and talk first. Yet encouraging children to skip the crawling phase by
plonking them prematurely in an upright position in a baby walker, for instance,
is not good. Baby walkers are used at a time when children do not have the
developmental capabilities to use them safely, and when they can, they
don't need them any more. They can delay steps being taken or even
lead the child to miss important parts of their development.
Natural developmental stages are there for a reason and it is
neurologically detrimental to leave them out.*

Penelope Robinson, Director of Professional Affairs,
The Chartered Society of Physiotherapy

Consider yourself

Your child won't give a damn whether you've cleaned the kitchen floor
or if his tops don't match his bottoms or if the house hasn't been dust-
ed for weeks. He will give a damn if you don't eat properly or if you've
had so little sleep, support and time to unwind that you're completely
exhausted.

It happens, often. Most parents go through stages when, out of
necessity or circumstance, their needs are completely subsumed by
those of their children. The trick is to avoid it when it is not necessary,
so you have the energy to cope when it is.

*Think of your body as a car, and rest and relaxation as the petrol it
needs to keep going. The giving to your self simply fills up the tank so you
are able to keep running smoothly and nurturing others. Think of three things
that you will do for yourself each day without feeling guilty – they may be
as simple as eating a chocolate biscuit, switching the phone off for an hour,
phoning a friend. But by doing this, and establishing a habit of
doing this, it becomes much easier to remember you have needs, too.
It is good for your self-esteem – it is saying to yourself you are worth it.*

Gill Wood, NCT ante-natal teacher

Introducing your needs into the equation may be in very small ways
initially – perhaps having your baby or a trusted friend babysit while
you have an uninterrupted sleep. A walk in the sunshine may give your

Relaxation through breathing

Lolli Stirk, pregnancy and post-natal yoga teacher

Being a parent, particularly first-time parents of a new baby or a toddler, can sometimes feel like being 'on duty' 24 hours a day. Taking time out to relax can make the difference between enjoying your baby or just feeling trapped and exhausted. Having someone look after your baby and going out with your partner to remember who you were before the child came along is vital. Shorter, concentrated, ten-minute relaxation breaks also help, and can be as refreshing as a couple of hours' sleep. What follows is a short visualisation exercise to encourage deep relaxation through breathing.

1: Lie on the floor, drawing your knees in towards your belly.

2: Wrap your arms around your bent legs and 'cuddle' them towards your body.

3: Stay like that for a couple of breaths and then put your feet down on the floor. They should be close to your bottom, hip width apart and slightly turned in.

4: With the next couple of exhalations become aware of your lower back releasing and dropping towards the floor. Then give yourself an enormous hug, slipping your fingertips under your shoulder blades to open the space between the shoulder blades.

5: To open them up even more, snuggle your chin down into your chest and for the next couple of exhalations feel the upper spine sinking down into the floor, drawn by gravity. Then let your arms drop heavily down to your sides, palms turned upwards.

6: For a few moments imagine you are lying on the sand on a warm, sunny beach with your feet just touching the edge of the water. Slowly bring your attention to your breath and observe how it enters and leaves your body, how it rises and falls just like the waves of the sea. Now, as you inhale, imagine you are drawing the breath like the waves of the sea, up through the soles of your feet through your legs, pelvis, chest, shoulders, head. The inhalation fills you with everything you need – oxygen, energy and lightness.

7: As you exhale feel the wave of the breath sweep down your body back towards the sea, taking with it your toxins and your tiredness and stroking you into a deeper relaxation.

8: Keep your attention focused on each cycle of breath and become particularly interested in the pause at the end of the exhalation. Let your body dictate the rhythm of your breath as it does when you are sleeping, while you observe and enjoy the benefits that come with spending time focusing on your breathing.

baby the comfort of your company and you the chance of fresh air, exercise and a change of scene.

Try to make at least a little time for relaxation (see Relaxation through breathing, opposite). This is not indulgence, it is an investment for you and your family. How you choose to relax is up to you – it may be by fulfilling your need for adult company, for solitude, for exercise, for a video and a takeaway – but try to include a bit of pampering and a bit of peace somewhere along the line. If you simply don't have the time, try to work out what needs to be done to get it.

CHAPTER THREE

SLEEP SOLUTIONS

*It's my weakest spot. If they don't sleep, I don't sleep and if that
happens night after night after night, I begin to fray at the edges.
I get ratty and unreasonable and desperate.*

Ruth H

C hildren need sleep and so do parents. Sleep deprivation is a very
effective form of torture and only those who have survived periods
without it will know what this can do to your brain, your body, your
patience and your sense of humour. Helping your child develop parent-
friendly sleep patterns will help you both have the resources you need
to appreciate life's high spots and deal with its difficulties.

Babies and sleep

Newborn needs

Young babies need feeding and attention through the night. They have
no control over when they sleep and when they wake and have yet to
spot the difference between night and day.

Some people do have babies who sleep for chunks of the night from
a very early age, but their ability to soothe and settle their child may
have very little to do with it. It is also partly circumstance – birth
weight, birth experience and so on – and partly luck. Just like adults,
babies have widely varying sleep patterns and needs and young babies'
sleep patterns can be particularly erratic.

So the first thing to remember is that your baby's sleeplessness is not
your fault. If this eases some of the guilt, anxiety and frustration most

parents carry along with the baby as they pace up and down the bed-room in the small hours, it's worth knowing.

We all have expectations and when things do not happen as we expect – for example, when the baby doesn't sleep at night – we see it as something to rectify. Sometimes it is better to be able to step back and recognise that the baby is just not ready for it yet. When a couple comes to me for advice it is because they feel something is wrong – that there is a problem with their baby or that they are bad parents or wrong parents. Mostly, however, what we are dealing with is a normal developmental pattern in a normal baby.

Ann Herreboudt, midwife and family therapist

If anyone asks, it *is* possible to get a baby to sleep for 12 hours through the night from a very early age. A few babies do this naturally, the rest are programmed to do it in early infancy by being bottlefed by the clock and trained not to expect either milk or attention at night – ie they learn that their cries will be ignored. To show a tiny baby that her cries will not be responded to, that her need for comfort, care and love are worth little, seems a peculiar path to take.

For most parents, the first weeks are rather a question of sleeping when they can, of gradually tuning in to how best their baby likes to be settled and soothed, of recognising and responding to her emerging patterns and holding on to the fact that these are early days and it will get easier.

Three in a bed?

Many mothers – out of considered choice or sheer exhaustion – let their babies sleep in bed with them. This is the accepted norm in many societies and cultures and it is an arrangement that has been around a lot longer than cots, so it is hardly a new or radical idea. There is much evidence that young babies cry less when in body contact with their mother.[1] Some parents believe putting a young baby in a cot enforces a premature separation and are convinced of the psychological advantages of 'co-sleeping'.

You may find that nights of light sleep, while your baby breastfeeds at will beside you, are more restful than nights broken by having to stagger out of bed to feed her, or you may find the very lightness of sleep

Settling for sleep: 0–6 months

Remembering where babies have come from – a dark, warm, sometimes noisy womb where all their needs were met instantly – may help us better understand their needs.

— Some babies like rhythmic rocking or gentle patting of their back, chest or bottom to mimic your heartbeat in the womb.

— Keep stimulation to a minimum, with lights low and no playing. Keep partners or visitors under control!

— Some babies like no noise, some like background noise (even vacuum cleaners), some like music.

— Relax your baby with baby massage (see p.12).

— Some babies like being wrapped in a blanket, especially newborns who may feel startled by freedom of movement.

— Remember babies get overtired, too.

If this is avoided they will be easier to settle.

— If you are breastfeeding, could any foods you are eating be upsetting your baby? For example, hot, spicy foods, citrus fruit and chocolate are known to affect some babies.

— What does your baby like best? Every baby is different, and every baby's needs will change. Some like gazing at mobiles, for instance, while others find them disturbing.

Important: *For safety's sake it is recommended that you place your baby to sleep on her back, in the 'feet to foot' position and ensure she does not get too hot (see FSID, Contacts, p.355).*

Consult your GP or health practitioner if you think your baby's wakefulness, particularly associated with crying, may be due to any medical problems (illness, allergy, etc).

together exhausting. Whatever your experience, it is your choice, but be aware that co-sleeping can become a fairly long-term commitment if your baby learns to depend on your physical closeness to settle (see Sleep clues, opposite).

While it is extremely rare for babies to be rolled on in bed (the risk is much greater if either parent is under the influence of drugs or alcohol), they can easily become overheated, so make sure your baby's clothes and covers are light enough and that nothing can be pulled over her head. You may have to put something beside the bed to stop her rolling out.

Sleep clues

All children have to learn to go to sleep themselves eventually. When your child learns this is largely up to you, but in time, when your baby seems generally settled (often around three months and over) and only when and if it feels right, it may help to remember these two rules of thumb:

Babies learn sleep clues If a baby is always fed, rocked, patted or cuddled to sleep as a matter of routine, she will soon expect and depend on these 'clues' until she can't fall to sleep happily without them. This isn't a problem if you don't mind. If you do, she can still be cuddled, comforted and fed, then put down and allowed to actually fall to sleep on her own.

This not only helps when your baby goes to sleep in the evening, but could also help reduce the number of times she needs you through the night. All babies and children move, wriggle and wake at night without even being aware of it. If your baby doesn't depend on you for her 'sleep clues', she can fall back to sleep again on her own and only cry for you if she is hungry or needs attention or comfort for some other reason.

If babies don't learn to be on their own, the problems can get worse as the baby gets older and she can fight sleep. We have endless calls about babies who cry the moment they are put down. Or you put them down, creep away and before you have even got to the door, they are crying again, because they know they are no longer in their parent's arms and they haven't learned to settle without them.

Louise Walters, Chair of Serene, incorporating the Cry-sis Helpline,
the support group for families with excessively crying, sleepless and demanding
babies and children (see Contacts, p.355).

Babies expect to wake up where they were when they fell asleep If your baby was feeding in your arms or lying in your bed when she nodded off, it can come as a shock to find herself in her crib or cot when she wakes. For this reason, it helps to put your baby down to sleep wherever you hope she will stay happily for the remainder of the night.

If she is calm, comfortable and content, then protests a little at being put in her cot, try to resist the temptation to pick her up immediately, but don't leave her to become distressed either (see Crying, p.16). 'Sleep training' (see p.44) – leaving babies to cry for five minutes or more – is not recommended for young babies (six months and under) and can be counterproductive. As always, do what works best for you and your baby. This will vary from child to child.

Complementary approaches

Many parents report success with complementary therapies for excessively crying babies or those with sleep problems. The two most commonly used are homoeopathy and cranial osteopathy.

It is important that you choose a reputable, qualified practitioner experienced in treating babies (see Contacts, p.355) and only do what feels right and appropriate for you and your child. Also be aware that some children seem more receptive to certain treatments than others.

Cranial osteopathy for babies
Gez Lamb, cranial osteopath

Cranial osteopathy (also known as paediatric osteopathy) is a very gentle, non-invasive treatment that involves holding the baby's head or body and making minute movements to correct problems. It is most recognised for correcting the effects of birth trauma, in the easing of 'mechanical' (circulatory, muscular, skeletal, digestive) conditions that may contribute to poor sleep and digestion in babies, and for speeding the body's own healing processes. The treatment is generally considered very safe and gentle, and most babies find it relaxing.

Cranial osteopathy can be useful for babies suffering from:
- Not sleeping/waking often
- Excessive crying
- Colic
- Restlessness/irritability
- Feeding difficulties
- Post-vaccination to alleviate shock

If you give it time, most of these problems will recede after birth. I would expect more than half of all babies to sort out these things for themselves. Where this does not happen, patterns can remain and cranial osteopathy help. I find mothers have a real instinct for when their baby is not settling or not quite right, and that is the best time to come.
Gez Lamb, cranial osteopath

I used to love being sung to by my mother and used to sing to my babies until one day, my three-year-old daughter said 'No!' when I started their lullaby, 'I don't like the noise!' It came in useful later, though, because I could say 'if you don't get to bed I'll sing'.

Helen D

Homoeopathy

Edie Freeman, homoeopath

Homoeopathy can be useful for babies suffering from:

- Any after-effects of the birth
- Constant crying
- Sleeplessness
- Colds and coughs
- Teething
- Digestive problems, including colic

Homoeopathy can be useful to maintain and improve children's health in a number of ways:

1: Building health, thus improving the immune response, making children less susceptible to infections and able to recover more quickly

2: Providing alternatives to drugs, such as antibiotics

3: Healing chronic conditions: asthma, eczema, ear infections, some speech difficulties

4: Vaccinations
i) Pre- and post-vaccination remedies to prevent and alleviate after-effects
ii) Alternatives to vaccinations if parents do not want their children vaccinated

5: Addressing emotional and behavioural problems, particularly through times of change

It is important that you feel comfortable with your chosen practitioner, that you have trust and rapport. Some are much better than others, and some will suit you and your family better than others.

Be Aware: you will know what your child needs better than anyone else. Take your child to hospital or call a doctor if your child's temperature rises above 102 degrees, looks to be losing consciousness, or has an acute ear infection.

Homoeopathy is a system of medicine that treats the whole person (mind, body and emotions) with a minute amount of a substance that is just sufficient to stimulate the body's own healing forces. Homoeopathy is very gentle and remedies do not have side-effects.

Edie Freeman, homoeopath

Patterns and routines

As sleep patterns begin to emerge, try gradually to establish a bedtime routine. This can provide your baby with the security of predictability, help prevent overtiredness and encourage her to distinguish night from day.

Aim for a situation that suits you as well as your child – there is no reason why she should be in bed by 7.30pm if she's getting enough sleep at other times of the day, and many parents are happy for their children to stay up until late in the evening. What matters is that each evening has roughly the same structure – say, food, play, bath, cuddle,

Parent-friendly sleep patterns: 6 months – toddlers

Some babies have fallen into parent-friendly sleep patterns by about six months. Some fall out of them again, some don't adapt to them until much later and many need a little persuasion. The tips for settling young babies still apply (see Settling for sleep: 0–6 months, p.38) and the following checklists may help:

Difficult settlers

— Do you have a regular bedtime routine? Try to introduce one if you haven't.
— Does your baby depend on signals from you to fall asleep? (See Sleep clues, p.39)
— Could your baby be teething?
— Is your baby overtired? Have a calm, quiet time together before you attempt to settle her to sleep, perhaps looking at a picture book. Think about the frequency of naps – is she getting enough sleep during the day? Babies' needs change as they grow and it may be that your routine needs revising.
— Is your baby tired enough? Perhaps she is having more daytime sleep than she needs.
— Does your baby have a comforter? Some parents find it helps to encourage one – a toy, a blanket, even the child's own thumb – if it helps the baby cope away from the mother's physical presence. If your child uses a dummy, try putting more than one in the cot so she is more likely to find one herself.

book, bed — at roughly the same times. A child can't be expected to know when it's time for bed if that time keeps changing.

Many children become particularly unsettled at around two months due to 'colic' (see p.19) and between seven months to a year, when they are old enough to force themselves to stay awake.[2] Babies who had previously slept for enviably long stretches may wake many times in the night at this stage. According to the support group Serene (see Contacts, p.355) one in three children are still waking regularly in the night at 12 months. Re-establishing routines when you can will help you all get back on an even keel.

Night wakers

Consider all of the above, plus:
— Is your baby waking for night feeds? If night feeding is increasing, it could be a sign that your baby is ready to go on to solid food if she hasn't done so already (see Feeding and food wars, p.52). Most babies of six months and over do not need night feeds for nutritional reasons, but many still enjoy them. If this isn't a problem for you, there's no reason to stop. If it is, try gradually to reduce the number of night feeds. If bottlefeeding, very gradually reduce the amount given at each feed.
— Is your child sleeping in your bed/bedroom? If you are disturbing each other, consider moving your baby into a cot or another room.
— Are you jumping to attention at your child's slightest whimper and snuffle? This can disturb a baby more than letting them drift off to sleep again.

Early wakers

— Try heavier curtains or black-out blinds.
— Cot activity toys, mobiles, etc, may encourage your baby to play in her cot for a while.
— If your baby wakes for her early morning feed at a regular but ungodly hour, try to move it, gradually and in five-minute jumps, to a more parent-friendly time.

Nap refusers

— If your baby won't sleep in her cot during the day but will sleep in her sling or pushchair, try taking her out at a regular time to establish her sleep pattern. Once established, you could try the cot again.
— Does she need the nap? If your baby is at an in-between stage, refusing a nap but getting strung out without it, try building quiet times into the day so at least she is calm and rested.

Sleep training

I was getting up ten times a night every night with my youngest, until he was 16 months old. I took it out on my other children because I was too tired to cope. We were referred to a sleep specialist by our GP, who made us write down everything we did, day and night. She said I needed to communicate to him that nothing exciting happens at night: no food or drink, no cuddles or play. But what she really taught me was how you have to make a decision about what your aim is, then work out steps that you can cope with to get there.

Sue B

I tried sleep training. The first two nights were just awful. He was so upset and I felt dreadful, but I was so incredibly tired I knew I had to do it. But the third night I put him in his cot, he made a token cry, then lay down. By the fourth night he was sleeping until morning.

Lindsay C

I thought about sleep training but realised I just couldn't do it. So I decided not to view my baby's sleeplessness as a problem I had to solve but as something I had to live through, a phase that would end. I feel quite liberated. Now I don't have a problem, I just have a child who doesn't sleep through.

Kathy H

Sleep training is troubleshooting. It can be extremely effective but it is not recommended for babies under seven months and it is only intended as a last resort, for use when the usual methods have not worked and either you, your baby or both are desperate for more sleep (see Parent-friendly sleep patterns, p.42).

First consider whether these are the right methods for you, your child and your circumstances. If they don't feel right, don't use them. If you wish to discuss her individual case in detail, contact your GP, health visitor or health practitioner. They may also be able to refer you to a specialist sleep clinic if necessary, although these aren't available in all areas.

Sleep training techniques

With both methods, it is important to put your child into her cot *awake*. Do not carry her to her room sleeping, as it can be very disturbing for a child to fall asleep in one room and wake up in another.

The checking routine (for babies 7–9 months and over)

This method has worked for many parents who have contacted the Cry-sis helpline, and can also be used for the older child.

1: Ensure parent(s) and baby are well. Give yourself two clear weeks when you are not going out in the evening or going away.
2: Babies and children need a routine, especially at bedtime. Set a bedtime and stick to it. Make sure there is a good 'winding down' period: quiet games, stories and a relaxing bath.
3: Put baby to bed, tuck her in, say 'goodnight' and leave. Make sure she has any comfort objects with her before you go.
4: When she cries, leave her for a set time (1–5 minutes) then go back, 'check' her, tuck her in and leave. Do this until she goes to sleep. You may wish to start with a short period between checks, leaving it a little longer each time.
5: If your child gets up return her gently but firmly to bed. Ensure she knows you mean business and that you are not going to give in. It may help to use

the same repetitive phrase and calm tone of voice each time you go in to your child.

6: Avoid drinks (unless the weather is very hot), cuddles or stories as these can be interpreted as 'rewards' for not going to sleep.
7: Be determined. If you give in now she will try much harder the next time as she knows you will give in in the end.
8: If your baby wakes in the night do exactly the same as before. Go back as many times as is necessary to 'check'. In this way, you and your baby know everything is OK.
9: Be consistent. If you have the support of a partner, make sure you work together.
10: Be prepared. This is a difficult process for you and your child.

The gradual retreat method

This method usually takes longer to work than the checking routine but is probably gentler on you and your child. This time, instead of leaving the baby, you stay and sit by the cot or bed until the baby falls asleep – stroking her as necessary. Over the next few nights, gradually sit further away from her until she will go to sleep with you outside the bedroom door.

Adapted with kind permission from 'Sleep Problems In Babies', produced by Serene, incorporating the Cry-sis helpline (see Contacts, p.355).

Sleep for toddlers and older children

The ground rules for bedtime change considerably for toddlers and older children who have moved out of a cot and into a bed.

Sometimes it is obvious that what your child really wants is comfort, or perhaps to tell you something that's been on her mind, which is when a few minutes' cuddling is often the most caring and the quickest way to settle her. But sometimes she may issue demands simply because it is a good game. This is when you need to tuck her in, kiss her goodnight and tell her, calmly and firmly, that it is time to go to sleep.

Sleep training can still be very effective. Other points to remember include:

Be boring Be as low-key and calm as you can. If your child hates hair-washing, try doing this in the morning to shift tensions away from bed-time.

Stick to routines If you have let them slip, try to re-establish them. If your child is spending time between two families, try to ensure that everyone sticks to the same plan.

Look beyond bedtimes Could any event or change in your child's life be unsettling her?

Be firm Try not to raise your voice, but mean it when you say it's time for bed. If she pops out of bed again, turn her around and return her to her bedroom. Don't let her sit with you, don't make it fun. Explain that she needn't go to sleep if she's not tired (which is what she may protest), but that she must stay in her bed.

Be honest Sometimes we all forget to explain to children why we want them to act in a certain way. Even with young children this is sometimes all that is needed to turn an unreasonable order into a sensible plan (see Communication, p.70).

I'd had weeks of my twins hopping in and out of bed, and I
couldn't get on with anything. Out of exhaustion more than anything one
night I sat on the end of a bed and explained to them, very quietly, that
I was shattered, I wanted to get to bed myself, that I couldn't until
I'd cleared up and that I couldn't clear up if they were running
around the place. My daughter said, 'All right then'. And that
was that, no more running about past bedtime.
They were only three.
Julia P

Give warning Advance warning gives your child a chance to get used
to the idea of going to bed. How long this should be depends on the age
and temperament of the child – five minutes before bed is enough for
a young child, half an hour will give an older child time to finish whatever she is doing and have all the moans she wants.

Allow sufficient time Rushing at bedtime often backfires. Just an
extra 15 minutes can mean the difference between calm and hysteria.

Get a clock A child's concept of time may bear little relation to
reality. Show her where the clock hands are when it is time to get ready
for bed and where they are when it is time to go to sleep. Also show her
the time when you think it's OK for her to get up in the morning.

Help your child to let go Some children find it incredibly hard to go
to sleep. Sometimes cuddles and reassurance do the trick. Children who
seem lonely or frightened in their bedroom may fare better if they can
share a room with a sibling. Some children need help to relax.

I help her imagine herself somewhere relaxing. She lies down still, and I
tell her she's lying in a field of lavender, the sun is warm as a hug and a
soft breeze is blowing. Then she adds her own bits, like imagining she's
wearing a pair of heart sunglasses. Once what she calls 'the picture in her
eyelids' is just how she wants it, she's often calm enough to drift off.
Aileen M

Praise whenever you can Try to praise success rather than criticise
bad nights (see Encouraging positive behaviour, p.143).

Food and drink Does your child eat or drink anything before bed that may be making her unsettled? Cheese, chocolate, even fruit and raw vegetables before bedtime are known to disturb some children.

Understand bed-wetting This may be one very obvious reason why your child isn't settling at night. Many children aged four and up will still occasionally wet the bed. Encourage dry nights by praising them when they occur and try to discover if there has been any upset or change in routine that might have prompted the bed-wetting. There needn't have been – sometimes it just happens.

Nightmares and night terrors

*I can still remember details of nightmares I had as a very young child.
I was just so scared by them.*
David P

*You do have to be careful if you begin to break the bedtime routine significantly.
I know parents who have set up problems by changing routines, such as having to
sleep in the child's room on the floor with them. If you respond like this you are
almost saying you have got something to be afraid of. You are also breaking
down the routines and boundaries they need to feel safe whilst they are
experiencing ordinary fears. You could be putting them in freefall.*
Pat Elliot, psychotherapist and bereavement counsellor

Nightmares and night fears

A child's imagination can be a scary place, and a child's nightmares so vivid that memories of them linger well into adulthood. You may not be able to prevent them happening, but you can provide the comfort and reassurance your child needs to recover from them.

Nightmares tend to occur most in children over three, but can begin earlier. It makes sense to consider whether any change in your child's routine or circumstance may be upsetting her or even whether anything in the bedroom is making her anxious – children's imaginations can transform familiar objects into all sorts of dark and threatening creatures at night. But there may not be an identifiable cause.

When you do comfort your child, try not to deny her fear by saying 'Don't be silly' or 'Don't be afraid' because she is afraid and it is much better she can express that (see Dealing with feelings, p.94). Also try not to compound her fear by looking under the bed and behind the door to 'check the monster has gone'. Over-reacting – 'Oh! How terrifying! You must be frightened out of your wits! Let me cuddle you!' – could also make your child more fearful. She depends on you to be calm and in control of the situation.

If she insists on you looking behind the door or under the bed, you could explain that monsters exist in stories and imagination but not in real life, and that you are doing it to reassure her, not to reassure yourself. Tell her she is safe and you are near and try to gauge what else may help. Some children like a lighter room, some a much darker one that doesn't cast long shadows. Make it clear that you do not accept it is a real situation but you do accept it as a real fear.

My kids like to know what to do in the dream if it gets scary.
We've talked together about what dreams are and how imagination isn't real,
but also how they can use their imagination to help themselves. My son
likes to hold a magic kiss in his hand to protect him and my daughter
likes to know she can tell any imagined creepy things that her mum
will sort them out if they don't clear off. It makes her laugh
which takes the sting out of the fear a little.
Jane P

It helps to ask open questions, such as 'How are you? I heard you crying', rather than specific ones such as 'Did you have a nightmare?' or 'Are you thirsty?' as these can be auto-suggestive.

If your child has a nightmare and isn't fully awake, it may be kindest to simply soothe her and let her know you are there. She will, hopefully, drift back off to sleep and have no recollection of her bad dream in the morning. If your child is fully awake, try not to question her about it because the mere process of recollection may set it in her conscious memory. It is often best to allow her to forget.

Night terrors

A child having a night terror may appear to be awake, with her eyes open, but is actually having a nightmare. She may be shouting or even screaming, and unable to respond to anything you do or say because she cannot hear or see you. This can be terrifying for the parent as well as the child, yet there is little you can do other than soothe her if she will let you. Some children are even more alarmed by being comforted, almost as if the parent's actions become part of the nightmare. Be guided by your child's reactions and if she is disturbed by your efforts, wait until she calms down, then soothe her back to sleep.

Waiting is extremely hard, especially as the terror can last 30 minutes or more. But remember your child is terrified, not in control of her actions or of what she is saying, and probably won't recall a thing about it next morning. Getting angry or trying to shock her awake could frighten her more and make her hysterical, so try to keep calm, stay with her and comfort her when you can.

Serene (see Contacts, p.355) suggests that if a night terror occurs at approximately the same time each night, it may be worth trying to gently rouse the child 15 minutes before it would normally begin, then allowing her to drift back to sleep again. If this is done for several nights, the change in sleep cycles may stop the terrors occurring.

If you are concerned about the frequency and intensity of your child's nightmares or night terrors, contact your GP, health practitioner or health visitor, who may recommend specialist help.

It was the most frightening thing that's ever happened with my kids. My son used to wake up sometimes just screaming, shouting, 'Mummy, Mummy, Mummy,' obviously terrified. I would try to get him to talk to me, saying 'It's all right, Mummy's here,' but he never heard me. It was like a blind terror and I just couldn't reach him. Once I tried to shake him awake, and another time I tried to get him to snap out of it, being quite stern and saying, 'That's enough, Mummy's here, stop now.' But both times he went completely hysterical. I had no idea what it was and had never heard of night terrors. Once I found out that he was actually asleep, it helped me deal with it better. Now I just say 'I'm here' in a really quiet voice, and wait until he's ready to be comforted back to sleep.

Helen P

Sleep and you

Sometimes a mother's condition can be radically improved by restoring a single, critical need in her life that has been damaged subsequent to her baby's birth. In many cases the decisive factor is sleep. Sheer, unalleviated exhaustion is one of the most commonly experienced symptoms and the restoration of a regular and sufficient amount of sleep may produce a very significant improvement in a mother's condition, even when other symptoms such as depression and anxiety are present.

Simon James, The Association for Post-natal Illness

Most mothers of young children understand the joke – 'What do women want in bed? Eight hours.' But sleep is a serious issue. Go without what you need for too long and the consequences can be extremely damaging. The Association for Post-natal Illness recommends every new mother has at least one proper rest in bed every day until her baby is several weeks old. As your child grows, try to catch up on sleep when she sleeps, or ask your partner or a friend to babysit while you rest.

Your options are largely determined by your circumstances but try not to let your sleep slip from your list of priorities.

Sleep v. sex

A good night's sleep is more important than good sex, according to a survey conducted at 15 World Health Organisation centres around the world.[3] In the quality of life study, which involved almost 5,000 people in 15 different countries, sex was rated as one of the least important priorities. Way above it came the ability to carry out ordinary daily activities, energy, restful sleep and personal relationships. Professor Michael Power of Edinburgh University, who presented the data to the British Psychological Society, said: 'We were somewhat surprised by this finding.'

CHAPTER FOUR

FEEDING AND FOOD WARS

*Breastfeeding is something that affects you at a very deep,
very fundamental level, which is why it is so wonderful when it is
going well and so upsetting when it's not.*

Anna P

*The hardest thing is being understanding when they reject a meal
you have lovingly prepared. I find that really, really hard.*

Laura M

From first milk feeds to family meals, knowing what to expect and what to do if problems arise will help ease your concerns and keep battles over food to a minimum. This is an action plan for the present and an investment for the future.

Breastfeeding

*At birth all the baby's senses are co-ordinated around the mother's breast.
It is no coincidence that the distance the baby has clear vision is about
14 inches, and the distance from the mother's breast to her face is this distance.
It is nature's way of helping the bonding process.*

Peter Walker, yoga teacher and physical therapist

The evidence continues to increase that breast milk is best for your baby in the first four to six months of his life. As well as being the perfect food, it also contains antibodies to fight infection and provides protection against asthma, eczema and other allergic diseases. Its quantity

Breastfeeding facts

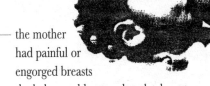

Breastfeeding is slowly on the increase in the UK and now stands at around 66% from birth (from 62% in 1990) and 14% at nine months old (from 11% in 1990). Yet we still have one of the lowest breastfeeding rates in Europe. More than 95% of Norwegian women, for example, breastfeed their babies at one week; 80% fully breastfeed at three months.[1]

Among women who give up breastfeeding within the first two weeks after birth in the UK, the most frequently mentioned reasons are:

— insufficient milk or that the baby seemed hungry

— the mother had painful or engorged breasts

— the baby would not suck or latch on to the breast[2]

As an inadequate milk supply is very rare and the other problems can usually be remedied relatively simply and quickly, it seems more women would continue to breastfeed if they had access to, or felt able to ask for, the advice and support they need.

and composition changes to meet your baby's changing needs, and it may even help in the introduction of solid food, as it can be flavoured by what the mother eats and thus familiarise the baby with a variety of tastes. Breastfeeding is also cheap, convenient and cuts down on the washing up. But it is not always easy.

The popular image of a breastfeeding mother is extremely potent and usually airbrushed, which can be guilt-inducing and frustrating when you feel less like Madonna and Child and more like Daisy the Cow. Many women give up after a short time because they have encountered difficulties and believe they must therefore be doing something wrong. The truth is that while a lot of mothers and babies take to breastfeeding easily, and most eventually find it a close and loving experience, many are surprised by the effort and energy it involves and find it a struggle at first. Knowing that this is not unusual may help more women stick with it.

Informed advice is readily available and may be all that is needed to make breastfeeding a happy, satisfying experience for mother and baby. The support of those around the mother is also hugely important – women whose partners strongly approve of breastfeeding are 33 times more likely to breastfeed than those whose partners don't.[3]

Patterns and balances

*I breastfed my first child in front of my mother-in-law and he was
still crying afterwards when she leant over him and said, 'Is your mummy
not feeding you properly?' I said to my husband 'Sort her out' and left the room.
The oldest and cruellest way to undermine a breastfeeding mother is to
wonder if the baby is 'getting enough'.*
Christine Chittick, NCT ante-natal teacher

The most successful way to encourage a predictable pattern of breastfeeding is to let your baby set the pace in the early weeks. If you let him
feed as often as he wants for as long as he wants, he will be getting what
he needs and, gradually, the gap between feeds should increase.

If the gaps aren't increasing, it may be that your baby delights in
comfort sucking and would quite happily stay snuggled up your jumper
for 24 hours a day. If you are happy that you have both got the hang of
breastfeeding, you might want to try giving him the comfort and closeness he craves without him suckling. Try carrying him round in a sling
for a while once he's had a good feed, or perhaps ask your partner or
trusted friend to carry him instead.

It can take three months or more for a predictable pattern to be
established. If pure demand feeding is working well for you, continue
for as long as you feel able and your circumstances allow. It's one hell of
an achievement and you have every right to be proud of it.

If, as time goes on, you are beginning to feel like you would kill for
another 20 minutes' sleep if only you had the energy, or if other
demands on you mean that you can't always feed the baby when he'd
like, it may be time to strike a balance between your baby's needs and
your own. Once feeding is established, you may want to give him occasional feeds before he gets hungry enough to demand one. This may be
before you attempt to sleep at night – feed him and he is less likely to
wake ten minutes after your head has touched the pillow.

If you are worried about producing enough milk, an occasional
bottle of formula milk will solve nothing as it may disturb your milk
supply. However, you could take a well-earned break and let someone
else give a bottle to your baby if you can express enough breast milk for
a feed. Every child is different, but a bottle used in this way seems to
cause least disruption to feeding patterns and meet with least resistance
if introduced after six weeks but before four months. The first six weeks

are considered crucial in establishing breastfeeding and a bottle before then may prove disruptive, but if you wait until after four months your baby is much more likely to refuse it.

I think it is helpful to occasionally get your partner involved, giving expressed breast milk in a bottle. It helps their relationship with the baby and helps you. If you are giving expressed breast milk it also gives the baby a gentler learning curve for going on to the bottle than if you were to introduce formula straight away if and when you decide to stop breastfeeding.
Paula Bell, health visitor

Common problems and solutions

Pain. Usually caused by the baby not latching on properly. If he sucks on the nipple alone he will get little milk and you will get sore. Hold him close and turn him so his chest is facing yours. Line your nipple to the top of his lips. Make sure he opens his mouth very wide (brush his lips with your nipple to get him to do this) and takes in not just the nipple but most of the areola (surrounding area).

Anxiety. Try breathing and other relaxation exercises (see Relaxation through breathing, p.34) before and during the feed.

Milk coming in late. This can occur when babies are born prematurely or by Caesarian section. Talk to your midwife and/or health visitor for information and support.

Baby struggling at the breast. Causes may include wrong positioning (see above); restricted breathing (make sure nose is free of the breast; if nose is blocked consult health visitor or GP); the force of the milk entering his mouth (try expressing a little before the feed).

Tight, lumpy or tender breasts. Firmly stroke affected area towards nipple while feeding to help unblock milk ducts. Don't stop breastfeeding as you need to drain milk away from any affected areas. Try a warm bath or soothe tender breasts with a flannel wrung out in warm or very cold water. If you develop flu-type symptoms, you may have an infection (mastitis) and should contact your GP.

If you have any concerns, consult your GP, local clinic, midwife or health visitor as soon as possible. Breastfeeding counselling services can also offer invaluable advice (see Contacts, p.355). Their advisors are expert, supportive and can sometimes arrange home visits.

Looking after yourself

If you are breastfeeding, it is extremely important that you have sufficient rest, food and peaceful time to feed your child. Rushing is counterproductive, as your baby will only need another feed sooner than if you took your time and allowed him to take his fill. Relax if and when you can. Remember this is an opportunity not only to nourish your child but to help him feel cherished and that there is rarely a better use of your time.

Feeding a baby can be draining. That's something that is rarely emphasised enough. If you don't take it on board you can push yourself too far, your milk will suffer, your baby sleep less, the more drained you will become and so it goes on. Mothers sometimes aren't very good at thinking of themselves, but you sometimes have to step back from the situation and see how important it is to look after yourself so you can look after your baby.
Careen H

Choosing to bottlefeed

Success in breast- or bottlefeeding will largely depend on how happy you are with the decision you have taken and how supported you are in that decision. It horrifies me that women can come to NCT mornings, hiding their use of a bottle and stuttering their way to justify their decision. Who are we to judge?
Christine Chittick, NCT ante-natal teacher

New mothers are constantly told two things: that breastfeeding is far superior to bottlefeeding for our babies and that 99.9% of women are able to breastfeed. This is a huge over-simplification. If you truly feel unable to breastfeed, or if you have tried breastfeeding and sought the advice you need and it still hasn't worked for you and your baby, then go with what feels right. Everybody's circumstances, needs and demands on them are different. A bottle and a happy mother seems a much better deal for all concerned than a breastfeeding, desperate, anxious or unhappy mother. If you are unsure of which route to take, it makes sense to try breastfeeding first and to seek any support and advice that may help.

Moving on to solids

*There is an important Hindu ceremony, Mook-e-bhat, when the
baby reaches six months and has her first taste of solids. It means 'rice
in the mouth', and in India it usually is their first taste of food because babies
there are breastfed for so long. Family and friends bring gifts and the baby
is dressed up – in her first sari, with a little golden crown and sandalwood
spots on her face if it's a girl. The ceremony is a very big deal, a rite
of passage to celebrate the fact that the baby has survived and is
now moving on to the next stage, taking food.*

Chitrita C

Some time between about four and six months your baby will probably
show he is ready to start solid foods, either by demanding more milk
feeds, remaining hungry after feeds, waking more in the night or all three.

Many mothers feel pride at their baby's first taste of food, others a
tinge of regret as their child becomes less dependent on them for
sustenance and turns from a suckling babe into Jackson Pollock in a bib.
It is, as many cultures recognise, a significant and symbolic step away
from infancy.

It is also a significant and symbolic step towards mess. As a society
we tend to encourage children to play with 'educational toys', and then
expect them to keep their fingers out of the mashed banana. This
seems a bit of a tall order. Your child will want to play with his food,
stick his fingers in it and smear it everywhere within reach. And within
reason (ie. up to the point you can stand), why not?

Your child's attitudes to feeding and food are influenced by your
reactions and his first experiences of it. To make the transition to solids
as stress-free as possible, it may help to remember that:

1   Babies soon learn the entertainment value of parental anxiety about
    what and how they eat. There is much you can do to avoid this (see
    Food wars, p.61).
2   Babies soon learn to use food as paint. There isn't much you can do
    to avoid this.
3   Your baby needs you to be relaxed and realistic about his eating more
    than he'll ever need your homemade papaya purée, so don't knock
    yourself out in pursuit of perfection.

If you offer a breast or bottlefeed after solids, the amount of food your baby takes should gradually increase over time and the amount of milk he takes gradually decrease. Some babies, however, especially those who get fretful without a breastfeed when hungry, might be more relaxed with a milk feed before solid food to begin with.

Introducing a variety of foods, say a new one every few days, will encourage your baby to enjoy a wide range of tastes.

What, when?

Paula Bell, health visitor

This is a cause of great anxiety to many parents, especially those with their first baby. Reassure yourself that there is not a lot you can do wrong. We have to empower parents with the confidence to use their own common sense, not to worry too much and to follow a few simple rules:

1:   Sterilise equipment until your baby is about six months of age. This will help ensure your child doesn't get an infection of the gut.
2:   Beware certain foods at certain ages (see below and Avoiding common allergies, p.60).

Try to wait at least 16 weeks before introducing solids, when your baby's kidneys and digestive tract are sufficiently mature to cope and his ability to use his tongue and swallow is sufficiently developed.

Some women and some babies are happy to fully breast- or bottlefeed up to six months, but by about this time the baby really needs to start using his chewing and swallowing reflexes. If you delay solid food beyond six months, your baby may have a less easy transition to solids when you do decide to introduce them.

First foods (4–6 months)

Move from sloppy to porridgy textures and purées.

You might include: Baby rice; fruit and vegetable purées.

Introduce foods one at a time. Mixing foods you know your baby has no problem with will often make meals easier to digest.

Avoid: giving cereal more than once a day; wheat products; milk other than breast or formula, even for mixing foods; eggs; citrus fruits; nut products.

Food refusal in babies

It's not worth spending a long time trying to encourage your weaning baby to take food – he will take it if he wants it. If you try to force him, the danger is that mealtimes will become a battle of wills. In the long run, you will be the loser, either because your child has discovered early that food refusal attracts attention, or because he associates eating with stress (see Food wars, p.61). Try to go at your child's pace, remember that a baby who turns his head away or holds his mouth

Six to 9 months

You may introduce lumpier textures. (Meat may need to be puréed to begin with.)

You might include: Lean meat; liver; lentils; white fish; eggs (well cooked); wheat products; milk products (yoghurt, cottage cheese, etc); finger foods (fruit, vegetables, bread, etc).

Milk: Cow's milk can now be used for mixing foods (breast or formula for milk feeds).

Drinks: From six months you can introduce a beaker or cup – offer water. (See Soft drinks, hard facts, p.68)

Iron: A baby's iron stores begin to run low from six to nine months. Ensure adequate iron intake with one serving of meat or fish a day and iron rich foods such as pulses and green vegetables. Vegetarian babies need two servings a day of alternatives such as grains, pulses and cereals. Vitamin C in fruit and vegetables increases the body's ability to store iron.

One year plus

You might include: Oily fish; cow's milk for drinking as well as cooking (most children over one need no more than 600ml of milk a day – more may affect their appetite).

It is best to introduce food containing nuts as late as possible; many experts recommend three years plus (see Avoiding common allergies, p.60).

By the end of the first year, your baby should be eating a good range of foods and, within reason, be having what the rest of the family eats. Support and help are available at the end of a telephone if you want to talk things through (health visitors may be contacted via your GP surgery or local health authority).

Avoiding common allergies

Most signs of allergy or intolerance to a particular food are evident within 24 to 48 hours of it first being introduced. Reactions can range from a very mild rash or a slight runny tummy, indicating that your child is not yet ready to take the food happily, to a true food allergy indicated by symptoms such as breathing problems, swelling of the lips and dramatic rashes. Such reactions are very rare.

If, however, there is a family history or sensitivity to particular foods, or of atopic conditions such as asthma and eczema, you may wish to proceed more cautiously in the introduction of foods.

'Timing is important,' explains early months specialist Ann Herreboudt. 'It is best to introduce one thing at a time for a few days at a time so you can have a clear view of how the baby is doing. There is a possibility that any of us can develop an allergy at any stage and, as the baby has never had banana or porridge in its stomach before, the risk of allergy seems to be higher.

'High risk foods include nuts [the government now recommends that children from families with allergic histories should not have peanut products until they are at least three and no child should be given whole peanuts until they are over five[4]], citrus fruit, eggs, strawberries, and shellfish. Each food should be watched, however.

'I have known babies allergic to potatoes, tomatoes and tap water. The very best thing to avoid problems is to introduce new foods gradually.'

---

tight shut has had enough, and that even young babies have likes and dislikes. Food refusal may also be a sign that your baby is feeling off colour (consult your GP, health visitor or medical practitioner if you are concerned).

Doing it for themselves

Your baby will show you when he's ready to start learning to feed himself, usually by grabbing the spoon. This is when the real mess starts.

Try to be relaxed, but if you find the mess hard to cope with, plan accordingly. This might stop you feeling overwhelmed, angry or resentful. It may help to have two bowls, one for your baby, one for you, and take full advantage of finger food. Try giving him only one or two pieces of food at a time, or giving him a small portion of something less messy while you deal with the runny, flickable stuff.

Food wars and how to avoid them

Eating can be a focus for conflict and tension at home and undermine the mother's confidence in performing one of the most basic tasks of motherhood, feeding the child.[5]

Jo Douglas, Consultant Clinical Psychologist, Department of Psychological Medicine, Hospital for Sick Children, Great Ormond Street

My dad's sausages are disgusting. They're the worst thing.
My favourite meal in the whole wide world would be prawn cocktail crisps followed by spaghetti with the red sauce, not the funny one, and ice cream with sweets stuck in the top and squirty chocolate sauce.
And apple crumble. And crisps.

Jemma, aged six

What our children eat is hugely important to their health and development and it takes much less parental effort to prepare good food for them than it does to deal with ill health and other consequences of a child's poor diet (see What's healthy?, p.66).

Yet preparing healthy, varied food doesn't mean your child is going to eat it. Most children go through phases of refusing certain foods. This is most common under five, but can occur at any age – a recent study found that children aged between three and 16 commonly had an 'arbitrary and despotic dislike of vegetables' and that many children only ate the recommended five portions of fruit and vegetables a day at Christmas.[6]

Food wars are a very common feature of family life. They can be fuelled by your child's early feeding experiences and their effects can spread to other aspects of your relationship and your child's behaviour. Yet it is possible to prevent them breaking out or to call a truce if the battle has already begun. The following points will help:

Realism Appetites vary between children, and even the same child's appetite may fluctuate wildly. Some children are simply pickier than others and this may be more a matter of temperament than bloody-mindedness (see Why children go 'Urggh'!, p.64).

Understanding your child's attitudes to food may not make life more predictable – what he liked last night may still be what he hates tomorrow – but it may make it a less likely cause of conflict between you.

One of my kids had an amazing appetite, one was picky but could
be gently coaxed into eating up, and the other one just shut his mouth and
would not eat what he didn't want. He was like that as a baby
and he's the same now. I was lucky he was third. If he'd
have been my first, I'd have panicked.
Jess T

Parental behaviour and children's eating habits

Your attitudes to food are an extremely powerful influence on your child's eating habits.

'Recent research[7] shows how mothers' concerns and behaviour at mealtimes influence their child's eating,' Dr Andrew Hill, psychologist at the Division of Psychiatry and Behavioural Sciences at Leeds University, explains. 'For example, a study of mothers with eating disorders and their 12-month-old babies found significant differences in how they interacted at mealtimes compared to other mothers. They were generally more intrusive and negative, and their infants were lighter.

'These interactions were filmed and make stunning viewing. The mothers seem to be both ambivalent about giving food and also find the whole ritual of mealtimes a fuss and a mess. There are examples where a child is literally force-fed and spits the food out, which upsets the mother who then cleans the child . . . basically both child and parent get more and more upset. Mealtimes, instead of being good fun and a time to communicate, turn into an adverse experience with neither mother nor child responding to the other's communication. This can inhibit the child's ability to learn self-regulatory skills around food.'

Keeping your cool

Children are beautiful behaviourists and far better at it than their parents,
so don't go into anxious overdrive if your child doesn't want what you've cooked
because your child will find great fun in watching your reaction and having your
concerned attention. I watch mothers, especially middle-class mothers, doing it
all the time; going into a long lecture to a healthy, robust five-year-old about
why they should eat peas. The child sits there thinking 'I don't understand a
word she's saying but I've got her attention'. Try saying, 'Fine, the rest
of us are having peas but you can go without.' It's a clear message,
they can get what they need from other foods and they'll probably
have peas again in six months' time.

Dr Gillian Harris, senior lecturer in Developmental Psychology, School of Psychology,
Birmingham University and Clinical Psychologist and Head of The Feeding Clinic,
The Children's Hospital, Birmingham

Keeping your cool is the key to minimising mealtime battles and largely depends on you not feeling incensed and/or hurt by your child's rejection of food. It may help to remember that it is your food that is being rejected, not you, and that food fads are a very normal part of growing up. Parents can only lose over food if they engage in a battle, and food refusal isn't half as much fun if your parent doesn't blow a gasket or give you their undivided attention as a consequence.

Try to gauge your reaction to your child's food refusal by his age and dietary needs. If a very young child rejects food, try offering something else in its place. It makes sense to offer savoury items first, or he will soon learn that making a fuss brings sweet things sooner.

If your child is old enough to have established the skills of eating and is generally healthy, yet refuses to eat certain items on his plate, try saying, 'OK, if you don't want it, don't eat it.' If he refuses to eat any more or even anything, calmly remove his plate. If he isn't hungry, it doesn't matter and if he is but is simply playing up, it will help you both in the long-term because he's much less likely to do it again.

Try to make mealtimes relaxed and low-key. Don't bother offering the rejected food again for a while as the child may consider this confrontational and reject it as a matter of course.

Introducing foods early The earlier a food is introduced, after four to six months of age, the more likely it is that your child will enjoy it (see What, when?, p.58).

A process takes place during the pre-school years, through which children decide what is food and what not (see Why children go Urrgh!, below). If they haven't eaten a food by about four years old, they won't have it in their food 'category' and are much more likely to reject it. This explains why children of four plus often turn their noses up at foods that are not exactly as their mother makes.

Understanding fads and rituals Food preferences and fads may become evident between one and two years old and can pop up without warning from then on. Some children decide they don't like 'mixed-up' foods, others don't like different foods touching on the plate, or want tomato sauce on the potato but never on the peas. How you react depends partly on how it affects your life – if the requests are simple and you are happy to oblige, fine; if you feel you are being given the run-

Why children go Urrgh!

Dr Gillian Harris, clinical specialist in children's feeding difficulties

'If I gave you a sheep's eyeball, you'd go urrgh! This is to do with the categorisation of foods, a process which occurs around three or four years old. By this time children have decided what is a food and what is not for them.

'That is why I like to get children into my clinic before four years old because after that their categories can become entrenched.

'Children also have different tempera-ments; some are easy and some are difficult around food. Think of Michael Palin in *Full Circle* eating strange fried things in strange places. There are some people who will do that, who will try everything, and some people who won't want to try anything other than the things they normally eat. It may be a matter of temperament which, comparatively speaking, is inherited, rather than the result of their parents bringing or not bringing certain child-rearing strategies into play.'

around and things are developing to ridiculous extremes, it's time to say no (see Keeping your cool, p.63).

Using alternatives and disguises If your child declares a pathological dislike of carrots, give him other vegetables next time. If he's off vegetables altogether try disguising them, perhaps liquidised in a pasta sauce. If he winces at the mention of milk, give him other dairy foods – yoghurts, cheese, custard.

As long as, over the space of a week, he eats different types of food (meat, fish or pulses; dairy foods; starchy foods; fruit and vegetables) he is likely to be getting what he needs. It does not matter much if he wants the same lunch day after day, as long as he gets the variety he needs overall.

Knowing he won't starve Offer your child the range of foods he needs (see What's healthy?, p.66), then worry less.

> *No healthy child ever starved itself to death. I usually have mothers say 'She doesn't eat a thing' and I say 'Write down everything that passes her lips for two weeks' and having done this they realise there is not a problem. Obviously if it is a very young baby and they are losing weight this is different. But most of the 'problems' and anxieties are around toddlers who are fit, healthy and growing yet 'don't eat'.*
> Carol Ann Hally, health visitor and clinical practice teacher

Offering small portions Large portions may overwhelm a child by the sheer enormity of the task ahead.

Treats and chores If you give food as a treat, a reward or a bribe it will go up in your child's estimation, because it is generally withheld and therefore considered special.

We reinforce differences between 'treats' and 'chores' without even thinking about it. 'Eat up your broccoli then I'll let you have your pudding' is a trap most parents fall into occasionally, and when was the last time you saw a parent give a child a carrot for keeping quiet in the supermarket? We reap what we sow.

Consider the example of children with cystic fibrosis who were asked to list their favourite foods.[8] They require a high calorie diet, so parents tend not to offer salads and to encourage Mars Bars etc. Topping their list of favourites were cucumber and lettuce and chocolate came near the bottom. The food that was withheld or discouraged

---

What's healthy?

Our desire for our children to eat well has, ironically, led to many well-meaning, health-conscious parents giving their children completely inappropriate adult 'health' foods.

One recent survey in Newcastle found that the highest total cases of children failing to thrive occurred in the poorest social groups, but the second highest was among top income families[9] – a phenomenon researchers have dubbed 'muesli-belt malnutrition'.

A growing child needs plenty of protein and higher levels of fat, sugar and carbohydrate than an adult. No-fat and low-fat foods, including skimmed milk and low-fat yoghurts, are not suitable for the under-fives (the Department of Health advises that semi-skimmed can be given after the age of two only if the child has a varied and full diet).

Added fibre or high-fibre cereals such as bran can compromise a child's vitamin intake because of the problems they have absorbing fibre in the bowel, while natural sugars are more suitable for babies and young children than chemical sugar substitutes found in many low- or no-sugar foods and drinks.

Most young children in the UK are growing well and are not short of nutrients. In recent studies[10], the most common problems found in pre-school children were:

— **Insufficient iron** (10% of those surveyed). Iron is found in meat, green vegetables and pulses, as well as more commonly child-favoured foods such as fortified breakfast cereals and bread
— **Low zinc levels** (14% of those surveyed). Zinc is found in cheese, eggs and bread as well as fruit, vegetables and nuts

With this range of foods to choose from, it should be possible to provide what a child needs without too much difficulty or resistance.

had become desirable and things they were most encouraged to eat were the things they didn't want.

For this reason, treat bans with care. It may help to think in terms of good or bad diet rather than good or bad food. The occasional portion of chips, chocolate or packet of crisps is OK if the general diet is good, and much less likely to do harm than making food a battleground.

Sticking to deals Some children do need coaxing to take a few more mouthfuls. If yours is one of them, avoid connecting the last bites of one dish with the imminent arrival of the next – 'two more mouthfuls then you're done' is storing up less trouble than 'two more mouthfuls then you can have your ice cream' (see Treats and chores, p.65).

Stick to your side of the bargain. If your child takes the mouthfuls don't then up the stakes by requesting a few more – a deal is a deal. Also be willing to accept and respect your child's right to eat when hungry and stop eating when full.

Letting children help Letting your child help prepare food, set the table, pour the drinks, may help diffuse mealtime tensions as he will feel part of the process rather than at the receiving end of it.

Offering choices Be wary of offering choices to very young children – some find decision-making hard and the choice between fish fingers or pasta too traumatic to contemplate calmly.

Yet choices can help older children feel they have some control over what they eat. Try offering a choice rather than a question with an open-ended outcome – 'Do you want baked potatoes or pasta?' is more likely to result in a reply you are happy with than 'What do you want to eat?'

Are they hungry? A child won't eat a meal unless he is hungry enough to want it. This might involve reducing snacks, giving your child a run-around before teatime or cutting back on squash and juice (see Soft drinks, hard facts, p.68).

Children's appetites can be re-educated to expect food at different times of the day if the process is done gradually over three or more weeks, so if your child is snacking but not eating meals it may be worth slowly reducing the amount he has between mealtimes.

Young children who are still drinking large quantities of milk may need these reduced if their need for solids isn't to be compromised (a pint a day is recommended for children aged five years and under[11]).

Soft drinks, hard facts

Squash and other soft drinks may damage children's health and appetite. One study,[12] by doctors at Southampton, found that 15% of two- to four-year-olds were getting nearly half their recommended daily energy intake from soft drinks, and that this was disrupting the normal development of hunger between meals.

The study was initiated after doctors reported growing numbers of children displaying similar symptoms – loss of appetite, diarrhoea, stomach pains and misbehaviour at mealtimes. The researchers have dubbed this 'Squash Drinking Syndrome', where the high sugar content of soft drinks stops children feeling hungry. Parents of children in the study reported frequent disputes at mealtimes because their children refused to eat.

Consumption of soft drinks by children under five is estimated to have doubled in the past 15 years, and expensive squashes and fruit juices were as problematic as cheaper squashes, the report stated. One of the researchers, Dr Chris Rolles, explained: 'Calories in fruit drinks are empty calories . . . If these children are getting half their calories from fruit drinks, they will miss out on the vitamins, protein, fats, calcium and minerals they need to build bones and muscles.'

The study also showed how consumption of water has plummeted in recent years – 72% of two- to four-year-olds and 50% of five- to seven year-olds surveyed drank no plain water at all. Parents were advised to gradually dilute squash or juice over time until the child was taking it very weak or, preferably, not at all.

Don't force it Forcing a child to eat, by making him sit at the table until he's cleared his plate or by threatening to punish or withdraw treats, is about the least helpful thing a parent can do (see Encouraging positive behaviour, p.143).

I don't believe in giving a child what they don't like because when we talk to adults about their memories of eating they can remember exactly the colour of the wallpaper when they were forced to eat mushy peas, liver or whatever. It is so traumatic and achieves so little, why do it?
Dr Gillian Harris, clinical specialist in children's feeding difficulties

Don't mention diets

Dr Gillian Harris, clinical specialist in children's feeding difficulties

'There is so much anxiety about healthy diet in this country that you have more people worrying about eating than eating too much. In a massive trawl of schools around Birmingham, we found more children failing to thrive than obese.

'I wouldn't mention the word diet to anyone under the age of 32! You shouldn't put children on diets at all, but rather increase their exercise. If you think your child is becoming tubby, you can do two things: the whole family can switch to semi-skimmed milk or cut down fat if the child is old enough (over five), and you could start a family exercise programme in which you all go for a walk, you all get on a bike, you all get fit. What you don't do is start reducing the child's calories, because they will get very miserable and anxious about food and it is not going to work'.

CHAPTER FIVE

COMMUNICATION

Listen to them: children are worthy of being heard. Try and help them find the right words to express their needs. Children are never too young for adults to start really talking to them and listening.

Stella Ward, nurse and Parent Network co-ordinator

Children should be consulted and their views respected. In terms of a child's needs and welfare I think listening is the lynchpin of parenting. If you don't make time to listen there is little hope of other communication, especially as they grow older.

Eileen Hayes, Parenting Advisor to the NSPCC

If you are able to talk and listen to your child and she is able to talk and listen to you, your relationship can grow into one of mutual understanding, respect and consideration. Good communication helps children and parents express their needs effectively, which in turn will help you both avoid potential problems and untangle those that do arise.

Sounds simple? Try telling that to anyone who has ached for their child to tell them what's troubling them or who has experienced the table-chewing frustration of children's selective perception (ie their ears stop working when their parents speak – an extraordinarily common phenomenon).

Railing against your parents and grunting monosyllabic replies are part of growing up, after all – very young children do it, school-age children do it, adolescents do it. Poor communication and simple misunderstandings have been the root of international conflict so it is hardly surprising that they can also cause friction at home. Words are complicated things, especially for relative beginners.

Yet you can help your child talk to you when she needs to, and listen when you have something important to say. This is what matters most.

First words and conversations

It is vital that children acquire speech, and good for their overall
development and relationships to do so comparatively early, but the child
who acquires words first is not necessarily the one who is going to
have the most interesting things to say later, nor is the child
whose speech is delayed necessarily 'backward'.[1]
The Commission on Children and Violence

New research on language development sheds much light on how children learn to talk and how parents can best help in this process. Encouraging your child's competence and confidence with words is not only important for your own relationship but, as she grows, will also play a crucial role in her behaviour, schooling and social skills. The benefits of this could be life-long, but the foundations are laid in infancy.

Interacting with your baby A parent's eye contact and responses to a new baby's sounds and movements are all vital precursors to speech (see Communicating with your baby, p.9).

Keep talking

Talk a lot – it's really important. If you get used to chatting a lot to a
small baby you tend to set up a communication channel that continues.
Some people wait until the baby can talk back – it's a bit late by then.
Dr Sally Ward, specialist paediatric speech and language therapist

Talk to your baby as often as you can – about all and anything. Describe what you are doing and why, explain that you need a cup of tea more than you need to do the shopping, or even why today you are too tired to string a coherent sentence together. Where possible, let your child set the agenda and try to talk about what she is doing and what she is interested in. If she is playing with the saucepan or a rattle there is little point in you talking about the bird outside the window because she will not be taking in the information you are giving her.

Even very young babies enjoy songs, rhymes and finger games,

Talking parentese

Babies and young children have difficulty figuring out meanings in long, adult sentences. Talking very simply, repeating words and emphasising sounds helps them isolate, identify and understand important words more easily. This can begin as soon as your child begins to understand her first words.

The aim is not to make the words sound 'cute', although this is sometimes the by-product and why some parents have such difficulty with it. Understanding the reasoning behind it may make it a little easier. Saying horsy or doggy, for example, emphasises the 's' and 'g' sound for the child to hear and repeat.

Focusing on individual words – 'spoon' instead of 'Look, here's your spoon, let's put it in your hand, well done' – helps your child identify and name objects much more easily.

Dr Sally Ward, a specialist paediatric speech and language therapist, explains:

'Parentese is very, very important. When you have a very small baby that you know isn't understanding your words, the natural thing is just to chat and tell the baby what you're doing, as you do it, for example "I'm putting washing in here". But when the adult perceives the child is beginning to understand the words, around eight or nine months, then mothers tend to modify the way they speak. At this point, you don't continue to speak in long sentences but use much shorter utterances, for instance "It's a cup, a cup". Mothers will speak slower and louder, hopefully, with lots of repetition.

'Basically you are helping the child map the meaning on to the words. If that modification of how the parent speaks doesn't happen, if the parent speaks to the child as they would to a much older child or an adult, then it causes big problems. Children have a lot of difficulty then figuring out what we mean.'

which all increase the richness of their linguistic experience (see Play and learning, p.275). It also helps your child to make a sound if she can see how you make it. Get down to her level or bring her up to yours to play and chat when you can.

Modifying your speech Once your child begins to understand words it is important to stop using the long sentences of adult conversation but to adapt your speech more to your child's level. Many mothers do this instinctively, some find it very hard to understand and even harder to do, yet the importance of 'parentese' or babytalk is one of the most significant recent shifts in the understanding of speech development (see Talking parentese, opposite).

Keeping just one step ahead In most areas of development, parents can encourage children most effectively by working with them at their level of ability. Speech seems to be different, however. Research suggests that children are encouraged most when parents pitch their verbal responses just one step ahead of the child's level.

If your child is not yet saying words, use single, simple words and repetition to encourage her; when she is confident in saying single words, link two together ('more milk', 'Jenny's toy' etc); when she is saying two together, link three ('put it here', 'big, red tractor' etc).

If your three-year-old is talking in complete complex sentences, you can talk back like that; if they are at the 3-4 word utterance level, you need to respond at the 4-5 word level to help them move on.

Dr Sally Ward, specialist paediatric speech and language therapist

Minding your body language

Non-verbal communication is the language of an infant.
A pre-verbal child responds more to the music of the words and to the expression than to words themselves. Even later when there is language, non-verbal communication normally still carries most of the impact. The meaning of the words will be interpreted by the sound of the voice and facial expression. It is rather like watching a film with different music tracks. The same visual can carry very different meanings with different music, be it frightening, relaxing or whatever.
The visual and audio messages override the verbal.

John Bristow, psychologist and psychotherapist

It's not just what you say but how you say it that matters (see Communicating with your baby, p.9). How else is your young child going to know not to touch something hot unless you screw up your face and suck, saying 'Ooch, hot!'? The word 'hot' will mean nothing, but your gestures and tone of voice tell the story and teach the meaning.

The importance of non-verbal communication in any relationship is well established – only about 7% of what we express as adults is communicated through words, the rest is through tone of voice, inflection and other sounds (38%) and body language and facial expression (55%)[2]. Just as you are receptive to your child's non-verbal messages, so you will use a whole raft of gestures, expressions and exaggerations to get your message across, emphasise a point or engage your child's attention – smiling, frowning, looking surprised, changing the pitch, tone and volume of your voice and so on.

Sharing books Books are hugely helpful in developing a child's linguistic skills and vocabulary from a very early age, but the key to using them most successfully is to choose ones that are not too far in advance of the child's age and ability.

I think we are all in danger of introducing things much too early. Good books for young children are very repetitive and about their life or environment, about the world as they know it.

Dr Sally Ward, specialist paediatric speech and language therapist

Turning it off Recent research has come to some frightening conclusions about the effect of our lifestyle on children's language development. The implications are enormous but the remedy is quite simple – if you want your child to learn to communicate as and when she should, you must allow her times without the background noise of television, CDs, radio and so on (see Quiet times, opposite).

Slowing down Just as it is important to leave spaces for a very young baby to echo back sounds (see Communicating with your baby, p.9), so it is important to give a child of any age a chance to respond. If she can't get a word in edgeways, she may give up trying.

Avoiding constant questions Otherwise known as the 'What's this? What's that?' trap. Your child will learn much more if you tell her what it is even if you think she knows already.

Some children I meet can only say 'What's this?' because that's about all they have heard. It is far more helpful to tell them, because even if they know the word they need to hear it many many times in order to recall it well enough to say it.

Dr Sally Ward, specialist paediatric speech and language therapist

Quiet times

A 10-year research project by Dr Sally Ward for the Central Manchester Healthcare Trust[3] found that children from homes with constant noise from TV, music or radio took longer to learn to talk.

The incidence of pre-school children with listening and attention problems which delayed their language development doubled to one in five between 1984 and 1990, according to her findings. Dr Ward linked this to the increase in background noise in babies' crucial first year of life and to the introduction of daytime television and videos for older children.

Dr Ward explains: 'The figures are really scary. I went into nearly 400 homes of one-year-olds and discovered that 89% of them had constant background noise, and I mean constant. It was mostly the telly, and in a few instances music or radio. In some homes everyone was watching the television, the furniture was in a row like a cinema, and some places it was even dark, and the infant would be in the corner of the sofa.

'The babies weren't actually watching but their attention would be attracted if something happened visually, a change of colour, a flicker or a sound so it was very definitely having an effect on their attention to anything else.

'The development of selective attention, the ability to focus on a sound and tune out background noise, is absolutely critical to speech development. It normally happens in the second half of the first year, but with huge amounts of noise it doesn't happen. Another precursor to speech is the parent responding to sounds the baby makes, which can be drowned out by TV. This is one of the most important reasons for having quiet times.

'I think that there have been profound cultural changes within people's homes over the last 20 years. People have not realised the deleterious effects. Of course, watching videos is the most wonderful babysitter if you want to get on with something else, but within reason, because they interrupt children's enjoyment and experience of the interaction of language. Last week I had a barrister mother who asked me if the fact that her child watched six hours of video per day had an effect on her speech!

'By the time children have language, around three years, watching time could possibly be up to an hour a day if the programmes are carefully selected and, preferably, the carer watches and talks about the programme with the child. I certainly wouldn't recommend any more than 30 minutes to an hour a day for a pre-school child.'

Getting Help

I do think developmental checks are a useful way of picking up if there are any areas where a child might benefit from help. There is no question that the vast majority of children fall in the 'normal' range, which is very wide — for a two-year-old, for example, 'normal' would be a vocabulary of anywhere between 20 and 200 words.

Sarah Darton, health visitor

If you are concerned about your child's speech, your health visitor can refer you to a speech therapist for assessment and further help if necessary. Early intervention is very effective in turning around language development problems in children. Paediatric speech and language therapist Dr Sally Ward found that talking to a baby or young child for half an hour a day, every day, preferably one-to-one in quiet surroundings, made 'a colossal difference to their speech and language abilities'.

Avoiding correction Reinforce your child's confidence with a positive statement (see Accentuate the positive, p.152) to show that you have understood what she is trying to tell you and also to teach her how to say a word correctly. Your child is desperate to please you and keen to learn. Think of these two examples from her point of view and imagine which would inspire her most to keep trying to get it right:

> *Child:* 'Dup.'
> *Parent:* 'No, not dup. Cup. Cup.'
> or
> *Child:* 'Dup.'
> *Parent:* 'Yes! Cup, cup.'

With older children, it often helps to echo back mistakes correctly. They get the message, but they do not feel criticised. This can be key to keeping communication going between you.

> *Child:* 'Miss Shones said I had to bring vis back tomorrow.'
> *Parent:* 'Miss Jones said you had to bring this back? OK.'

Have fun Words and sounds make children laugh, and encouraging delight and confidence in language and expression can do nothing but good. Your child will enjoy fun for fun's sake and shared pleasure is healthy in any relationship, so find the time to join in when you can.

> *My daughter had one word that made her collapse in giggles from about two and a half. It was 'seaweed'. She'd say 'seaweeeeeeeed' and fall about laughing.*
> Joanne H

Encouraging your child to talk to you

> *I am incredibly passionate about the importance of a child being able to talk to somebody. If children learn from an early age the ability to talk to someone I think this is the foundation of emotional well-being.*
> Camila Batmanghelidjha, psychotherapist and Director of Kid's Company, a charity providing caring adults to listen to children in their school or home

> *The main benefits of listening to our children is that it is fun and you get to know them as people.*
> Dr Sally Ward, specialist paediatric speech and language therapist

As your child grows, good talking and listening skills will be key to your relationship. Without them, communication channels may begin to close – which is when problems can escalate beyond an easy point of return. Such problems may be easier to notice when children hit adolescence but most have their roots early in a child's life.

All the following skills and approaches will help you encourage your child to talk. Some are adapted from techniques used by professionals to help children 'open up'. Others are straightforward tips and pointers that parents and professionals alike have found useful. But for any of them to be effective, your child has to believe that you want to listen to what she has to say.

Seizing the moment

It is so important to be emotionally available for our children and by that I mean being around in a peaceful and responsive way. You can be certain the most important piece of information comes when you least expect it, not when you schedule 'a talk'.

Adrienne Katz, author and researcher

Making time to talk is important, but don't expect this to be at your convenience. Life is rarely that neat. Your child is too young to understand the varied demands on a parent's time and is just as likely to need to tell you something as you're about to fly out of the door or take the dinner out of the oven. Try to keep your 'antennae' up for any signals that she wants to talk, take her lead and, whenever possible, listen.

This means giving your child your full attention. Think of it from her point of view. If you were trying to share something important with a person who was doing something else at the same time – answering the phone, cooking, shouting at the dog, telling another child to put their coat on – you would probably feel unheard. You might lose your thread and would probably stop sharing and disclosing even if you managed to keep talking. If you do want to do something else at the same time, try to make it something you can do together (see 'Sideways' talk, below) and focus on what she is saying.

If it is not possible to listen at that moment, say so:

'I'm so tired/rushed I don't think I'll be good at listening right now, but I really want to. Can we have a cuddle and a chat at bedtime when I can listen better?'

or

'I want to listen to this, it's important to you. Let me just finish this then I'll be able to listen to you properly.'

A deal is a deal, so give her the time she needs as soon as you are able.

'Sideways' talk

Often parents want to talk about the burning issue when children are not able or ready. When children reject the offer to talk, parents can get frustrated and annoyed which makes the child close up further. Using different ways to approach the subject can help. It is often a question of being available and not forcing the issue. Often in therapy I find it useful to have an outside focus, to be doing something together with the child so you have 'sideways' talk at the same time. A lot of eye contact can be too intimidating – waiting and listening for openings is the most important skill.

Jim Wilson, family therapist, Cardiff Institute of Family Therapy, Barnardos

Some children find face-to-face conversation too intense, especially if they have something difficult or uncomfortable to say. If you are worried that something is troubling your child, or if you have had a conversation along the lines of:

Parent: 'How did it go today?'
Child: 'Fine.'
Parent: 'It doesn't look like you're fine.'
Child: 'Well I am!'

try doing something together: cooking, going on a trip, playing football, plaiting her hair, anything that reduces the intensity of the situation. This will give you a valid reason for being together, and will allow you to bring up the subject lightly and skilfully. Or it may enable your child to relax sufficiently to bring up the subject herself.

If you have more than one child vying for your attention, it may help to allocate each child a little time every day to do some activity together – reading, playing, pottering about outside, anything that means each has your undivided, relaxed attention. Even ten minutes a day may work wonders. For the child who isn't being focused on at the time, it helps to set up something to do – paper ripping, drawing, pretend cooking – whatever it takes for them to feel treated rather than ignored.

There are many fun things you can do as a parent to encourage your child to open up and talk things through. You can even have a special place in the house where you both sit to talk, having special mealtimes where you can both go under the table in a tent, creating a place. It is so often difficult for children to talk because an adult is looking at them and asking or demanding them to. It comes down to spending time and doing things with them – making a cake, doing washing up, painting. Whatever you are doing the focus is on something else, something enjoyable and that has a way of cutting down the tension.

Camila Batmanghelidjha, psychotherapist, Director of Kid's Company.

Are you listening to me?

According to research by Prof. Philip Zimbardo, an American psychologist of Stanford University, presented to the British Psychological Society in 1997, working parents spend an average of just eight minutes a day talking to their offspring 'but it isn't even meaningful talk – it is mostly them giving commands to the children'.

In an NSPCC survey of 1,000 children and young people, most respondents believed adults in general did not listen to what they had to say. Most children said they had at least one person to talk to when they had worries or problems, and mothers were overwhelmingly the most popular confidantes. However 22% of younger children in the survey felt they had no one they could turn to.[4]

Let your child tell you anything

Be tellable. Your children need to be able to tell you anything and know it won't get them into more trouble than they are already in.
Steve Biddulph, psychologist and author

There were things in my growing up that I could never have told my mum and dad, not because I thought they'd be angry but because I thought they'd be so upset, so disappointed that my childhood and adolescence weren't as happy as they'd hoped or that I wasn't who they thought or hoped I was. So I kept a lot to myself.
Chrissy M

Your child needs to know you will listen, however uncomfortable you find what she is saying. For our own peace of mind, our children's safety and the richness and honesty of our relationships, children need to be able to describe their thoughts and experiences and we need to be able to listen to them.

This is not the same as agreeing with or approving of what you hear, and it does not mean you won't want to do anything about it. But it does mean that you shouldn't do anything at that moment. That moment is for listening and for listening only, not jumping to conclusions or pronouncing judgements. Do that and the child may stop talking. And often the most important things for our children to tell us are the hardest things for them to say.

Think back to the way you communicated with your own parents. Did you feel that they listened to you and that you were able to express anything that worried, concerned or even interested you? Were there reasons why you did not tell them more? Was it to avoid disapproval? Punishment? Disinterest? Humiliation? Did you do it to protect them because you thought they would be unable to cope? Or be disappointed? Or value you less?

The key skill for getting a child to talk is listening in a very non-judgemental way. If you are going to listen you are actually saying to the child that they can tell you negative things as well as positive, otherwise it cannot be an honest and full dialogue. Otherwise it is like tricking the child, saying 'I want to listen to you but I do not want you to say anything that is upsetting to me'.
Camila Batmanghelidjha, psychotherapist, Director of Kid's Company

Resist interrupting

Try to listen to all your child has to say. This involves putting aside your needs for the moment, even those inspired by the best of intentions – ie. your need to interrupt to express how you feel, to get more information, to give advice, to make it 'better', to pass judgement, to finish that half-completed sentence.

Once your child trusts she has your full attention, gaps and silences in her conversation can actually help her order her thoughts, become clearer and calmer and thus put things in perspective. If you do fill them with your words, try to ensure it is because you are responding to her tension and not your own.

Parents are often so anxious about correcting their children's behaviour or having a 'good' child that often they push essential information and communication underground. Listening is not to say we approve of everything children do, but listening time isn't the time to step in and correct. Behaviour education can come later. This keeps the channels of communication more open. Often we do not listen to our children because we cannot bear to hear, especially if they are in pain.
Camila Batmanghelidjha, psychotherapist, Director of Kid's Company

Ease the pressure

Vivienne Gross, Clinical Director of the Institute of Family Therapy

'I think car rides are wonderful. You can talk about things – with the environment flashing by – with a lot less intensity and the child might appreciate that.

'Don't just sit children down in a room eyeball to eyeball and say, "Dad and I have been thinking, we need to get close to you right now". You don't want to leave them with a feeling of no escape, or they may stop listening and talking altogether. Little children actually put their hands over their ears if they don't want to hear something. Older children may not use their hands but they may still stop listening if the conversation feels over-intense. You may have to come up with different ways of getting a message across. Reading books together and other "slightly to one side" ways of talking can be very effective.

'It is not a matter of doing either one thing or the other, but actually paying attention to what you all feel is right. It can be that a child almost floats off, that you realise three weeks have gone by and you haven't a clue what they've been doing at school or whatever, and that you have actually lost your focus on them because there's been so much other stuff happening. You can sort that out by having a relaxed chat in a relaxed situation without being too deliberate or intense about it.'

Use open questions and statements

We generally ask questions for our own curiosity – 'Was Rachel there?' – or to pass judgement – 'Why did you do that?' If you genuinely need more information to understand or to encourage your child to continue talking, it helps to ask 'open' rather than 'closed' questions. Consider which of the following are likely to elicit a longer reply:

> Open question: 'Anything interesting happen today?'
> *or*
> Closed question: 'Good day at school?'

You can also feed back incomplete statements, leaving a gap to encourage your child to continue: 'You said John was mean to you . . .'

Show your child you are listening

*If I'm cooking and Josie wants me to read a book, she may
say 'Mummy, Mummy' and pull at me a bit, or whine. If I get down
to her level and either ask her what she wants or show her I understand
and acknowledge how she feels by saying something like 'I know you would
like me to read that book right now and I can't because I'm cooking dinner'
she is much more likely to be OK about it than if I try to ignore her or
tell her to get off my leg. It is a matter of acknowledging and
respecting their needs while also asserting your own at that moment.
And you can only work out what they need if you listen.*

Stella Ward, nurse and Parent Network co-ordinator

*We argued every single morning about getting ready on time.
I would go crazy because I felt he was stalling on purpose. Then one
morning, he said he didn't like school and instead of saying the usual 'Of
course you do' or 'We all have to do things we don't like doing' or 'It will get
better', I just said 'Really?' It was hard to resist the temptation to say more,
but I didn't. After a short while he said his friends all wore blazers and he
didn't. I asked him how that made him feel and he said 'stupid'. All that
time we'd been arguing and I hadn't known the root of the problem.*

Helen S

Pitch your responses appropriately. If you are having a chat with your child about something not particularly serious, you can respond to show you have heard what she is saying but you don't have to drop everything. The world does not and should not revolve around your child every minute of the day.

If, however, your child seems to want to talk more seriously, or if you haven't had a good talk for too long, your attention should focus on her, and she should know your are listening. You can signal that she has your attention by:

Looking at her while she is talking Eye contact can show that you are interested in what your child has to say, but it has to be comfortable for both of you (see 'Sideways' talk, p.78). Should she need it, make yourself available for relaxed eye contact by being close to her, on her level and looking in her direction, rather than crawling over the furniture to catch your child's gaze.

Responding so your child knows you understand what she is saying Simple, low-key responses can be clear but unobtrusive enough not to interrupt your child's train of thought or flow of speech. They can be non-verbal, such as gestures and facial expressions to show you have understood what she is saying, or verbal, such as 'Really', 'Uh-huh', 'Sounds scary'.

Reflective listening

I see listening as the foundation of close relationships and understanding in families on which all other things are built.

Doro Marden, Chair of Parent Network Executive Committee
and Parent Network co-ordinator

At its worst, he'd stop talking altogether and just shout 'Aaarrrghh' at me when he was angry and storm off. He'd just turned six and this had been going on for ages, these temper outbursts. I tried to talk to him, but after a while you just give up, don't you? There's only so much of your life you can spend trying to communicate with a caveman. Then I tried reflective listening, didn't say anything until he'd stopped shouting then said something like 'You sound really angry'. There was a pause and he shouted back, 'I AM.' I couldn't think of anything else to say so I just said 'Really angry . . . Poor you. That must feel bad,' and he crumpled. I can't remember the last time he'd let me hold him when he was upset like that.

Melanie M

This is one of the master skills of communication. It is frequently used by family therapists and other professionals but it can be learned by any parent keen to encourage better family communication. It is just as effective with surly adolescents and grumbling partners as it is with young children.

Reflective listening takes time and energy to practise to a point where you feel comfortable. Time and energy are what most parents don't have much of, but stick with it if you can (see Shock of the new, p.88). Put most simply, it involves repeating or 'reflecting' back to a child what she has said to you, so she knows that you have been listening and that you understand.

Watch out for communication traps

The key to getting children to talk is to listen. Some parents are very good listeners. Some think they are listening when they are not. It may help to check that you are not doing something else instead, such as:

Advising 'Lucy wouldn't let me play with her today.' 'I'd take no notice if I were you. Go and play with Polly tomorrow instead.'

Criticising 'Joe took my key-ring and lied and said it was his and Mrs May believed him!' 'Well I told you not to take it to school.'

Dismissing 'Emily broke my shell.' 'Oh, it doesn't matter. We can always get another one when we go on holiday.'

Correcting 'It wasn't fair at lunch time. You are always nicer to Jason.' 'You mean tea time.'

Ignoring 'I need Daddy to take me to football on Sunday.' 'Would you help Lucy with that balloon.'

Distracting 'I've not been picked for the school play and everyone else is in it.' 'Come and look what I got you today, that will take your mind off it.'

Reassuring 'I'm scared of the monsters in my room.' 'There's no need to be scared.'

Praising 'I hate him playing with my toys.' 'Oh, you don't mind, you're such a good big brother.'

Most parents do all of these from time to time, but none of them involve real listening and none will reap the same results. They are used most when parents have run out of patience or time, because they can be very effective at stopping a child talking. Listening has the opposite aim – to encourage a child to talk.

But first a word of warning – this is a technique to use sparingly. It is only really useful when your child needs some help to work out how she is feeling or what has happened to her. Use it in everyday conversations, exchanges and situations and you risk making a drama out of a crisis and sounding like a wally:

Child: 'Mum. Take Charlotte into the other room.'
Parent: (Trying to reflect her child's feelings) 'Take Charlotte away? Sounds like you're finding it hard to be with her right now.'
Child: 'No. She's just standing in front of the telly!'

Observe your child and her situation, so you know when reflective listening is appropriate. Sometimes your child will be helped to talk most by your silence; sometimes, especially if she seems to be struggling or stuck and needs help to keep talking, she needs some expert help from you.

When circumstances are right for you both (times when you are very tired or rushed are best avoided), what you 'reflect' back can be split into two key elements – the meaning and content of what your child has said and the underlying feeling she has expressed.

Reflecting back your child's words Repeat back what your child has said, briefly and simply, so she knows you understand. At its simplest level, this involves you feeding back your child's own words, adding no personal comments, observations or judgements.

> *Child:* 'I got told off today.'
> *Parent:* 'You got told off?'
> *Child:* 'Yes. And it wasn't my fault . . . I told Miss James we were playing not fighting but she didn't believe me.'
> *Parent:* 'Oh.'
> *Child:* 'No. And . . .'

True reflective listening is one step up from this, and requires the parent to summarise, in their own words, the gist of what the child has said. It may feel like stating the obvious, but it shows you have listened and understood. This can make things clearer in your child's mind, help her focus on what is troubling her and move on.

> *Child:* 'Katie said I wasn't her friend any more. She said I had silly hair and my teddy had a silly name and my bike was silly.'
> *Parent:* 'Katie was unkind to you.'

Listening in this way passes no judgement upon the teller and so encourages children to tell us what is really going on, not what they think we want to hear. It also gives them a sense that their view of a situation is recognised and acknowledged. To a child in pain or crisis, this can feel like a lifeline.

Feeding back the underlying feelings At the same time as summarising your child's words, you can briefly describe the feelings you think she may be experiencing. The above example, for instance, could continue something along the lines of:

Child: 'Katie said I wasn't her friend any more (and so on).'
Parent: 'Katie was unkind to you.'
Child: 'Yes, and she stuck her tongue out.'
Parent: 'Sounds like she hurt your feelings.'

This needs to be done sensitively, without pretending you know exactly how she feels but rather offering suggestions that may help her feel understood and also help her make sense of her own emotions. Once that is achieved, she will find it easier to let those feelings go. For example:

Child: 'I was the only one without a Chelsea kit.'
Parent: 'Sounds like you felt left out.'
Child: 'Yep and Michael said I wasn't any good in goal.'
Parent: 'I guess you've had a tough morning.'
Child: 'I hated it,' or perhaps, 'Oh, it wasn't that bad. I did a cracking free kick.'

Suggesting how children feel gives the sense that you are helping rather than taking over. Children quickly indicate whether you are on the right track, often with much passion. If you guess right, they will be pleased. If you are mistaken, it is much less likely to draw the conversation to a close. Stating, rather than suggesting how children feel, on the other hand, risks your child's incredulous scorn if you get it wrong.

Child: 'I was the only one without football boots.'
Parent: 'You must have felt left out.'
Child: 'No. I just kept slipping over! Don't you know anything about football?'

For this reason, steer clear of comments like 'I know just how you feel' because you probably don't. Phrases like 'it sounds like', 'I expect', 'I guess' and 'I imagine' are much safer ground. If you haven't a clue what your child may be feeling or even what he is talking about, be honest. Ask 'How did that feel?' or better still, 'I don't know what that must feel like', 'I'm a little confused about what you were doing' or 'Let me see if I've got this right . . .'

Shock of the new

*It really used to irritate, when he'd use these
listening techniques and put on a certain voice.
It was his 'now children, your caring father is listening'
voice and it would either crack me up or drive me mad, depending
on how I was feeling. He doesn't do the voice any more. I suppose
because he's more relaxed about it. Thank God!*

Anne M

*When I first started reflective listening, I felt a complete
idiot and very vulnerable to ridicule. I thought my children would
just burst out laughing, but they didn't. I struggled to remember what
I was supposed to do, but the kids kept me at it. They talked to me.
Over the first few weeks I found out loads of things that
I didn't know were going on. Now I'm much more at
ease with it and do it without even thinking.*

Terry S

New skills do take a while, and lots of practice before they feel natural. Reflective listening, for example, won't feel as easy as making judgements to begin with. In a reasonably short space of time, however, it will be second nature.

If, after about four to six weeks, there is still no positive change, the technique may not be right for you and it is probably best to move on. Not all skills discussed in this book will work for all relationships, because relationships are as unique as the individuals involved. But most will. As Parent Educator Peter Mellor explains: 'Most of the skills will work for most of the children most of the time, depending on the commitment of the parents.'

*Learning to drive, wearing a new pair of shoes, anything new is
awkward, anything new is uncomfortable when you first try. I guess you
have to go through the difficult bit to get to the good bit. But the children
seemed to respond better even when I still felt awkward. It was
hard for me but not really for them.*

Kathy A

Help your child describe emotions

Encouraging your child to talk about her feelings will allow her to recognise, express and manage her emotions (see Dealing with feelings, p.94).

Beware adult word play

Irony, sarcasm and the like are way above children's heads until they are at least five or six, and even then they can cause problems. Superior, adult reasoning powers can also inhibit a child's confidence in conversation. Of course you can express your opinions more clearly and effectively than your child, but that does not deny her the right to have her views respected and considered.

She was two and a bit and had wiped the paint all over the table top and I remember saying something like 'Oh great! That's really marvellous, that is' and her little face! When she turned round she was beaming, she really did think I thought it was great. That got me thinking and I realised we all used sarcasm. It must have been hard for her to work out the difference between what was said and what was meant.

Suzanne T

Mirroring

I did think it was weird, but I was desperate enough to try anything and I have to say it seemed to work. It seemed to reach him when I was at a loss what else to do. It calmed him down. Me, too.

Mark O

This is not an everyday technique and is another to hold in reserve until your child really needs your help to unlock genuine distress and talk about problems.

To do it, simply copy how and where your child is sitting. For example, if she is sitting on the stairs, feeling sad, sit with her. Sometimes your child may be upset but still 'accessible', in which case you could look into her eyes to show her that you are there, concerned and supportive. But sometimes this is the last thing in the world she wants. A hug or even a touch may be shrugged off as inappropriate or overwhelming. In which case, sit by her or near her and match what she does. If she is hunched, hugging her knees, hunch and hug yours. If she is holding her head in her hands, do the same.

It is the body language equivalent of reflective listening (see p.84) – showing that you acknowledge how she is feeling, that you are respectful of her feelings and willing to go at her pace, taking her cues. Once the child sees you are not going to impose or invade, physically or emotionally, she will often begin to relax her body. As she adopts a more 'open' position, so can you until, eventually, you are both relaxed enough to get closer, either to hug or to talk or both, whichever seems right at the time.

Keep it up

If you can listen well in everyday, ordinary circumstances your child is more likely to want to talk to you when a problem or extraordinary situation arises. If you are both used to talking and listening, you will not have so many barriers to break down.

Encouraging your child to listen

Your child will learn to listen if she is listened to. All the points discussed above are therefore important. It will also help if you:

Pitch what you say to your child's level of understanding
Language is complex and a child's level of understanding will depend on her age and ability (see Modifying your speech, p.72). If your words and means of expression are way over her head she may, quite understandably, stop listening.

Try not to witter on Less extreme but much more common is the trap of overwhelming a child with words. It is very easy to jabber on about how and why and where, especially when you are frustrated by your child's lack of action or expression, but this flood of information is likely to result in inaction for the simple reason that the child gets lost among all the words. She can't listen to what you are saying if you are giving her too much to take in at one go.

> *She's five, and I was having a go at her last week for not listening to what I'd asked her to do when she shouted back, 'I'm trying to tell you I'll do it.'*
> Martin G

Say your child's name before you tell her what you need her to hear A teachers' trick, and especially useful for attracting a child's attention when there is a lot of background noise. Simple, but effective.

Choose your moment An argument or time of conflict, for example, is the wrong time to expect your child to listen to a word you say.

Be in the same room Your child is much more likely to listen to you speaking quietly in the same room than shouting from somewhere else in the house.

> *This has been life-transforming. I used to shout up the stairs endlessly every morning. 'Get ready. Get your shoes on. Have you brushed your hair? Come on.' And none of them took a blind bit of notice. Then I went upstairs, and stayed with each one until they'd done what they needed to do, saying 'Well done, now the next thing'. They do it themselves now. It's been much quicker and much less stressful than the old shouting routine.*
> Leslie M

Mean what you say This is particularly effective for getting your child to co-operate (see Encouraging positive behaviour, p.143) but will help get any message across. On the simplest level, it means that your body language and non-verbal signals should match your message. If they don't match – perhaps you are trying to smile sweetly while you are seething inside, or trying to be stern when you feel like laughing – your child will pick up conflicting messages and won't know which one to follow.

> *When I first heard about matching the messages it was like a light going on in my head. Because I've got a sweet tooth I always found it hard to say 'No' to my kids when they wanted sweet things. They'd sense that and would just go on and on until I either gave in or blew my top because I really didn't want tea spoiled again. Once I realised I had to sort out how I felt, then let them know clearly, it was much easier. Did I want them to have one or not? If yes, then OK as a treat and none of this posturing. If no, then I really meant no and I had to make sure they got the message. It sounds so obvious, but it worked like magic.*
>
> Sophie P

Message received?

> *I must have asked my son to put on his trousers six times and he said 'OK'. I guessed he wasn't really listening to what I'd said so I asked him to repeat back what I'd asked and he replied, in all earnestness, 'Yes, I want peanut butter on my sandwiches'! At least I knew why he wasn't getting dressed, he hadn't been listening at all, but neither of us realised he hadn't until I checked.*
>
> Anne M

Sometimes a child won't listen because she doesn't understand, and sometimes there seems no better explanation than that it is going in one ear and out the other. If in doubt, check that your message has been received.

Try to avoid the 'What did I just say?' approach which can sound like a reprimand and make children unnecessarily anxious or lose the thread. Little children can be helped by direct questions: 'Put this in the bin . . . Where does this go? Yes, put it in then. Thank you.' Older ones may respond best to a straightforward check: 'Can I check what we have agreed here?'

Use different means of communication If your child doesn't seem to listen to a word you say, not using words may help. A note in your child's lunchbox telling her you love her can get a very important message across, especially if she is going through a tough patch at school. A note by her bed, reminding her of an agreement struck the day before, may push a point home.

As ever, do not presume that because an approach makes sense to you it will make sense to your child or work every time. Many parents report success, but there will be glittering exceptions.

*I tried leaving a note by her bed on the advice of a friend.
It asked her to clear up her room, like we'd agreed. Next morning I gave
her enough time to tidy up, then went upstairs all eager to see how it had
worked and saw she'd stuck her own note on the front of her bedroom
door. It said one word. 'No'!*
Claire H

Be careful about what you say Don't presume that because your child does not always listen, she does not always hear. Most children have an uncanny ability to home in on parental expletives. Much more importantly, they will also pick up any conversation regarding themselves. In particular, try to avoid criticising your child to others in her presence or within her earshot. Every word you say may be remembered for a very long time to come.

Encourage turn taking Children can easily be drowned out by siblings or even loud friends. Granting each child the time to say their piece will not be achieved without the occasional protest from those being asked to stay quiet for a moment, but the objections should decrease as allowing others to speak becomes a family habit. All will come to realise that they will have their turn (see Modern manners, p.313).

CHAPTER SIX

DEALING
WITH FEELINGS

*Children need to have the opportunity to express their feelings and
be valued for who they are and how they feel, not who they have to be to
gain the love or approval of their parents.*
Kitty Hagenbach, psychotherapist

*The more a child is made to feel good about herself, the more she will
want to be good. The more she is humiliated, made to feel tiresome, wicked
or helpless, the less point she will see in trying to please.*
The Commission on Children and Violence[1]

*If we cannot tolerate our children's upset, they will learn this and not tell
us when they are upset. So the line of communication will be blocked.
And if we can't handle the upset, how the hell can a child?*
John Bristow, psychologist and psychotherapist

Responding to your child's emotional needs is the nub of parenting, the
core issue from which all others flow. Your better understanding of
it will enable you to help your child feel good about himself, encourage him to risk reaching for success, help him respect other people's
emotions and to manage the expression of his feelings. These abilities
are crucial to his behaviour as a child and to his healthy development
into adulthood.

Helping your child feel good

*Self-esteem is a bottom-line sense of self-worth. It is not the same
as bumptiousness or precociousness, or being selfish or self-absorbed. It is
the kernel, the child's core belief in their own value. It is not about telling
your child 'you are a marvellous baseball player' or whatever, it is about
your child having masses of experiences that enable them to appreciate
that their life has value, that they are a worthwhile person, that
their opinion has some validity and that they have an
entitlement to a place in society.*

Vivienne Gross, Clinical Director, The Institute of Family Therapy

If we show our children that we love them unconditionally, that they
and their feelings and wishes matter and that we value, acknowledge
and care for them, we will boost their sense of self-worth. From this will
spring the confidence and security they need to understand their feelings and manage their behaviour, to get along with others, to grow in
independence, to seek assistance when they need it, to cope with life's
knocks and imperfections, and to love. In other words, it sets them up
for life.

Much research now confirms that children whose emotional
needs are chronically rejected will begin to distrust others, will have
difficulties forming friendships and stable relationships, will have more
problems at school and are at increased risk of mental and behavioural problems. At the extreme, children subjected to insensitive care and
harsh treatment are more likely to develop conduct problems and
display aggressive delinquency in adolescence and beyond.[2]

This knowledge doesn't require you to grin benignly at your child
in all circumstances, ignore his misdemeanours or be a slave to his every
whim. It does require you to:

— love him for who he is, not who you'd like him to be
— recognise and respect how he feels and allow him to express this
— listen to what he has to say and show that his opinions matter (which
   is not the same as agreeing with him all the time)
— understand that horrible behaviour is often a normal and necessary
   part of growing up (see Horribly normal, p.119)
— show you dislike certain behaviour, but love him

— help your child negotiate problems, but not always negotiate them for him

Experiences of loss, deprivation and other circumstances and external factors beyond your control may impinge on the way your child views himself and his world. Yet even in extreme situations, it is important to be aware of the influence you have on your child's view of himself and his future (see Coping in hard times, p.229). You can make a difference.

Consider how key your own responses are to how your child views himself and his actions. At a simple level, if you show pleasure in your child having done well, his own pleasure in his achievements will greatly increase (see Encouraging positive behaviour, p.143). If he behaves in a cheeky way and you laugh, he will see himself and the situation very differently than if you had shown anger or irritation.

Yet how you respond to your child's worst moments can influence his sense of worth and his own reactions as much as your responses when he is deserving of praise. You help build your child's self-esteem by responding to his needs, and all children need to know what behaviour is expected of them and when they have overstepped the mark. It is up to you to make those boundaries clear (see Horribly normal, p.119

Simple pleasures

Think about treasured moments of your own childhood. What made you feel loved and special? Often it's not the grandest days out, the biggest presents or the organised activities that make the most impression, but the more simple times when a child and a parent can find delight in each other's company.

Spending time with your child matters hugely. But being with your child to enable such moments to unfold is not only a matter of time, but of being emotionally available. You can be with your child 24 hours a day and still not tune into his needs or actually share time together, talking, going for a walk, rolling around the carpet, cuddling up together with a book or even letting him 'help' with the household chores. What you do matters much less than that your child knows you have enjoyed being with him. This isn't about po-faced parenting, this is about pleasure.

and Effective discipline, p.170), yet also to let your child know that your love is not conditional on his 'good' behaviour.

Let your child know they are allowed to make mistakes and you will still love them. If a child feels they are in a loving, caring environment but not one in which they are over-protected or stifled, if they are allowed some independence, allowed to make mistakes, that speaks volumes about the sort of person the child will turn into.

Hugh Foot, Professor of Child Psychology and Social Development, Strathclyde University

This message of unconditional regard can be reinforced throughout your child's life, from his very first weeks when you made him feel secure and valued by responding to his cries, caring for his needs and showing your pleasure in his company (see Baby's needs, your needs, p.7).

Of course, it will not always be easy. Every relationship hits rough patches and there are bound to be times when you wish you had handled matters differently. Building a child's sense of worth is a continuum rather than a set of isolated incidents, however, and children do not require their parents to be perfect, but responsive and loving.

Children also need to be accepted as unique individuals rather than reflections of parental wishes and aspirations. Your relationship with your child may be the only opportunity either of you has to love unconditionally, but do you really know who it is you are loving? You may have looked forward to your child sharing your pleasure of sport and he may turn out to hate it. You may want him to be an academic high-flyer when he's just not made that way. You may appreciate calm and quiet and have given birth to a firecracker. Accepting your child for who he is involves tolerating and appreciating the differences between you, creating opportunities for him to shine at what *he* is good at, developing *his* potential and helping him make the most of *his* world.

We need to help children become skilled, find what they are good at and build up a self-esteem bank from which they can draw at times when they're not able to do something particularly well. One of my daughters was poor at anything sporty but over time we found she loves singing and drama. Because she excels at these things it gives her the ability to cope in areas she is not so good at.

Eileen Hayes, Parenting Advisor to the NSPCC

Your self-esteem matters

I think too much attention has been focused on the birth.
When you think 40% of families in the UK will be split within
ten years of the birth it is clear there are much more important issues to address.
We are so abysmally uneducated about the importance of emotions in our lives.
The single most important thing we can do for our children is to strengthen
and develop our own self-esteem. This equips us with huge resources to
draw on when the going gets tough as a parent and provides a role
model for our children to feel good about themselves in the world.
Little is more important than this.

Yehudi Gordon, Consultant gynaecologist and obstetrician, specialising in holistic health

If you wish to show your child how effective good self-esteem can be, consider how good you feel about yourself and how you could treat yourself better.

If you work at your own sense of worth, the job of boosting your child's self-esteem will be that much easier (see Your needs, p.23).

If a parent has low self-esteem they are likely to place greater expectations
and demands on their children to behave in a way that will reflect positively on
themselves; they will be less accepting of their children as they are.

Kitty Hagenbach, psychotherapist

I was never quite good enough. Even when I did something right
there was always a mistake pointed out, a something I could have done
better, another hurdle to jump.

Doug C

A bedrock of love, understanding and appreciation is crucial to your child's sense of worth. Specific approaches to help you boost his self-esteem are detailed later in this chapter, but your respect for your child's feelings and individuality and the effort you invest in monitoring and responding to his emotional needs will be what turns these skills from potentially confusing bolt-on extras with a short shelf-life into effective strategies with profound benefits now and for years to come.

Naming emotions

It's not what he feels but how he expresses it that really winds me up – it's moan, moan, whinge, whinge. He just presses all my buttons. It's not my one-off reaction that concerns me but the cumulative effect of me getting irritated and saying 'Oh, for God's sake'. That does worry me. Is he going to think he shouldn't let me know how he feels?

John T

I think parents these days have this expectation that their children have to be happy all the time and you feel something is very seriously wrong if they are not, but it is just life, it involves happiness and sadness, ups and downs.

Marina C

Aaaaaaarrrrrrrrrggggggghhhhhhhhhhhhhhhh.

Joe P, five, on being told to turn out his light

Your child's ability to recognise and express his own feelings will help you both. You need to know what he feels and why, within reason, and he needs to be able to communicate his needs and learn to control his behaviour.

How children express their feelings can sometimes be a problem – for them and for others. If they express them in ways that are too aggressive, too timid, too loud, too confused or simply inappropriate, they risk being told off, fobbed off or ignored. Yet with your guidance, your child can learn to show his love and assert his needs and opinions without going haywire.

To do this, he first needs to know what emotions are, how they feel, what they are called and what can be done with them. Sounds obvious? Remember you are an adult with an adult's experience and grasp of language. A child may never have felt such jealousy, hate, fear or unbridled joy before, or at least not so intensely or mixed in such a maelstrom of other emotions. Even if he has, he may not know what the feeling is called or even that other people feel it. If you identify, name and describe an emotion, you show your child that you know this feeling, too. You've handled it, and so can he.

Try not to wait until a problem or crisis is looming, but bring the subject of feelings, or at least the recognition of emotions, into everyday conversations. Naming positive as well as negative emotions also makes talking about them feel less peculiar.

The best of parenting is when you are helping children recognise their emotions and express them on a day-to-day basis, not just when there's a problem. If they come hurtling down the slide and they are shrieking with delight, you can say 'That looks fun'. You can talk about what is going on for them all the time so they are able to name their emotions, and express them, so that when they come to express anger it is not the only emotion they have had to express.

Vivienne Gross, Clinical Director, The Institute of Family Therapy

Parents can help children express emotions effectively if they:

Allow children to feel Avoid telling your child not to feel or how to feel. Think how many times children are told 'Don't be sad', 'Don't worry', 'It doesn't hurt', 'You do like it', 'Don't be daft'. . . They trip out of our mouths before we've had time to think, but they can easily make a child feel misunderstood, confused, ignored or rejected. Yet acknowledging your child's feelings may be all the help he needs to begin to deal with them.

Robert fell over, I was in a rush and my first response was 'Oh, you're all right, come on, we've got to be quick' and he started howling and going into one. So I tried again. I said 'That must have hurt' and he stopped crying and nodded. If you try to squash their feelings, they can explode right back at you. Once he realised I knew how he felt, he calmed right down.

Leslie B

If you tell a child repeatedly not to feel how he feels, he may stop telling you. A communication breakdown between parent and child often becomes most obvious in adolescence, but the process can begin in a child's earliest years. Children whose emotions are denied may also, over time, lose confidence in their ability to recognise their own feelings, which makes them more likely to be easily led and influenced by others. Ultimately, and most destructively, they may withdraw from emotional life.

So try to take your child's expression of emotion as a compliment,

Talking about emotions

Your ability to give your child emotional support and to talk to him about how he feels will enrich the relationship between you way beyond his childhood years and provide him with benefits that extend far beyond his emotional develop-ment. US psychologist and author John Gottman's 20-year study of 100 families[3] indicates that children of parents who give emotional advice have better health, fewer behavioural problems and better academic results.

even if it is an emotion you could do without at that moment. Most children show behaviour and emotions to their parents that they would not show to others because they know their parents' love is uncondi-tional. This is how it should be, and much better that than they show no one at all.

Accept how children feel With the very best of intentions, parents often try to steer their children away from expressing anger, fear or unhappiness towards happier thoughts and pursuits. But stopping the expression won't stop the feeling. The sooner the feelings are expressed and accepted, the sooner they can be dealt with and disappear. Feelings that are not accepted do not disappear. They simply hide to erupt again another day, often in ways that are harder to handle because neither parent nor child can locate the cause.

Help children to identify emotions

All scrumblywumbly.
Bea, three, when asked how she felt about her first day at nursery

You will need to acknowledge a child's feelings.
For example: 'It sounds as though you are upset about something.'
Labelling emotions is very helpful to children, specific names for emotions
can help them recognise, acknowledge and manage their feelings.
John Bristow, psychologist and psychotherapist

Children sometimes need adult help to identify what it is that they are feeling and why (see Reflective listening, p.84): 'I can see you're very angry that Kate has broken the toy,' for example, or 'You seem frightened of going to school today.'

Labelling children's emotions may feel artificial to begin with, but like most techniques it will become second nature once you've practised it enough. Its inherent danger is that you impose what you believe your child is feeling when in fact they are feeling something else. For this reason, when in doubt or when you think your child has a mixture of conflicting emotions, say so: 'You must be feeling lots of things at the moment. Perhaps you're a bit excited and a bit scared?' or 'I'm confused. Could you tell me a bit more about how you feel?' Even describing the situation – 'This must be hard for you. Your toy is broken' – shows some understanding and encourages the child to explain.

Show you understand Let your child know that you understand and recognise what he is feeling (even if you don't agree with the reasons why). One effective way of doing this is to 'reflect back' his emotions, in context. For instance:

> *Child:* 'I hate her.'
> *You:* 'I can see she was getting on your nerves.'
> or
> *Child:* 'I hate you.'
> *You:* 'I know you are angry that I made you tidy your room.'

You are not saying your child should not feel the emotion, neither do you need to agree with his response, you are simply saying 'message received' which, with any luck, will stop another louder message following on (see Reflective listening, p.84).

There may be times when it's simply not possible to discuss a situation in detail with your child at a particular moment. Letting him know you understand how he feels will help him cope until you have got time to talk. Compare these three exchanges.

1   *Child:* 'I hate Miss Adams!'
    Parent: 'No, you don't.'

2   *Child:* 'I hate Miss Adams.'
    Parent: 'Oh darling, do you? Poor you. Are you all right to go to school?'

3 *Child:* 'I hate Miss Adams.'
Parent: 'You hate Miss Adams right now. Can you tell me why?'
Child: 'She told me I wasn't trying and I was!'
Parent: 'That must have been hard. We have to go to school now but let's talk about it again this afternoon.'

In the first exchange, the child's emotions were contradicted. In the second, the parent collapsed under their weight. In the third, the child's emotions were acknowledged but not inflated, and avenues were left open for further conversation.

Let your child know that feelings are OK, but there may be better ways of expressing them It is important that children know that their feelings are valid, but that this does not give them free rein to express them in any way they choose. Your child will need your guidance on what behaviour you find acceptable and what not, and most are able to understand the basics of this from the beginnings of toddlerhood on. Take time to explain that being angry is OK but hurting is not, for example, or that you understand why he is disappointed, but shouting in your face is not going to help him or you. He should try talking.

Respecting what children feel does not require you to give in to the power of their reactions. If you don't like how your child is behaving, tell him and ask him to think of a better way – 'I can see you are angry and tired of waiting for your turn *and* you know it is not OK to pull Katie off the swing. I won't have that. How could you do it differently?' (see Encouraging positive behaviour, p.143 and Effective discipline, p.170).

Sometimes you may want to suggest alternative ways of behaving that will help you both cope better. If your child is wailing because of a tiny bump, telling him not to cry or that it doesn't hurt will not help. What might is to say: 'Oh, that must have hurt. Sometimes it helps me if I hold my knee after I have banged it. Do you want to try?'

How and when to express how we feel is a balancing act we all get wrong sometimes, so don't expect perfection from you or your child. The important message for him to receive is that he does have a choice in how he communicates his emotions.

Exploring emotions

It helps if the underlying message is that when you are faced with difficulties you are courageous and do the best you can; that the world is an interesting place and even though bad things happen, lots of good things happen, too. All the old fairy stories show that even though you are a little person, you are strong and courageous and so these are wonderful to share with children.

Dr Dorothy Rowe, psychologist and writer

You cannot accept and acknowledge your child's emotions until you know what they are. But what if your child cannot put his feelings into words? Sharing stories can help children explore, identify and understand the feelings of others, which may help them understand and express their own (see Exploring tales together, p.337).

Some parents encourage their children to paint or draw how they feel. This can be very effective and reinforces the message that even negative emotions can be expressed non-aggressively. It may be more appropriate for less violent emotions such as sadness or longing, however, or after the storm has passed. Few children in full-throttle rage would respond well to a parent suggesting: 'Would you like to draw how you feel, darling?'

Try to be alert to times when your child describes feelings through symbols, images, even gestures, when they don't yet have the confidence or vocabulary to use specific words.

This mother's story is a graphic example of how parental responses can help a child struggling to understand emotions and experiences. 'We were chopping vegetables and my son (six) said "You know there's a difference between this time this year and this time last year? Like someone with a big axe comes and chops time into two different bits?" We had no idea what he was talking about but I knew he was trying to tell us something important, so later I asked him how he felt about the two "bits of time". Asking how he felt rather than what he meant seemed to help. It turned out he was talking about his new teacher. This year he feels understood and understands, last year he felt neither. His experience is so different, to him it felt like time had been split into two bits – then and now.'

Once children have expressed an emotion, it is much easier for parents to help them cope with it.

The reassurance needs to come after the emotion has been released otherwise it cannot be heard. When the emotion is there it needs to come through.

Kitty Hagenbach, psychotherapist

Thinking about how he must feel has helped me stop flying off
the handle so often. I see him more as a kid who's tired, nervous, muddled,
or angry and not just a kid who's being horrible and getting on my nerves.
It's also helped me explain things more clearly. I think I used to just say
'No, don't'. Now I'll say something like 'I know you are feeling such
a way but you are not allowed to hit your sister, just like she's
not allowed to hit you'. It has helped.

Dave G

Try not to confront but to talk Acknowledging and naming your child's emotions requires you to be calm. If you are confrontational, your child will clam up, won't talk and won't hear. He might shout, but he won't listen.

There will be times when you are justifiably angry, but don't expect these to be the times when you can discuss your child's feelings or your own. Be honest about it – 'I'm too angry to talk right now,' or 'If we talk about this now I'll lose my temper and I don't want to. Let's leave it for a while.'

Sharing feelings

Your emotions have a right to be acknowledged, too. We all get angry, happy, sad, confused and if you do not show your child your feelings or how you deal with them, you will deprive him of a crucial role model.

Anger, for example, is an emotion most parents experience, often with good reason. Show your child that anger is not the same as aggression and that it can be used positively to change situations for the better. If you can express it in a way that shows you controlling it rather than it controlling you, without becoming abusive or threatening or crushing your child in the process, you have taught your child a powerful lesson.

Some issues are not appropriate to share with your child, so try to ensure you tell him how you feel in ways that respect his age, vulnerability and understanding (see Coping in hard times, p.229). Neither blame him nor burden him with responsibility for your happiness (say

'I feel angry/tired/sad,' rather than 'You make me angry/tired/sad') and remember to tell him when you are feeling great and loving towards him, as well as when you are feeling angry or low.

The catch, of course, is that you can't let your children know how you feel unless you know yourself and are willing and able to admit it. Being emotionally honest with yourself will help you:

Better understand your relationship with your child How you feel is key to how you respond to your child and thus key to parenting.

Parenting involves an almost endlessly diverse and shifting mixture of care, affection, control, and stimulation. All this is supported by a complex array of feelings and interactions which reflect partly the parent's internal world and partly the child's temperament and reactions. [4]
Christine Puckering, clinical psychologist, Senior Research Fellow, University of Glasgow, and co-founder of Mellow Parenting

Better manage your responses Your responses will take you less by surprise if you are aware of your own emotional state. Not admitting how you feel, even to yourself, will only make you more tense and increase the chances of you blowing your stack in ways you do not wish.

The first stage for parents to do it differently is to become aware of their own emotions sufficiently to moderate them while experiencing them. We may learn many tactics and skills but not be able to use them because of our state of mind. Being in touch with our own feelings is in a sense a master skill. Without it, we cannot use others.
John Bristow, psychologist and psychotherapist

Remember that communicating your feelings honestly will help your child:

Express his emotion Instead of bottling up and lashing out, your child will learn the confidence and the vocabulary to tell you how he feels and to begin to recognise and consider other people's feelings in what he says and what he does.

We need to accept feelings and be flexible in the ways these are expressed. Families who have problems around expressing anger tend to fall into one of two groups. One group is where everyone is angry all the time and the other is where no one ever gets angry whatever happens or admits to the slightest bit of irritation. It would be more helpful to talk to our children about how we feel and give guidance on how to behave with those feelings. It is helpful to show different ways – shout, go quiet, write a letter to those we cannot challenge directly. It is important to show children different ways to express anger.

Dr Dorothy Rowe, psychologist and writer

Increase his understanding Knowing how you feel gives your child a more realistic view of the world and of people's strengths and weaknesses. This allows him to be more accepting of his parents' inability to control the universe perfectly (as important a knowledge for a seven-year-old who wants new state-of-the-art trainers every fortnight as it is for a toddler who wants the rain to stop). It also gives children the opportunity to view themselves in a more accepting light, warts and all.

Throw off his guilt Honest and appropriate communication of your emotions can help your child realise he is not to blame for everything that happens. This will help protect him from the potentially devastating vulnerability and responsibility children can feel when something very painful or serious happens in their lives (see Coping in hard times, p.229).

I thought my mum had left home because I was untidy and she was so unhappy about that. I had no understanding of her real feelings or reasons for leaving. It is not protecting children to hide how you feel if they still have to cope with the consequences.

Jane S

Get the message If you say one thing and feel another, your child will intuitively sense the contradiction and not know which to respond to – your words or your feelings (see Minding your body language, p.73). Smiling while saying 'Come on sweetie, let go of Grandma's curtains' as you fume inside will only confuse him. This is more likely to result in him gripping on tighter than letting go, until *what* you say and *how* you say it communicate the same, clear message – ie. you shout a firm 'Get down!' It is far easier for your child and for your nerves if your feelings are clear from the start.

Let them know how you feel. Without this, it can just feel like a nag. If you find what they are doing a problem – perhaps they are being unbearably loud or playing football in the house – explaining how you feel will help motivate them to change their behaviour because they understand the consequences for you.

Brigid Treacy, Parent Network co-ordinator

Ripping up labels

When children's behaviour is unacceptable, adults should criticise the behaviour, not the child. They should say 'That noise is giving me a headache', not 'You make me ill'.

The Commission on Children and Violence[5]

It can be very unhelpful when children get polarised in families into being 'the good one' or 'the troublemaker' or 'the child from hell' or even 'mummy's little sunshine boy'. Children pick these labels up and it is very restricting. We don't see the half of our children's qualities, we tend to focus on a few and then narrow them down into a very constrained role.

Vivienne Gross, Clinical Director, The Institute of Family Therapy

I got so sick of being the 'good' one. Still am.

Julia M

Labelling emotions is useful (see Naming emotions, p.99). Labelling children – 'bad girl', 'clumsy child', even 'clever boy' – is not.

Turning around the way we use labels can be hard. The thinking behind it is often difficult to grasp and may require you to break habits of a lifetime. But stay with it. Once you have the hang of it, it will become second nature. It is acknowledged by all respected professionals dealing with children's issues as an important and powerful skill and is one of the most effective ways to protect and promote your child's self-esteem and to help him manage his own behaviour.

Avoiding labels will help your child because:

Labels describe the child rather than what he has done. Your child can think you disapprove of *him* rather than his *behaviour*. This can crush, confuse or even scare him and result in more negative behaviour, not less.

Labels can stick. If children begin to feel *they* are, say, 'bad', 'stupid', 'lazy' or 'slow', they can begin to feel unloved or even unloveable. If repeated or reinforced over time and in different situations, the label can become part of the child's view of himself and therefore self-fulfilling. It may convince him that he really is 'stupid' or 'thoughtless' or 'crazy' and so he will begin to behave accordingly.

A label does not communicate anything helpful. It fails to tell children what it is we approve or disapprove of in their behaviour, or how they could do things differently.

By placing a label on your child you take away his ability to put the situation right. If he sees the problem as who he is rather than what he is doing, he may feel powerless to improve matters.

If ripping up labels is so liberating, why do so many parents use them? Most of us have done so and there are many reasons why. The first is their familiarity – it is the way we were brought up. They are a short-hand means of expression, which saves time and effort. They can also be used as an expletive: an emotional release to make us feel better, almost like swearing – 'Oh you horrible child!' or 'Naughty boy!' Yet labels can be positive or negative.

Negative labels These are the most common and tend to be used in times of exasperation – 'bossy', 'lazy', 'stupid', 'selfish', 'naughty', 'rude', 'cheeky', 'bad' are common currency and you might have been called a few of these yourself as a child.

Adults feel angry or hurt if value-judged in this way, and so do children. If they feel unable to express that anger, they can become resentful, unlikely to want to listen and even less likely to want to co-operate. If this still sounds bizarre, think of it from an adult perspective. Which would you respond to best – a boss calling you 'hopeless' or a boss pointing out calmly that you had made a mistake?

Positive labels These can be restrictive, inaccurate and potentially damaging for similar reasons. Your child will need to know when you think he has done well (see Descriptive praise, p.154), but will suffer if he comes to believe that your attention and acknowledgement of him depend on his 'good deeds' or achievements. Children may come to feel over time that the love they receive is conditional on them being a 'good girl' or a 'brave boy', the 'funny one' or 'the clever one'.

A child can also become hooked on receiving praise rather than experiencing the satisfaction of doing something for himself because he enjoys it or because he knows it to be the right thing to do. This weakens self-reliance. Children may feel manipulated with the use of generalised praise of the 'Oh you're such a good boy, I'm sure you'll let your sister have your new book' kind. This can lead to resentment and resentment can lead to rebellion. You have been warned!

Labelling is usually a generalisation, be it negative or positive.
Both can be as damaging. In talking to parents and parent groups, it is
clear that even the good labels attached to people as children were unhelpful.
If praise was general it could lose its meaning. Sometimes, the child also came
to regret that the message they received was that love was conditional – if
they were good they were loved. Children are not born with a view of
themselves and what is said does tend to be believed.
A child is highly suggestible.
John Bristow, psychologist and psychotherapist

Avoiding labels can turn around how your child views himself and his actions. Doing so requires much understanding and practice and many parents find it easier to proceed in steps.

Step one: **Separate the doer and the deed.** In other words, comment on the behaviour rather than the child, for example: 'Your bedroom is a mess' rather than 'You are so messy'. You have communicated what you need to without labelling him.

Step two: **Describing behaviour.** If you have managed to label your child less often, you are doing well. The next stage is to stop labelling his behaviour and to describe it instead. A specific description of exactly what you see and hear – for instance, 'You have spilt the milk on the

Sticky labels

John Bristow, psychologist and
psychotherapist

'Labelling must be put in context. We are
not perfect parents, all of us can easily slip
into it at times. However it is a very low-level
form of influencing, controlling, condition-
ing and educating our children. You have to
ask yourself what your aim is.

'If the behaviour of a child is over-
generalised – for instance "You are a bad
boy" – that child may enter another experience thinking "I am bad" and will therefore
not behave very effectively. Then the child
will feel even worse about themselves. If it
remains generalised, expectations are built
that things are not going to turn out well, the
child becomes more anxious and therefore
does not perform well. It is a vicious circle.

Very often as parents
we find ourselves behaving
as our parents did or even
hearing our parents' words
and being quite shocked by
that. Parents may also label
as a vehicle of emotional release,
like a swear word – it is often considered
more acceptable to say "You idiot!" than
"Oh bloody hell!" if a glass of milk has gone
over the carpet.

Yet specific praise and criticism, focusing
on the behaviour rather then the person,
can be a very useful tool to help educate
children's behaviour whilst maintaining
their self-esteem (see Effective discipline,
p.170). We do have a responsibility to both
educate our children about the world and
help them feel good about themselves in
their interaction with it.'

carpet and it's made a mess' – gives a child much more information
about what is wrong than saying 'That's so clumsy' or 'Clumsy girl'.

The technique can be just as effective with young children – 'Leave
it! The cup is hot!' gives them more important information than 'No,
naughty!' 'You are so rude' might make an older child feel crushed.
Either that or he'll ignore you completely. On the other hand, 'You are
shouting and I cannot hear what Grandma is saying' tells him exactly
what it is you object to without humiliating him. This increases the
chance of him putting it right.

Without specific descriptions, the world can be a confusing place
for a child. A child can be praised as a 'Good boy' for putting a cup by
the sink, only to be told he's a 'Naughty boy!' two hours later because
the same cup is now full of hot tea. A simple description of what it is
about the behaviour that you approve of or object to would be far more
informative. For instance, 'The cup was empty. Thank you for putting
it there,' and later: 'The tea is hot (taking it away). Look.'

Specific descriptions of behaviour may feel strange. Surely we are just stating the obvious? Yet children do respond differently when given this sort of information. They often talk more because they feel less threatened and co-operate more as they have understood the effects of their behaviour.

Step three: **Describing the consequences of your child's actions.** This will give your child a greater understanding of how and why a situation should be put right, or why he should avoid the same thing happening in future.

'You have forgotten to feed the rabbit and he is hungry,' gives the child more to go on than, 'John, you are so selfish, that poor rabbit!'

'You are using your spoon, well done!' might be the most appropriate response to a baby's messy attempts at spoon feeding.

'You've poured porridge down your school uniform and I'm going to have to wash it again,' might be a more helpful response to a six-year-old if you want him to understand why you are gnashing your teeth.

How your child's actions affect other people's feelings is another important consequence for him to understand and consider, so try to include it in your description. This is how children begin to understand that a specific action is not always the problem but rather who is doing it, the environment in which it is done, who it is done to, when it is done and the feelings of the person receiving it. How else is a young child to understand that you love to be tickled, but baby brother does not; or that you love to be tickled, but not when you are eating; or that your sense of humour plummets when you are tired? This is complex and sophisticated territory for a child and he will need your guidance.

Over time children do understand the concept of appropriate behaviour, ie. it is OK to have feelings and it is only OK to behave in certain ways with those feelings. So even, for example, the joy of splashing through puddles in the park can be separated out at quite a young age so that this same behaviour is not OK in different circumstances, eg. on the way to school. That is appropriateness. In a sense this is socialisation.

Pat Elliot, psychotherapist and bereavement counsellor

Such guidance can be used in praise as well as criticism. Compare 'There's a good boy' with 'Thanks. Grandma really appreciated you being quiet tonight because she was very tired.'

With your child's increasing self-awareness and sense of self-worth will come a growing ease with the knowledge that he is fallible. He knows he will sometimes get things wrong and that this will affect others, and he also knows he has the capacity to put many things right. This balanced sense of himself will allow him to take responsibility for his mistakes and do something about them rather than relying on the constant approval of others, denying his mistakes, blaming others or becoming aggressively defensive.

Common fears and anxieties

Doubts, fears and anxieties are there in life. The important thing is to equip a child to cope with them.

Pat Elliot, psychotherapist and bereavement counsellor

I used to see a snake in my wall. My parents would tell me not to worry, there weren't any snakes in my bedroom, which didn't help at all. Years later I realised it wasn't a snake but the light from the lamppost outside, shining through the curtains. We left that house when I was four, and I can still remember that snake.

Sean C

Research increasingly points to the fact that young children and babies can cope with their anxieties, fears and bad feelings if they know those feelings are recognised and accepted by those caring for them[6] (see Separation anxiety, p.116). The key to helping your child cope with everyday fears and anxieties is thus to accept and acknowledge them, no matter how inconvenient, uncomfortable or irrational you consider those fears to be.

Far from pandering to negative emotions and encouraging weakness, as many parents once believed, acknowledgement of children's fears actually makes them more emotionally resilient and better able to cope. It equips them to recognise and work through their anxieties themselves.

Looking at situations from your child's perspective will help you see that what seems trivial or even ridiculous to an adult may terrify him. It will also help you understand how best to proceed.

Take one very common young child's fear – the bath. If a baby seems frightened, it makes sense not to force the issue. Skip the bath for a few days and top and tail or wash in between. Get in the bath with him, encourage water play with toys. Playing in a swimming pool can reassure older babies and children that water can be fun – try to pick a quiet time in a training pool. If your child is scared by running water on his head and creates a fuss when having his hair washed, try a shampoo shield, wet and rinse his hair with a flannel, let him rinse it himself and praise him when he manages any of these.

If children get very frightened usually something has happened – perhaps they have slipped badly in the bath or anxiety for their safety is being communicated by the parent. It is better to give them less water and more freedom than lots of water and still the need to hold on to them. It is very wrong just to keep going in an effort to overcome fears. We do have to expose children to things they are frightened of but in a safe, gentle way.

Carol Ann Hally, health visitor and clinical practice teacher

---

A fundamental fear?

Peter Wilson, child psychotherapist and Director of Young Minds

'I think, right from the outset, children are terrified of not belonging to anybody. You can have different names for it, but basically infants are frightened of not being fed or nourished. Then they also fear there is nothing out there for them that cares about them, that the things they need – the nourishment, the pleasurable experiences, the sense of attachment, the sense of feeling held and protected – will not be there, and they will be left abandoned, isolated, uncared for, unheeded, unacknowledged and unfed.

'These are the primary fears and underlie others – fear of the dark, of separating from Mummy, of parents arguing and rowing, of what's going to happen to them.

'At a higher level, the fears are: not being approved of, being rejected, being humiliated, put down, being made to feel no good, being hurt or damaged, fears which build on each other the more the child is aware of the world. But behind them all is the fundamental fear of being left.'

Every child has fears and vulnerabilities, some of which may be obvious, others less so – dogs, loud noises, new places, the list is as varied as children themselves. There will be times when the cause of the fear is beyond your control and you can do nothing more than reassure him that you are with him and will help him deal with it.

Children often worry about 'adult' concerns, from crime to family breakdown, for instance. Just under three in four children are concerned about poverty and homelessness according to recent studies of attitudes among 9- to 15-year-olds,[7] and awareness of such issues begins at a much younger age.

As children are so alert to the information they pick up from their parents and other sources, and are so attuned to parental anxieties, it seems only fair that we recognise this and support and reassure as necessary rather than dismissing their concerns as inappropriate to their age – the 'Don't worry your little head about it' trap. This doesn't mean providing your child with information he doesn't need or which may disturb him further; it does mean that honesty as well as positive reassurance are often the best policy.

Wherever possible tell your children the truth and go for the straight line because in the long run your children will trust you. I think you can protect them best that way. If a child asks, 'Can a burglar get in?' we can say, 'We've locked up, it is very unlikely. I really don't think it will happen.' That reassures but acknowledges it is a small possibility.
Peter Wilson, child psychotherapist and Director of Young Minds

Beware ridiculing fears. Even well-intentioned, gentle ribbing of the 'You silly sausage, there's nothing to be afraid of' variety may sound loving to you but can be devastating to a child who is trying to express a very real anxiety. Children experience intense emotions and wild imaginings – it is obvious to you that a strange swamp thing couldn't fit into the bottom of the airing cupboard, but not to your child (see Nightmares and night terrors, p.48); you know from experience that a bath is a safe place to be, but to a baby still getting to know the world, it can be a very scary place.

Far better to respect how he feels and respond to his need rather than ignore, dismiss or fuel it. Compare these two responses:

Child: 'There's a witch in the cupboard.'
Parent: 'Don't be silly, there are no such things as witches.'

and

Child: 'There's a witch in the cupboard.'
Parent: 'That's a scary feeling. Witches are in stories and thoughts, though, not real life. What would make you feel better?'

If your child is having difficulty identifying his fears, talking to him about how you felt as a child in a similar situation may help him better

Separation anxiety

We expect 18- to 30-month-old children to begin exploring with the absolute certainty that they can return to their carer in a group situation. They are often desperate to get in there and play but they need to know they are not on their own and they can run back to 'Mummy' when they need to. There would be cause for concern if the child will not leave the side of the carer at all, and I would be equally anxious if a mother says her child just runs off without ever batting an eyelid. It is perfectly understandable that a young child would not want to stay with strangers.

Carol Ann Hally, health visitor and clinical practice teacher

Separation anxiety at your absence is a perfectly normal and healthy response from a young child. You are his emotional anchor and he is bound to feel sad and confused without you.

The importance of acknowledging the child's distress is one of the most significant findings of new research into handling separation anxiety. Many parents and carers try to stop children expressing their sadness at separation, which may help the adults but

does not help the child (see Choosing childcare, p.219).

Think of it from the child's point of view and this makes great sense. If a child is comforted, he knows he is in a place where his feelings matter. If he is encouraged or told to hide how he feels, he is not only without his parent but in a place where people do not understand his sadness.

'Nurseries sometimes view child upset at this time as an indication that there is a

understand his own experiences. This may enable him to express his worries and, at the very least, will show him that he's not alone in feeling as he does. Try not to put words into his mouth or to focus more on your feelings and fears of the past than on his in the present.

After her first morning at school, my daughter was in a state. It was almost as if she wasn't sure which emotion to have so she tried them all out for size, in rapid succession. She sang, then shouted – at me – then announced that she hated her drawing paper then had an astonishing tantrum and ended up sobbing and she didn't know why. We cuddled, then I told her about how

problem or that something has gone wrong rather than seeing it as a normal reaction to the stress of separation,' state Peter Elfer and Dorothy Selleck, senior development officers at the National Children's Bureau's Early Childhood Unit.

They have studied the responses of children under three in nurseries. This has included the anxieties children feel when they are brought to nursery, and how these can be handled more sensitively by parents and staff.[8] Their findings throw much light on managing children's anxieties in general, and on adults' tendency to try and brush them under the carpet.

'Sometimes staff consider that the best strategy is to move the child away as quickly as possible. We have seen many examples of staff wanting to distract a child by showing him something out of the window or wanting to distract him with a toy.

'Where we did see examples of staff who were able to "tune in" especially skilfully to a child's emotional needs, they would instead take the child to a quiet part of the nursery and just reassure them gently that they would be OK, that Mummy or Daddy would be returning at whatever time, and they would talk about what Mummy and Daddy may be doing whilst the child was in the nursery.

'It really is better that the distress is acknowledged, tolerated and managed. It is not helpful to pretend it is not here or not real or too dangerous to be talked about. It is upsetting to say goodbye to someone you love and that should be recognised. A very young child may not have a real sense of when their mother is going to return and they do need comforting and reassuring about that.

'It is important to remember the pressure on nurseries to appear to be happy, jolly sorts of places – you can understand that from a business point of view. But the transition into nursery is a very important one and the nursery and parents need to think through how it is best managed.'

strange I'd felt on my first day at school, because there were some bits of it
I liked and other bits that felt very odd and other bits that were scary.
I didn't know all the people, I'd only just met my teacher and I wasn't
even sure where the loo was. She seemed amazed that I ever was a child,
then said she'd felt a bit like that, too. It seemed to help her calm
down enough to talk rather than explode in all directions.'

Lindsay C

Whatever your child's age, try to listen to what he is telling you, through either his words or behaviour, and show that you are listening (see Communication, p.70). Don't dismiss how he is feeling by ignoring, contradicting or even diverting attention, but show you understand. Even if you can't take away the source of his concern, knowing you understand his fears and take them seriously will help him express them, and once they are expressed, he is more likely to be able to cope with them better.

CHAPTER SEVEN

HORRIBLY NORMAL

Parents have a huge vested interest in their children being a credit to them and therefore anything their child does to show them up they find really hard to handle. We have found this to be a huge problem for parents.
Eileen Hayes, Parenting Advisor to the NSPCC

It is an age thing, mostly. Almost all children really start to understand why and how things are wrong after the age of three or four years.
Carol Ann Hally, health visitor, clinical practice teacher

I used to lie when my first child hit any other children – 'I can't believe he's done it, he's never done it before.' He'd been doing it for months but I wouldn't admit it, especially to other mothers.
Mel M

Much of the child behaviour parents worry about most is perfectly normal. Horrible, but normal.

Most children lie, cheat, hit, bite, snatch and throw tantrums at some stage for the simple reason that they haven't yet learned how to behave differently. It's up to us to provide them with the direction and experience they need to know better – and to keep a healthy sense of perspective (see When to worry, p.120). A child who dabbles in whopper fibs is not destined to become a compulsive liar; the child who stuffs stolen banknotes up his jumper in a game of Monopoly is not a cheat for life; the child who bites is not Vlad the Impaler. All need parental guidance and patience. And you will need your sense of humour.
It also helps to:

Be realistic If you expect too much too soon, you will be frustrated and your child will have less incentive to achieve because your aims are out of reach. The process of educating your child's behaviour starts young (see Encouraging positive behaviour, p.143), takes time and involves a great deal of repetition.

Be clear Is the behaviour really that bad? It may be driving you demented but that may be more down to your mood than your child's actions. Remember, too, that if a child of any age isn't aware that her behaviour is wrong, she needs educating, not punishing (see Effective discipline, p.170).

A very young child may bail out the bath or bite your backside because she thinks it's fun. So much fun that she thinks you'll enjoy it, too. Leave her in no doubt that you don't, but avoid being too harsh or severe as this can confuse or terrify her to a degree you never intended

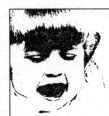

When to worry

Hilton Davis, Professor of Child Health Psychology at Guy's, King's and St. Romans' Hospitals, Medical and Dental School and The Lewisham & Guy's Mental Health Trust

'No behaviour is abnormal by simple virtue of it happening. That's important for parents to know. Almost everything that could be described as abnormal behaviour — in a child actually occurs in normal development. Behaviour only becomes abnormal in its frequency, its chronicity and its intensity. So parents should ask themselves how often it happens, how it is developing and whether it is hurting the child or anyone else.

'An adult might be deluded on occasion, thinking "God, they're all laughing at me". That doesn't mean they are psychotic; the frequency and intensity of the experience is well within the band of "normal".

'In the same way, if something's hap-pened that worries you about your child's behaviour, don't panic but wait to see how and if it develops. It might well just go away.

'As part of that process you also need to be able to go to someone and say, "Hey, what do you think about this?" It may be a friend, your health visitor, someone you can be honest with about your concerns and who may be able to provide helpful advice.

'Unfortunately there is still a stigma attached to seeking help. We are seeking to change that, to say we know it is difficult raising children, that everybody needs sup-port and that support ought to be available to parents very easily and in a way which isn't stigmatising.'

and still leave her unsure of what she did wrong. She may even try to cheer you up by bailing out the bath again.

Be positive Shorten the journey to better behaviour by building your child's self-esteem and her ability to express feelings without going bananas. Make it worth her while to behave better by praising her when she does (see Encouraging positive behaviour, p.143).

Learning to be 'nice' or 'good' often means that a child
must learn to act against her own best interests: if she does not snatch
the last cake, she will not get to eat it. If he does not hit his friend on the head
with that toy brick, the friend may snatch it. It is up to adults to balance
cakes and toys with praise, hugs, gold stars or whatever constitutes
the 'feel-good factor' in their particular group.
The Commission on Children And Violence[1]

Be observant Let your child know when you don't like what she is doing. Even very young children care if another person is hurt, but they may not realise it is their own actions that caused the pain (see Encouraging positive behaviour, p.143). It is up to us to tell them.

Children suffer natural empathetic responses to another's distress.
Parents' failure to confront the child about actions that harm
others may extinguish such concern.
Professor Diana Baumrind, research psychologist[2]

Be sociable Children as young as 22 months have been found to 'work' at friendships and change their behaviour to influence their friend's responses.[3] This awareness of how their actions and moods affect others is the root of understanding the importance of acceptable behaviour. Providing opportunities for your child to mix with others will help her develop this understanding (see Encouraging play with other children, p.281).

Pre-toddler mood swings

He does these cartoon leg-pedals when I pick him up from where he shouldn't be. He has an iron will, an iron grip and has perfected a screech like a dog whistle when he's not getting what he wants. And he's not yet 16 months.

Paula C

As a baby edges towards toddlerhood, she will begin to put her dawning sense of independence to the test and try out her developing physical capabilities. And sometimes they just won't work in the way she'd like them to.

As your child becomes more aware of what she can do, she also becomes more aware of what she can't. She wants to crawl forwards but her body goes backwards. She wants to walk but she falls down. She wants to climb on a chair but she just can't reach. She tries to open the fridge door and her mother shuts it. Where once she was easily distracted, she may now grip on to objects she shouldn't have as though her life depended on it, and shouts at every attempt to untangle her fingers.

Growing up is often confusing and frustrating for a child who begins to realise she can't control the world, other people or sometimes even herself. How your child responds to this realisation will depend largely on her temperament but also how you handle this stage in her development. Some babies take frustrations in their stride, are quite content with their lot and seem to wait for the world to come to them. Others want to go out and grab it and become desperate when it is beyond their reach. How soon this phase begins can also take parents by surprise – you may see tears of frustration or flashes of steely will and determination even in children under one year. Now is not the time to discipline but to understand:

Never underestimate the intensity or integrity of your child's feelings Little children experience powerful and passionate emotions. What may seem fickle, farcical or 'put on' to an adult is a child's very real and fluid emotion, whether it be frustration, rage or joy. To her, at that moment, dropping her toy may be The Worst Thing.

This passion is a driving force behind her development – if she cares enough about the brick she will attempt to crawl across the room to get it. Such extreme emotion is not always negative – watch a child's thrill at a new-found skill, see her race around in delight at her new mobility.

Understand the emotional seesaw She will swing dramatically from wanting to be with you to wanting to strike out for independence. She is not being 'naughty' or 'difficult', but simply hasn't a clue what she wants most so ends up wanting both with equal passion – hence the child who doesn't want to be picked up but doesn't want to be put down. Your child is on the cusp between infancy and toddlerhood and will have practice runs at progress then regress into needy dependency. It's all part of growing up.

Provide comfort and reassurance when she needs it Children experience new fears and anxieties as they become more aware of their world and their place in it. From around eight to nine months, for instance, your child may become wary or scared of strangers and cry or protest when she sees you leave a room.

The reassurance she needs is a reflection of the bond between you and the security she feels in your presence – all the things she'll need to become confident and increasingly independent.

Encourage when appropriate If your child is attempting a task that seems beyond her capabilities, help her but try not to take over – she may surprise you and be able to do it. If she has no chance of success, it may be best to encourage her to try something else.

Perfect the art of distraction A few well-placed toys could save you both the anguish of further frustrations. For a short while. Tempt her with a favourite game, show her the aeroplane, the bird, your watch, how you can touch the end of your nose with your tongue. Consciously shift the focus of your attention and your child is much more likely to shift hers.

A nanny I met told me a trick. It's a box of special, little things that's only brought out on special occasions or when I really need to get things done. We've got a toy box full of plastic so this is full of natural things or things made of natural materials that are good to feel – some wood, wool, a little loofah. Little ones are intrigued by it.

Helen O

Tantrums

Embarrassment in supermarkets? I have been there and got the T-shirt. My children thought they could do anything in supermarkets – demanding this, that and the other and protesting loudly if I refused – because they picked up that I would be embarrassed. Once they got the message that I was not going to be embarrassed any more and that regardless of what they did I was not buying it, they stopped trying it.

Vivienne Gross, Clinical Director, The Institute of Family Therapy

It wasn't the confrontation but the fact that he seemed so angry and desperate that I found so hard. It felt like I couldn't reach him. He wouldn't even let me touch him when he was in the middle of a rage. It was like he found life so hard in a way I couldn't understand and couldn't make better, and that made me so sad. Once I just sat on the bottom of the stairs and cried.

Caitlyn M

Tantrums can be divided into two basic types. At the root of one is frustration and anger that the child isn't getting what she wants when she wants it. At the root of the other is confusion and fear, prompted by the child's limited understanding of the world and its ways, and even herself. These two intertwine and feed off each other, but understanding the twin forces involved may help you decide how best to respond.

The essential difference between tantrums and earlier mood swings is the intensity and the level of confrontation. For the most part, she used to get angry with herself and her limitations. Now she may get angry with you.

Tantrums vary hugely from child to child, in type, intensity and timing. Some children never seem to rage, some wait until later (even school-age children do it – a foot-stamping, teeth-gnashing five-year-old is a formidable sight) and others have storm-force explosions from around 18 months. However and whenever they manifest themselves, children need to learn, for their own safety and healthy development, that they can't always have or do what they want, when they want. And they won't like it. They may scream, shout, kick or roll around the floor, often do all at once and usually perform best in public.

Your child may like running away in the street, for example. She may not even know the difference between this and a chasing game, until you let her know. But when you do she may get very, very angry at being controlled. So be it. You have to ensure she's safe and she has to be shown where the limits on her behaviour lie for her own sense of security.

It's hard on you, but imagine it from your child's perspective.

— She doesn't have the language to communicate all she wants to express, especially when she is excited or upset.
— She can't predict or control much of what happens in her life.
— She is beginning to be more independent of you and aware of this separateness, which can be pretty frightening as well as thrilling.
— Her abilities won't always match her desires.
— Her world is bewildering, with new freedoms and a growing consciousness of limits to that freedom.
— On top of all this there is the unpredictability of her own needs. At times she will swing madly between needing and rejecting you, clinging to you for reassurance then refusing to hold your hand. It can be tough being a toddler.

Your task is to help your child master her increasing powers and skills and to let her know this does not mean she is master of the universe. By not giving in to her every request you will also begin to teach her to consider other people and their needs – a hard and confusing concept to grasp but essential if she is going to socialise happily with others.

Prevention

Our evenings were hellish. I'd rush to the childminder's after work, but couldn't get there until gone six. He'd then fall asleep in the car on the way home, get hysterical when I got him out of the car, and sometimes carry on screaming and protesting until he fell asleep again. But I couldn't stop work so we had to think round it. I tried to get him to bed on time so he didn't start the day tired and my childminder restructured her day a bit to allow him an extra nap. She also built in quiet time in the afternoon, where the kids sat down with her while she read them a book. It didn't stop his outbursts, but it did help.

Claire M

You do have to maintain yourself as parents. You need enough rest and enough breaks to be able to stay calm when things are not easy.

John Bristow, psychologist and psychotherapist

The easiest way to cope with a tantrum is to prevent it. Try to ensure your child has rest and food when she needs it. It also helps to time shopping trips and other high-risk activities to fit in with her feeding and sleep patterns. But life isn't always that neat. Which is when other tactics are necessary.

1   **Allow your child to be physically active** Few toddlers will sit happily in a buggy or car, then happily in a supermarket trolley, then happily in the buggy or car again for the journey home. Before you go into the shop, walk around a little, go to the park, anything that uses a little of her energy reserves.

2   **Avoid unnecessary confrontations** Avoid refusing reasonable requests simply because saying no has become a habit. At other times, try rephrasing your replies to accentuate the positive (see Encouraging positive behaviour, p.143), especially if you are having to ask a young child with no concept of time to wait a while. To her, 'just a minute' means 'never' unless you make it clear that you really do intend to act. Compare:

> *Child:* 'Can I paint now?'
> *Parent:* 'No, not yet, I've got to . . .'

and

Child: 'Can I paint now?'
Parent: 'Yes. What a great idea. I'll just do xyz then we'll get the brushes out.'

It's the same message, but the different emphasis makes it more likely that your child will understand.

3 **Plan a trip to the shops as you would a long car journey** Take nibbles, your child's favourite book, a drink, a sandwich. Let her hold things, count things, chew things. Talk to her about what you're doing, ask her opinion, let her choose the bananas.

4 **If trouble is brewing, try to find out what the problem is** while there's still time to talk through or round it.

5 **If this isn't working or there simply isn't time, divert attention** Quickly. The 'Oh! I almost forgot! I've brought your crayons' trick sometimes works. Two Crayolas and a small scribble pad can mean the difference between peace and pandemonium.

6 **Avoid difficult situations** If going to the supermarket with your child is unspeakably awful, for instance, try to time trips for when she can cope best, or go at a time when a trusted friend or relation can babysit. If you're having a *really* bad day, try to make do with what you've got in the house. This isn't cowardice, this is survival.

7 **Set clear rules and expectations – and expect the best** Certainly avoid the trap of telling your child you expect the worst – 'Don't you go screaming the place down.' There is little more likely to give her the idea and children tend to fulfil our expectations. Instead explain, in language she understands, what it is you would like her to do. Even very young children understand much more than we tend to imagine. Underline this by showing pleasure at any co-operative behaviour.

8 **Encourage her to ask rather than to demand** This not only equips her with the beginnings of necessary social skills but is also less likely to wind you up.

9 **Keep out of view any sweets, biscuits etc** that you do not want her to have.

10 Make sure you have enough support and rest Dealing with tantrums is hard enough without adding your emotional or physical exhaustion into the equation.

Action

It may be tempting to try to prevent tantrums altogether, but you are unlikely to succeed and it should not be your aim. Most children have them and need to have them to express their emotions in the only way they know how. It may help to know that a child going through a particularly tantrum-prone time is often on the edge of an important developmental leap. So it's painful, but it's progress.

Children often have these difficult times prior to leaps of development. It is not always the case, but it is my conviction that they very often precede a big leap, say from not being able to walk to walking, from apparently not being able to read at all to being able to. It's almost as though the child is thinking, 'The world is not how I thought it was, but I'm not yet sure what it is.' It is an awareness of the problem before they find the solution, which often brings frustration.
Professor Hilton Davis, clinical child psychologist

Stay calm and in control Try not to match her behaviour, shout over her or crumble under the force of her temper. A child may become frightened by the intensity of her own emotions. If you are to help her not be overwhelmed by them, you must show that they don't overwhelm you.

Speak quietly and explain Try lowering the temperature by lowering your voice and expressing your confidence in her ability to behave better. (If she's screaming, save your breath until she's calmed down because she won't hear you.)

Avoid giving in to unreasonable demands Standing firm will re-educate her behaviour, giving in will encourage it big time.

Go to a quieter place If the tantrum is in public, take her to a quieter spot where you are both less likely to be embarrassed by other people's reactions.

Acknowledge your child's feelings This shows that you don't disapprove of your child's emotions but rather how she has chosen to express them. Simply stating the obvious – 'I know you feel angry' – shows not only that you've understood how she feels but also that you can deal with it without hitting, stamping or screaming (see Dealing with feelings, p.94). It is a powerful lesson.

I went to seek advice about my daughter's tantrums because they seemed so extreme. She was three, nearly four so I thought she would have grown out of them by then. I was told that all periods of transition are hard for kids because they are unsettling – she'd just started nursery and I'd just had another baby. The advice I was given was not to always meet the tantrum head on or always try to control it, but let it come out and say 'I understand why you are feeling angry, it must be very hard for you and you must be feeling very scared'. It's hard, but I am trying and it has helped me understand more what's going on for her.
Maggie C

Express how you feel If you are angry, tell her, calmly but firmly, and reflect this in your tone of voice and body language. If you pretend to be unaffected while you are seething inside, your child will pick up two conflicting messages and become even more confused and volatile. Recognising your feelings also helps keep them under control. It is hard – try counting in your head or breathing exercises if you feel about to blow a gasket.

Ignore behaviour? Depending on what's happening and why, your best response might be to ignore your child's excesses, if you can. You are the best judge of when this may be appropriate. Acknowledge her feelings, state your case, then avoid eye contact until she has calmed down.

Hold your child? Some children respond well to being cuddled when distressed. Others may be in such a rage that a cuddle will only make matters worse – they want to be heard, not soothed.

What if she holds her breath?

Some children hold their breath in anger but it is self-limiting – if you hold your breath for too long you pass out, which means you start breathing again. It is very frightening and parents need to feel assured the child will come to no harm.

Sarah Darton, health visitor

A tantrum's grand finale may be breath-holding. It can be terrifying, especially if parents have no idea what is happening and why. Some parents manage to trigger a gasp reflex before the child passes out by blowing in their face, but this is not always possible. If you are concerned, contact your health visitor, GP or health practitioner.

The first time it happened I was absolutely terrified. I had no idea what was happening. She always came round, but in those seconds you're waiting, your blood runs cold. It really scared me.

Lotti M

When the tantrum is over Once your child is calm, she may be willing to be cuddled. If not, at least explain gently that you are pleased it has passed. When the time is right, your child also needs to know that you love her, that you are on her side and that you understand how she was feeling, but that you do not like that behaviour and you are not going to give in to things you know to be unfair, unsafe or unreasonable. Suggest different ways for your child to show when she's angry. Perhaps let her draw a picture of how she felt, talk about words she could use or even faces she could pull (always a good one for taking the sting out of post-argument atmospheres. When the mood's right, try pulling a face, too, or doing them together in a mirror).

If tantrums are happening often and with great intensity, think through whether anything specific may be disturbing your child – simple changes of routine can sometimes knock a young child off kilter. Also ask yourself whether you are expecting better behaviour from her than she can deliver.

Perhaps you need to loosen up a little and allow her to be the young child she is, or perhaps tighten the reins a touch and establish clearer

Tidal-wave tantrums

Kitty Hagenbach, psychotherapist

'After the tantrum, children often need a hug and call out for mummy. At that stage the child just needs to be hugged unconditionally without any "No, you've been a naughty boy". They just need to be held. Then if things need to be talked about or boundaries set, leave a space, wait until everyone is calm, then talk about it.

'I think there is a tendency towards tantrums in toddlers because there are few other ways to release their aggression, frustration or anger – they can't just take themselves outside and kick a football. Also, when they are in their twos, their feelings are so much a part of their bodies and a tantrum shows itself like this with kicks and screams and flying arms.

'Often, if they are allowed to have the tantrum, it's like a wave of energy that is then gone. If this is stopped it can get pushed down and maybe this leads to later problems.

'It takes someone with good self-esteem and maturity to allow a tantrum, especially in a public place.'

boundaries. Only you will know the answer. Think it through, sort out the possible from the unrealistically perfect, and try again. Crucially, remember this is a phase. It does get better.

Biting

I've got a picture of my twins as babies with what look like glorious rosy cheeks. They're bite marks. They'd go for each other like terriers.

Jane P

All my children have gone through biting and out the other side and they always bit other children they loved passionately. It was funny, they never bit people they were not sure of.

Anne M

For many children, biting is as much a part of growing up as trying on their first pair of shoes. So is hair pulling, thrusting digits up a parent's nose and taking exquisite delight in pinching. If you turn a blind eye or otherwise condone it, you'll be pulled, bitten and pinched all the more, but your response should be guided by your child's age and understanding.

If a baby or toddler bites you Show your disapproval by putting her down immediately. If she has hurt you, show it.

If she bites another Remove her or, better still, leave her where she is and remove the victim so she does not receive extra attention for unacceptable behaviour (see Effective discipline: removing the victim, p.178).

Either way, calmly and very firmly tell her what she has done and that it is not to happen again.

Don't bite back. It may stop your child in her tracks but sends such a confused message ('My parent says this is wrong yet does it to me/my parent thinks it is OK to hurt me') that it should be avoided. It is up to you to show your child different ways of responding to provocation.

The defence to biting a child back – that they need to know how it feels – is just not valid. They do not know that a flame hurts but we are not going to stick their hand in it to teach them, neither are we going to stick them in front of a moving car. If a toddler is hitting, kicking or biting because they are angry or frustrated, the best way to deal with this is to acknowledge their feelings and show other ways of behaving in that situation. For example: 'I know you are angry because you wanted to play with what Johnny's got and you can't bite him. The next time you want to play with a toy he has, you ask him.'
Sarah Darton, health visitor

Hitting

*I didn't hit my first child. I always found him very easy to reach.
There was never any need to. So by the time my second came along we had
a house rule – no hitting – and it worked. I used to be able to say 'I do
not hit you, you are not to hit me' and it really helped. I felt lucky to have
it so well established because my second is so much wilder and it has
helped stop me lashing out at him.*

Abby H

*A lot of toddlers hit out in frustration. It is also very common between
siblings. Of course it will occur more if they see this behaviour around them.
Sometimes even in a household where hitting is only used in play, it can
still be a bit confusing to a young child. It takes quite a while for
children to learn limits and appropriate rules.*

Carol Ann Hally, health visitor, clinical practice teacher

The advice on biting applies here, too. In general, however, hitting can
remain a problem for much longer and the reasons are fairly obvious –
children are surrounded by images of heroes who hit, they may see
their siblings or even parents hit, they may be hit themselves. It is also
a quick way for them to get what they want – a toy, more attention, a
release for their anger or frustration.

If hitting is allowed to continue, the risks increase for the hitting
child as well as those hit. The best predictor of violence in adulthood
is violence in childhood,[4] so parental disapproval and action is vital
if the child is to be spared long-term problems (see Checklist for non-
violence, p.134).

If your young child hits, try to keep it in proportion (almost all
do it sometimes) but do act (they must be taught to stop). Show your
disapproval in ways appropriate to the child's age, remembering
that very young children who hit have no idea it hurts (see Effective
discipline strategies, p.175).

All children can benefit from very clear messages – 'We use words
in this house, not fists' or 'Being angry is OK, hitting is not' – and very
clear instructions on alternative ways to behave – 'Yell if necessary but
do not hurt'; 'If you feel that angry and you can't sort it out come and
get me and I'll help you' (see Dealing with feelings, p.94). Older, school-

Checklist for non-violence

The Commission on Children and Violence was convened to review the known causes of child violence and to make recommendations about violence prevention. Its members – all leading experts in childcare and welfare – commended the following basic principles:

1:　Expectations of, and demands made on, children should reflect their maturity and development.

'Children's development is a process, not a race . . . Children cannot do, or be, what is developmentally out of their reach. Adults who have unrealistic expectations of children therefore jeopardise the positive relationships on which non-violence depends and lack the basic understanding they need to keep children safe.'

2:　All discipline should be positive and children should be taught pro-social values and behaviour and non-violent conflict resolution.

'Negative discipline takes violence in the relationships between adults and children for granted by focusing on "bad behaviour";

age children can begin to think of ways to be assertive without being aggressive and to resolve conflicts peacefully (see Assertion v. aggression, p.314).

Understandably, children who are hit are much more likely to think that physical punishment is right than those who are not. The most important way to teach a child not to hit is to not hit them (see Smacking isn't the solution, p.196), and none of the alternatives will cut much ice if you do.

Refusing to share

This is very normal, especially between about 18 months and 3 years, yet parents have very high levels of expectation. They want children to grow up quickly, easily and be perfect. Children do not often come with all these social skills built-in, they need guidance and training.

Carol Ann Hally, health visitor, clinical practice teacher

expecting it, watching out for, and punishing it. In contrast, positive discipline leaves violence on the sidelines by focusing on "good behaviour"; expecting it, making sure it is modelled, understood and achievable, and rewarding it.'

3: Non-violence should be consistently preferred and promoted.

'It is useless to tell children not to fight (or snatch and grab, hit or kick) without giving them effective alternative ways of getting what they want or holding on to what they have. All children should be taught to use (and to respond to) verbal requests and protests. If children are to listen to each other, they must be confident that adults will listen to them.'

4: Adults should take responsibility for protecting children from violence done to them, but also for preventing violence done by them.

'Although adults perpetrate the extremes of violence in society, adults also represent children's only hope of safety from it, because without adult supervision and control, children's lives can be dominated by each other's violence.'

This is a phase all my children have been through. It begins when they start realising they are a little person in their own right – before they have realised other people are too!

Anne M

Young children need sharing demonstrated so they know what it means. They also need practice at it, so encourage them to hand round biscuits or other treats or offer a toy to a friend, and praise them if they succeed.

Expecting your child to share everything seems unrealistic. Most adults would happily share their food, their hospitality, even their clothes but might draw the line at their car or their mother's wedding ring. Children have precious objects, too, and it seems only fair that these are accorded special status and the rules explained to siblings and friends ('That blanket is her most special thing and no one can take it without her permission'). Keeping it out of sight of others is the easiest way to avoid disputes, especially when children are too young to be expected to understand the rules.

With pre-school children and older, granting some element of choice to the combatants often helps, so the holder is asked for an object rather than it being grabbed away. For example:

> *Parent:* 'Please let go. I'm sure he will let you have a turn when he's finished if you ask.'
> *Child One:* 'Please can I have a go?'
> *Child Two:* 'OK then' (possible) or 'I haven't finished yet' (more likely).

Your possible options now include:

Letting them sort it out Tell them you think children ought to share, ask them to think of how they could do so, retreat and make yourself a cup of tea (see Encouraging positive behaviour, p.143).

Counting This isn't counting of the 'I'm going to count to three and if you don't hand it over I'll . . .' variety, but rather 'OK. I know you want to play with it a bit longer and I know Tom wants to play with it, too, so let's count to 20 (or whatever number best suits the situation), then you have to hand it over. That's fair.' Twenty seconds is a long time in child politics and by then she may feel she has made her point and be happy to hand it over.

The rules of sharing are complex and demand a level of social sophistication way beyond the capabilities of most young children, so it helps to be patient, understanding and encouraging, and to provide your child with opportunities to practise by mixing with other children. Avoid asking older children to always give way to younger ones as there is nothing more likely to breed resentment.

> *Parents can too easily pander to a younger child's needs because it is easier when you are under stress. For example, a toddler wanting the older child's toys all the time and the parent saying 'Just give it to her, she is your baby sister and she can't understand.' Parents should try to avoid this. For a child to hear 'I understand it is your toy and you have every right to play with it. I can also see your baby sister wants a go very much. When you're ready, perhaps you'd give it to her' is so much easier. It helps her feel more motivated to share.*
> Brigid Treacy, Parent Network co-ordinator

Stealing

*A very young child may take something that does not belong
to them because they don't yet realise it is wrong. A warning sign
with an older child, who knows it is wrong to steal, is repeated, secretive
behaviour. I have seen examples in schools of a child stealing from coat
pockets, even stealing other children's lunches. They were not hungry,
but the theft was an expression of a need. It may be they felt they had
nothing, so wanted to take extra rather than appreciate what they had
and work for what they wanted. They may have the material things
they need, but feel neglected personally. Or they may be feeling that
other children are better than themselves and so they want to
deprive them of something. It is these feelings
that need to be addressed.*

Vivienne Gross, Clinical Director, The Institute of Family Therapy

*It's the game my boys enjoy best. Stealing the biscuit tin from under
my nose and dashing upstairs with their spoils. I only know they've got it
because it goes quiet.*

Clare M

Your response to your child's light fingers should depend on her age,
her understanding and the circumstances surrounding it.

If your child is pre-school or younger, remember that most very
young children have no notion of property or, when they do, their
notion is that all property belongs to them. If you overlook incidents,
however innocent, you are wasting an opportunity to explain and educate, but don't go overboard if it appears she did not know it was wrong.
Instead, talk about favourite things and how stealing hurts people's feelings. Express your confidence in her leaving other people's things where
they belong.

If you suspect your school-age child of stealing:

— Try to establish the facts
— Let her tell her side of the story (see Communication, p.70)
— Keep a sense of proportion. Many children take things that don't
belong to them at least once
— Calmly make your disapproval clear

— Tell her you love her and want to help before her situation becomes more difficult
— Discuss how people feel when their things are taken (books may help if direct discussion of incidents stops your child talking)
— Avoid labelling her a thief (see Ripping up labels, p.108)
— Let her decide what she may do to improve matters (apologise and return any property is the answer you are after. If she doesn't come up with it herself, suggest it)
— Be vigilant, and also let the matter drop once the issue is dealt with. If you keep bringing it up your child will feel she can never leave it behind, which gives her little incentive not to do it again.

She was always taking her older sister's jewellery and bits and squirrelling them away in her room. I was getting worried because whatever I said or did didn't seem to make a lot of difference, then it struck me that her big sister was actually quite clever and cutting and always got the last word. Perhaps taking her things was her only way of getting back at her? So I had to tackle the way both girls behaved.

Claire T

Lying

You might be worried that your three- or four-year-old appears to tell lies. Children of this age find it hard to separate reality from their fantasy world and may quite genuinely believe in something which they may have been daydreaming about.

Eileen Hayes, Parenting Advisor to the NSPCC

I told whoppers as a child, I think mainly to make my rather normal existence more exciting and exotic. I told friends my dad was in jail, even though they could see him coming home from work every night, that my mother used to lock me in a cupboard and push my food in through a trap door on a stick and that my brother was a smuggler.

Michelle C

Lying and spinning yarns is something most children grow into and, generally, grow out of again. Within reason. Very few adults tell the truth all the time yet very many expect their children to display total honesty – except when Grandma asks if they liked the jumpers she knitted.

A healthy dash of realism will help you keep your children's transgressions in perspective. The reasons children lie are as varied as the reasons adults lie – to impress, to embellish, to dodge, to conform, to please, to protect, to provoke, to delay consequences, because they don't understand the line between fantasy and reality or because they don't understand the question.

Very young children rarely lie – until they are old enough to realise that other people have different experiences from themselves, there's little point. The first step in the fantasy league is usually imaginary play (from one year), then vivid dreams, daydreams and nightmares (especially around three years), then denial that misdemeanours or broken ornaments have anything to do with them (around the time they realise they may get away with it). By the time they have had a year or two at school, most children have witnessed the art of telling whoppers even if they are not skilled practitioners themselves.

It is very important that your child knows the difference between fantasy and reality, that she tells the truth when it matters (ie most of the time) and that she feels she can tell you anything. If nothing is unspeakable, the incentives to lie reduce dramatically. To achieve this, it helps to:

Talk about lying Be clear that telling the truth is important. Discuss how lying can hurt others and hurt the person who lies. Tell the story of the boy who cried 'Wolf' so many times when it wasn't true that he wasn't believed when it was.

Recognise the power of a child's imagination Wild imaginings are not lying and should not be treated as such. Talk about dreams and thoughts, explain what is real and what not, and help your child see the difference.

Encourage truth-telling Avoid punishing your child for telling the truth, however hard it is for you to hear (see Communication, p.70). Praise when it happens and help your child feel she can tell you anything: 'If you were to tell me that you broke that vase, I wouldn't be angry. I would be sad, because I liked the vase, but I would also be very pleased that you admitted it.'

Set the example If your child catches you telling a white lie, explain why you did it. Or don't do it in front of her. Think long and hard before covering up a lie for your child – it is usually much healthier for children to face the consequences of their actions.

Let them know you know This is important, as lying and story-telling can become a habit. If she is making up harmless stories, let her know gently – 'I used to wish things like that happened, too.' If you know something to be a lie, say so clearly and calmly. 'I saw you hit her. What do you want to do to make things better?'

> *I say 'Ouch' and pretend I've got poked in the eye by a long nose if one of the boys starts spinning a tale. It's just a good-humoured way of letting them know what they're up to. Once they know I've got their number, they usually stop.*
>
> David Y

Know how literal children can be Some young children can be so excruciatingly literal that they tell a truth but miss the point. The only solution is to be aware that it may happen and to ask very clear questions.

> *My son was told off for running in the corridor at school. He denied it, the teacher said she saw him do it and so he got into trouble for lying as well. I was stuck in the middle, with my son insisting he didn't run and her insisting he did. About a week later, when he was still really upset, he said 'I was not running'. So for the first time I asked him what he was doing and he replied 'Skipping!'*
>
> Jane P

Know that children rarely lie about sexual abuse If your child indicates that she has been abused, you must take it seriously. Tell her that you love her and will help her, and contact a helpline immediately for guidance and support (see Contacts, p.355).

Cheating

The moral high ground of playing fair rather than playing to win is unfamiliar territory to most five-year-olds and under. Many children cheat. You must teach them not to because there's no surer route to unpopularity, but be prepared for a few tempers and loud expressions of outrage and frustration along the way.

— Encourage children to think how they would feel if someone cheated on them. Let them know that games are more fun if people stick to the rules – and make sure they are clear what the rules are.
— Explain how to win and lose well – shaking hands and/or congratulating your opponent, not gloating. This may sound more suited to the MCC than Mousetrap, but some children like the ritual and most appreciate clear guidelines.
— Stop cheating when you see it, but try to avoid humiliating the culprit – 'Oh, I think you've picked up one too many cards by mistake.' If the cheating persists, have a quiet, private word with the child involved and say you will stop the game if you see anyone not playing by the rules. Keep to your word.
— Play board and other games with them until they learn how to behave. It may help to have an adult on each 'team' to begin with.
— Praise children who do not cheat. It is very tempting, and those who do not do it deserve to be told how well they have played.

Saying they hate you

It should be OK for them to hate you in the moment. The love–hate relationship you can have with your siblings or children is actually the same for your child towards you. Just as you hate their behaviour rather than them, they are protesting and hating what you are doing, rather than hating you.
Brigid Treacy, Parent Network co-ordinator

Your child saying she hates you in the heat of the moment is usually nothing more than a healthy, passionate and instant response to you doing your job. Not every child says it aloud, but most show it at some stage with a withering look or a slamming door.

> *Parents sometimes don't follow consistent rules with their children because they are worried about the child not loving them, yet a great deal of what goes with the territory of parenthood is being the person your child can hate. Having them tell you that they hate you is what you are there for, in a way, just as much as putting the fish fingers and baked beans on the table. It is much safer for you to take it than for them to tell their teachers that they hate them or the policeman on the corner because you are also the one doing the loving and the care-giving. Their relationship with you is where your children work out how to deal with aggression and restraint.*
> Vivienne Gross, Clinical Director, The Institute of Family Therapy

Your job as a parent will involve drawing lines and taking action that your child doesn't like. Some of her worst excesses of behaviour will be kept just for you and that's as it should be. At least it shows she knows your love is unconditional.

CHAPTER EIGHT

ENCOURAGING POSITIVE BEHAVIOUR

Parents sometimes find it hard to believe, but children are essentially co-operative. They want to behave in ways that make them feel good and their parents feel good. The key to encouraging positive behaviour in your child is to build on this natural desire to please (see Ready to care, keen to please, p.144).

As a first step, we need to recognise and respond to the very basic needs that may lie behind a child's more ghastly moments – attention, comfort, reassurance, guidance, even sleep and food in the right amounts can go a very long way (see Highs, lows and outbursts, p.146).

Beyond this lies a long, rich process of education and relationship-building. It is an investment which pays huge dividends and requires parental time, effort and understanding. Before you begin to apply the approaches suggested here, try to read the chapters on Communication, p.70 and Dealing with feelings, p.94 if you haven't already as these contain important information about encouraging positive behaviour and are the foundation stones of all effective behaviour strategies.

You can also make a huge difference to your child's understanding of and capacity to behave considerately and co-operatively by being:

Clear Your child needs to know what is expected of him, where, when and why. To guide effectively, you will also need to understand and consider your child's emotions and viewpoint.

Caring You care enough to be firm and/or compassionate as required. You also know that a child who feels loved, appreciated and respected is more likely to behave better than one whose self-esteem is low.

Consistent However you want your child to behave – and this will vary between families and cultures – all children require predictability of expectation and response.

But let's get real. No child should be expected to behave impeccably at all times because that's not what people do. Burden yourself and

---

Ready to care, keen to please

For a child to develop positive, considerate behaviour, he has to recognise and appreciate the feelings of others. Incredibly, this capacity is evident in a newborn child.

Gavin Nobes, a psychology lecturer and researcher, explains: 'Newborn babies can show a capacity to empathise with others. For example, babies will often cry when they hear another baby cry. This response to others' distress is similar to an adult's who sees another person or animal in pain.

'By two or three years most children show frequent signs of empathy. A toddler who cuddles another child who is distressed shows a sensitivity to other people's pain.

'So it seems likely that humans are born with a capacity to recognise other people's emotions. Their understanding of others gradually increases through infancy and childhood by observing people's actions and responses.

'Parents also help children understand and interpret what people do and what they mean through clear and consistent explanation and communication. So children arrive with an innate potential to acquire social understanding that parents can build on.'

Your child is not only increasingly sensitive to other people's feelings – he also wants you to feel good about the way he behaves.

'What gives you a handle on your children's behaviour isn't simply a neat set of behavioural techniques,' says Vivienne Gross, clinical director of the Institute of Family Therapy.

'If things have gone more or less well between you in your child's early years, in terms of you paying attention to their needs, the sleeping, feeding, changing, keeping them warm, cuddling them and so on, your child will want to please you. They have become "attached" to you, the caregiver, and this allows them to think about you, as well as themselves.

'It shouldn't simply be that children are like prisoners who obey the prison guard for fear of punishment, but that they have a regard for you, from which all sorts of other social and relational possibilities ensue. If there isn't that attachment credit in the bank, it is going to be far harder to impose a behaviour regime that works. If you do it in a cold state rather than there being warmth between you, these regimes can feel very uncomfortable for you both.'

your child with unrealistic expectations and you could tie yourself in knots (see Horribly normal, p.119). You could also make your child feel a 'failure', which will make him even less likely to behave as you would wish.

All the skills outlined in this chapter are important ways to encourage and teach positive behaviour, but don't expect to get the hang of them all at once. Some simply involve a little thought while others require a lot of practice; some will help in specific situations while others can change family life dramatically. Decide which you and your child need most, do what you can, when you can, and you will all reap the benefits.

The basics
Rules and boundaries

Without boundaries a child is completely at sea. If they push those boundaries and they collapse, this is a very scary situation for a child to be in. They can become very aggressive.

Brigid Treacy, Parent Network co-ordinator

Kids need to have some control, but it is distressing for children to believe they have ultimate power. If they feel they can do anything, they are terribly unhappy because the world then becomes a frighteningly uncertain and unpredictable place. Part of being a parent is allowing your child to experiment, to test what the boundaries are and where they lie, because your relationship is the safest place for them to do this. Much, much better that they do it with their mum or dad than outside.

Professor Hilton Davis, clinical child psychologist

Setting limits on your child's behaviour and making it clear where you have drawn the line is crucial to your relationship with your child, to his future and to your sanity.

Some parents feel uncomfortable about this, fearing that it veers towards authoritarianism and outmoded codes of social conduct. The truth is that it should be a natural extension of your love, concern and regard for your child. This is not the opposite of warmth, nurturing and mutual respect, but part of it.

Highs, lows and outbursts

My son seems to need refuelling with food every
couple of hours. If he doesn't have a little to eat,
often, he gets grumpy.

Anne M

I heard a foster parent on the radio. She took the kids in her care
for a daily trip to the playground because, she said, kids with excess
energy are much more unruly than ones who've had sufficient exercise.
I tried the same with my kids and it's really helped.
They still fight, but it's much less frequent.

Sandra B

Your child is most likely to behave in ways you find difficult when he is bored, frustrated, rushed, tired, hungry or poorly. Or when you are bored, frustrated, rushed, tired, hungry or poorly and therefore less able or willing to be guide, nurturer, entertainer, cook, social secretary, servant and butt of any low-flying frustrations.

If you recognise and respond to such needs, including your own, your chances of your child behaving as you'd wish improve dramatically.

Some children have energy dips during the day when they are more likely to become belligerent and bloody-minded. Some school-age children have particular times of the week or term when they need extra sleep if they are not to fray at the edges. Others have astonishing bursts of energy and may need to play outside like puppies at least once a day if there's any hope of them settling down.

If you have children with wildly different physical needs, it may be worth organising your home as well as your routines to take this into account. A room in which rough play is not allowed can be a sanctuary for a child who feels swamped or threatened by a sibling's exuberance. It can also be a sanctuary for you.

Your child won't see it that way. Part of parenthood is being the butt of your toddler's outrage at not being allowed to stick his Teletubby down the loo or bite your arm, or of your six-year-old's eye-rolling contempt when it's time for bed.

As ever it is a balance, between being firm enough to guide your child's behaviour and not being a doormat to his every whim and will, while also helping him feel loved, appreciated and respected.

Every family will have their own expectations and rules to guide their children's behaviour, but once you have decided what these are, the following approaches should help you maintain that balance.

Setting rules and boundaries

Set First decide the boundaries that apply to behaviour in your house. *Boundaries* are the guiding principles, for example: your child is to be safe. These principles do not change as your child grows. *Rules* are how these principles are put into practice, for example: Leave the plug socket alone. These can and must be appropriate to your child's age and circumstances, so may need to be adapted over time.

Explain Both rules and boundaries have to be explained if your child is to fully grasp what is expected of him. This is key to positive behaviour, for the obvious reason that a child who knows what is expected and why it matters is much more likely to do it. You could, for example, explain that he is not to hit (rule) because in your family 'We respect and look after ourselves and others' (boundary).

Chatting with your child about what the rules and boundaries mean and the different ways they could be put into practice will help get your message across. This is important as they may contain abstract terms such as 'safety' and 'care', which will be of no use if your child hasn't a clue what you're talking about.

I sometimes tell my kids 'I love you too much to let you do that', and then explain that part of my job is to keep them safe and that's why I won't let them play football on the pavement or go over the road without holding my hand. It seems to make it less of a power struggle. It doesn't mean they always like it, but it helps them accept it a bit more.
Debbi B

Remind Be prepared to remind your child of the rules again and again until the message has sunk in – 'Remember, no hitting', 'We have a rule about that, can you remember what it is?' Assume your child is basically co-operative but not quite getting the gist of what you are saying – this will help you stay patient and realistic. Sometimes children protest or ignore because they don't like the message, sometimes because they've forgotten it and sometimes because they still don't understand it. Check which it is – if it is the latter, explain again. If not, keep it simple – 'You know we keep the balls in the garden.' Over-wordy or over-worthy explanations are unlikely to be listened to.

Try to keep boundaries and rules simple and few. A small number of basic and age-appropriate ground rules that everyone can remember and agree to abide by are more likely to be effective than 101 things to forget by breakfast.

If you have been able to communicate and reinforce these rules as your child grows there will be less need for anything more than occasional reminders. If, however, you feel you have all lost the plot, it may help to draw up a list of rules with your child so you have a chance to discuss what they mean and why they matter. You can stick the list somewhere where every family member can see it, if you think it would help. Remember, though, that the most important and effective reinforcement is your positive response when rules are followed and your firmness when they are broken. There's little point having the house festooned with lists that even you take little notice of.

Consistency

Lack of consistency is the main reason why rules sometimes don't work. You can minimise the risk by:

Standing firm A young child is not a miniature adult. He needs to test, to show aggression, be unreasonable and say 'No' to his parents' eminently sensible requests. He is not being 'bad', but rather going through an essential stage in his development – learning how far he can go. And it is up to you to teach him.

This requires you to stand firm and not cave in under the pressure of his protests, rages or whines. A child's very act of pushing against the limits often reflects a need to know that his world is secure and does not crumble or break down if challenged. It is hard to believe when faced with a full-throttle temper, but children need and want you to say 'No' and stick to it. If your child's behaviour forces you to wobble from what you believe to be right, you are creating an environment of uncertainty from which neither of you will benefit.

A baby is hard work to look after but there is no mystery — they are dependent and we have to be dependable. Then it changes, somewhere around 18 months to two years, when a child sends out their first message that they need their first bit of discipline or limit-setting. It is almost an invitation from them. In some way or other, with a look, a gesture or a phrase they say: 'What are you going to do about it?' They want you to engage them. They begin to need attention, guidance, limits and discipline. It should be a relaxed struggle through this stage — with you relaxed and them struggling! That's the point. The limits a parent sets and sticks to are essential for growing up. We all know how painful people are who didn't get this parenting at a key stage and still think they are centre of the universe. They have not learnt that other people have feelings, too.
Steve Biddulph, psychologist and author

Try to keep listening, for the sake of kindness and safety. Standing firm and not caving in to protests is not the same as ignoring what your child is saying — he may be protesting over the lack of a biscuit one minute and the next be shouting 'Isobel's fallen in the fish pond'.

Developing self-discipline If you set new rules or drop them at whim, your child will have problems knowing what matters. We all do it on occasions, but it helps to limit such lapses to as few as humanly possible.

I went through a stage when, for all sorts of reasons that had nothing to do with the children, I was pretty erratic over this. I would insist on something one day and let it go the next, or suddenly blow up about something that hadn't been an issue before, like clearing away the table or taking their shoes off when they came through the door. I realised it was happening and even apologised for contradicting myself and expecting them to mind-read and we managed to get back on track. But I know I made what was a bad time for me a very tricky time for them because they never knew where they stood. Things calmed down incredibly once that predictability was re-established, once I was able to be a bit more self-disciplined, I suppose.
Jeanette R

Consistency between adults

We are so different in what we expect of our children, and this will vary between cultures, families, even within couples. There are so many arguments between couples, for instance, about how long you can expect children to sit at a table and eat a meal. That is a real old chestnut.

Vivienne Gross, Clinical Director, The Institute of Family Therapy

I know, I know, I know. We're supposed to show a united front, never disagree in front of the children about how we deal with the children, divided we fall and all that. But she thinks I'm too strict and I think she lets them get away with things too often. We don't agree and when tempers are high that's pretty obvious, I'm sure.

Mark D

Consistency between you, your partner and any other adults who care for your child makes a huge difference to your child's behaviour for the very obvious reason that one message is easier to follow than many conflicting ones.

Disagreement between parents can rock a child's sense of security and leave him unsure of what behaviour is expected. This is true of any age, yet especially when he begins to socialise with other children in situations outside the home. Different messages about accepted behaviour will be flung at him from all directions now, and he'll have little chance of negotiating this successfully if he is uncertain of his own family's expectations.

Let's inject a note of realism here. If the government's spin doctors can't manage to keep all its spokespersons singing the same tune, you can hardly be deemed unusual if you occasionally slip 'off message'. There will be times when your child realises you disagree with how your partner or another carer does things, just as there will be times when you give in to your child too easily. It's not great, but it happens.

What matters is that you keep these times to a minimum, and you can do this by regularly discussing your approaches with your partner or others and agreeing common ground and strategies. This also reduces the risk of your child spotting the gaps between you, or of one parent becoming the 'bad guy' for taking discipline seriously and the other becoming the soft option. Agreements take time and energy but think of them as an emotional investment that will help prevent future rows and uncertainty.

Revising rules Rules need to be adapted over time, as your child develops and his needs and your expectations alter. Many rules that apply to a toddler, for instance, would be totally inappropriate for a child of six. If rules are updated so they remain right and relevant for your child's development and circumstances, they are easier to stick to. In this way, strange as it may sound, allowing rules to evolve and change can sometimes be the best way to remain consistent.

What stay firm are the principles from which those rules spring, and this is where your child's understanding of these really helps. For example, he knows that one general principle is that he is kept safe. 'Always hold my hand as we cross the road because you must be safe' can change, eventually, into 'Look both ways as you cross the road' without you appearing to contradict yourself, because that general principle remains. All that has altered is the best way to put it into practice.

Such evolution is a sign of strength, not weakness, because inappropriate rules are all too easily ignored. Understanding boundaries and the need to apply them in ways that best suit each child may also help you negotiate some of the more common sibling battles: 'I know you're angry that he goes to bed later than you but the younger you are the more sleep you need to stay healthy. You go to bed when you need to, and he goes to bed when he needs to. And you can do the same as him when you're older.' Different rules, same principle, no contradiction.

Revising rules is very different from caving in under the pressure of a child's temper or your own indecision. To make it clear to your child that you have updated a rule because you think it is right, not because of his fuss or protest, it helps to:

1   Not change the rule on the spot. Giving way in the heat of the moment may give your child the impression that a good outburst will see off any rules he happens not to like. Don't justify, but stick with the rule you know for the time being.

2   When the situation has calmed down, consider if the rule does need revision. If the rule doesn't need changing, explain why it still matters. If it does, acknowledge it. Explain that you have thought long and hard and decided what the new rule should be (it may be useful to include the child in the making of the new rule, where appropriate). He thus feels you have responded to the new circumstances rather than his negative behaviour. He will also feel that he has a voice in the rule-making process, which will increase his sense of responsibility.

Making exceptions Consistency in the rules you set for your child does not mean they can never be bent. Most good rules have good exceptions. It is hard for children to understand priorities and urgencies and it is up to us to help them. If you take the time to explain why and how an exception is being made, the general rule can still hold good.

Support skills
Accentuate the positive

This is so important, I can't stress it enough. We always tell parents it takes three positive comments to every one negative comment to change behaviour. It's not easy – it's not very British to accentuate the positive, after all. We tend to just tell children off when they're not behaving. But then they get attention for being 'bad' and not for behaving well.

Jenny Oberon, Deputy Headteacher seconded to the Leeds Attendance and Behaviour Project

If you describe to the child what you would like from them rather than what you do not want, it gives them an image of what could be, so it is quite creative.

Barbara Dale, Parent Network co-ordinator and counsellor

Children's lives are filled with instructions on what not to do. Which is a great shame, because if they were told what to do they would be much more likely to do it.

Accentuating the positive has two basic strands:

1   Telling your child what to do rather than what not to do.

2   Noticing and commenting when he does something right (see Descriptive praise, p.154) rather than only noticing and commenting when he does something wrong.

The approach takes time and practise but can bring about dramatic improvements in a child's behaviour. Compare the following examples. Which one gives a child the information and education he may need to behave differently in future?

'Not like that, you'll cut yourself!'

or

'If you hold the knife like this it keeps it away from your fingers.'

Even the most urgent instructions can usually be given positively and effectively. Compare:

'Don't cross the road!'
with
'Stop. Now!'
or
'Don't run off with those matches'
with
'Put the matches in the drawer.'

Negative instructions have a nasty habit of turning into self-fulfilling prophecies: 'Don't! You're going to drop it all over the carpet!' can undermine a child's faith in their ability to do otherwise. Instead, try 'Hold the cup tightly when you carry it'. An anxious or angry 'Don't do that, you'll fall' may result in the child doing just that. You could tell the child what he needs to know specifically and positively, as in 'Turn around and come down the stairs backwards'.

Count up the number of times in a day your child is criticised or told what not to do, and the times he receives a positive comment. The results may surprise you. Yet simply turning around your language won't work unless you also believe in your child's intention and ability to co-operate. Children can spot insincerity and tend to do what is expected of them, not simply what they are asked to do.

This can be a hard shift to make if you see your child as 'trouble-some' or 'difficult' but it is worth the effort. Continual lack of trust can breed resentment and even rebellion as a child gets older. He will see no point in improving his behaviour if the worst is always seen and mis-takes are always highlighted.

Telling your child what not to do also risks giving him the idea in the first place. 'Don't you dare throw that water over me' may introduce an option he hadn't even considered. Negative comments can also be more provocative, especially for older children. 'Don't think you're going to come in here and drop your things all over the floor young man' is far more likely to result in conflict than 'Put your things away before you go out'. Even an implied 'Don't you dare' can be taken as a challenge!

Accentuating the positive, like all skills, is not appropriate to every occasion. Negative language – especially 'No!' – can sometimes be the quickest and most effective way of getting your message across, while there will be other times when you simply don't use the skill as well or as often as you would wish. Don't aim for perfection but do aim to increase the positive and reduce the negative comments in your child's day. This is what matters.

Descriptive praise

Its effect was like getting a drink when you are really parched.
It turned things around from a situation where we were at each other's throats,
when you ask yourself 'How did this all go so horribly wrong?', to one in
which you re-establish the links with your child. It was the most fabulous
tonic for both of us at a time when everything seemed hopeless.

Kate K

It worked even at tea time, a time of day that usually brought out the
worst in everybody. Instead of noticing what she hadn't done, like eaten all
her carrots, I said what had gone OK, like 'You've eaten two sausages already,
you're doing well.' It affected her behaviour around food straight away,
which I hadn't expected. Instead of pushing her food around,
she ate more than she had in weeks.

Lindsay M

Praise is a great motivator, and the most effective form of praise is descriptive. Descriptive praise – saying precisely what your child has done and why you approve – educates him in what you like and why you like it and thus increases the chances of him doing it again.

This is a simple and extremely powerful skill that you can use to encourage every aspect of his behaviour, from the way he cleans his teeth to the way he treats his friends. It may take practice until you feel comfortable with it, but it is worth every bit of effort.

Consider the following examples. Which provide your child with the most useful information?

Descriptive praise: 'Thank you for putting the glass on the side, it stopped it getting knocked over.'

or

Non-descriptive praise: 'Clever girl.'

Descriptive praise: 'It was kind of you to kiss Matthew, he was feeling a bit sad.'

or

Non-descriptive praise: 'Good boy.'

Repeated, non-specific praise of the 'Good boy' type soon loses its currency, while descriptive praise shows that what your child has done matters enough for you to take proper notice. An absent-minded 'Oh, lovely, dear' or 'That's nice' when shown your child's latest picture, especially when you've not taken the time to look, conveys little more than disinterest. 'That's beautiful' will not mean as much to your child as 'I love the way you have done the mountains so big and the people so small'. Children know when you haven't paid attention, and this can be worse than not noticing at all. It is usually safer to be honest and say 'I'm up to my eyes at the moment, but I really want to see it. Can you show me after tea when I'll have more time for a proper look?'

You can use descriptive praise whenever your child has done something worthy of a mention – painting a picture, sitting for a meal, finding shoes, putting the toothpaste back. Look hard enough and any step in the right direction can be appreciated and commented upon. The approach is particularly helpful when:

— A child is 'stuck' in a certain pattern of behaviour
— His confidence is low
— You have hit a rough patch and are aware that your child is getting more negative attention that is helpful for either of you
— Your child has done something he previously found difficult
— He has turned his behaviour in a more positive direction

As ever, don't fake it. Insincere, overused or inappropriate praise at best loses its currency and at worst undermines your child's trust in your honest opinion or focused attention.

Children do know the value of the praise they are getting and some know that whatever they do they will be praised by their parents and thus it becomes meaningless and is a waste of time. 'Mum, I've just murdered someone' –

'Oh that's marvellous, darling'. Praise is also often used to cover some sort of deficiency in the child or his environment. If used in this way, to compensate for not being very able or suffering a loss, a child will know this.'

Dr Dorothy Rowe, psychologist and writer

It's getting the balance that's the tricky bit. Between noticing and commenting on the good things, that he's sitting calmly or picking up his toys or whatever, and not going over the top and saying, 'Wow! You've picked up your toys!' Because that sounds so insincere. It's got to be somewhere in the middle, so you're comfortable with it. But once you are, it really works.

Anne M

Clear messages

I realised I had to be more precise with my instructions after the baby was born and I found my daughter dragging him down the hallway by his feet. This very sorry child said 'But you told me not to carry him when you weren't in the room. I didn't carry him. I pulled him.

Jane P

The clearer your message the more easily and quickly your child can respond. Being brief and to the point, making sure your body language matches your verbal message, leaves less room for debate and negative reaction. Compare:

'Deborah, where's your coat? You know you have to put it on so what are you doing looking at your comic?'
with
'Deborah – coat.'
or
'How many times have I told you not to do that? I can't believe you're still at it.'
with
'Joe – stop.'

Children can be excruciatingly pedantic. Giving simple, positive messages, rather than negative ones (see above), usually leaves you less open to contradiction and lets your child concentrate on carrying out your instruction rather than nit-picking. 'Keep the noise down' sends a clear message. 'Don't shout' risks a reply such as 'I'm not shouting, I'm singing'.

It helps to check first that you have your child's attention – saying his name then pausing helps him realise that you are addressing him – then check back that he has listened (see Communication, p.70). Be as specific as you can – 'Time to pick up your toys' – and avoid vague requests to 'be nice', 'be tidy', 'be kind'. Also avoid dressing up instructions as requests. Ditching the niceties of social etiquette can be hard, yet 'Please' or 'Would you?' may give children the impression they have an option not to do as asked. 'Would you brush your teeth, please?' may be less effective than 'Time to brush your teeth'.

Experience and example

STOP SHOUTING!
Parent, shouting

You cannot teach a toddler not to bite by biting her (whatever you may say) or teach a five-year-old not to hit other children by hitting him . . . If you do not listen to her, why should she listen to you? If you slap his hand when it goes where it shouldn't, why should he take care not to tread on your foot when it gets in his way? . . . Children take far more notice of what adults do than of what they say, so 'do as you would be done by' is good practical advice as well as ethical exhortation, whereas 'do as I say, not as I do' is neither.
The Commission on Children and Violence[1]

You can run but you can't hide. Your child will echo your behaviour and reactions and, from birth, his greatest role model is you.

How you respond to your child and to others has a far stronger impact than anything you say, so if you want to encourage your child to behave positively it only makes sense to reflect on your own behaviour, what that may be teaching him and whether it needs to be modified.

Aim for your actions to reinforce your expectations, not undermine them. If you shout, for example, your child is more likely to shout. If you stick to agreements, your child is much more likely to trust you, stick to agreements himself and know that you mean what you say.

Consider your parenting style and what that may be telling and teaching your child. It may help to split common parenting styles into three categories:[2]

1 **Authoritarian** This parent is overly strict, tending to pick their child up for every minor misdemeanour. They are often harsh and sometimes aggressive, depending on their mood. They are likely to impose rules on their children with no explanation other than 'Because I said so'. Their children are unlikely to be involved in decisions or rule-making.

2 **Permissive** This parent is not strict enough. They pretend not to have seen or heard even serious misbehaviour, either because they are unsure of how to tackle it or, for some other reason, don't want to. They often become resentful. Their children are usually sheltered from the consequences of their actions.

3 **Assertive** This parent is vigilant in observing their child's behaviour and responding appropriately. They are usually calm, assertive rather than aggressive and have good self-esteem. Their words and body language convey an expectation of compliance. They tend to believe every family member has a right to be considered and heard, explain and discuss rules with their children and revise them where necessary (see Consistency, p.148).

Children raised in authoritarian households are likely to miss out on opportunities to develop the skills of negotiation, co-operation, sharing and competition. They will also tend to see rules as absolutes that are imposed from above and must be followed without question, regardless of whether they are fair, in order to avoid punishment. They are unlikely to understand the point of rules and so will break them if they think they can get away with it. Children do have the potential to develop an understanding of rules as agreements and of right and wrong. How this potential is developed is largely a function of how they are parented, and whether they are encouraged to talk about rules and occasionally challenge them.

Gavin Nobes, lecturer in Psychology, University of East London

Extra time

People today are always in a rush. The enemy of love is hurry.
Love returns when we spend time together. If you want things to go well
with your children you need to win back some time. Children are in the
here and now. If you talk to anyone who has had something scary
happen with their children, they all say 'Enjoy them now'.

Steve Biddulph, psychologist and author

This is at risk of sounding like magic wand-waving. Talk to most parents about having more time for their children and the most polite response is 'Chance would be a fine thing'. Time is what many parents have much too little of, often for reasons way beyond their control. Yet that does not deny its importance.

If you can, grab some and hold on to it tight. The importance of spending time enough with your child to properly enjoy each other's company and understand him, his experiences and his emotions is obvious; less obvious may be the importance of allowing extra time to help your child behave co-operatively, which will help you both enjoy each other's company.

A tantrum-prone toddler is less likely to blow a gasket if he is allowed a bit of wobble, allowed to take great interest in every gate hinge on the way to the bus stop, allowed to walk to the shops and back for once or choose his own jumper after great deliberation. A few minutes playing with your child, starting off a game, rigging up a sail on the end of the sofa or chopping up an apple for his plastic animals can bring you more peace in the end than ignoring his cries that he's nothing to do. Morning hysteria – the 'I can't find my vest/where's my book bag?/I'm not taking this banana it's got a brown bit' routine – can sometimes be reduced by simply allowing an extra 20 minutes.

It is not going to work every day – sometimes you will need that extra 20 minutes in bed – and rushing against the clock is often unavoidable. But rushing ups the emotional stakes with children of any age, which means they are more likely to behave in ways that drive you to distraction. An awareness of this may help you make extra time a greater priority.

Almost everything with children requires effort, time and giving.
You will either give it up front or after the event, trying to sort out
conflicts and upset. In my experience, it's easier to take time to
think and head in the right direction than head off in the
wrong one and have to turn everybody around.

Claire H

Face-saving

Adults don't respond well to ridicule or loss of face, and neither do children. If you want to avoid confrontations, backlashes and damaging humiliation, you need to avoid shaming or embarrassing your child in front of others unless absolutely necessary.

Time is a useful face-saving device. If you give your child a choice or instruction, try giving him a little time to comply or think the matter through. Say what you have to say, then physically turn away to lessen the sense of confrontation and to indicate that you expect compliance without any further fuss.

Very young children may forget what they are supposed to be doing if you leave the room, but slightly older ones (school age and possibly younger, depending on the child) may respond well if told 'I'll be back in a minute to see how you are getting on/what you have decided'.

For similar reasons, advance warning of a situation may save public clashes and be all a child needs to think through how best to behave. 'We are going to Grandma's house soon. Can you remember the deal we made: if you take the toys out of the shed you put them back again before we leave?'

Helping

Don't do anything for children that they can do themselves,
including their thinking. Children are not grateful if you do. Their natural
urge is to become self-reliant and we as parents become resentful if
we do not allow them to be.

Noel Janis-Norton, Director, New Learning Centre

Your child can help you in many ways, from putting on his own shoes to buttering his own bread, tidying away his toys or setting the table. Children generally like to help and encouraging language may be all that is needed to prompt them into action. Compare:

> *Parent* (irritated): 'Didn't I tell you to put your shoes on? Do I have to keep telling you?'
> with
> *Parent* (calm): 'What's next? Is there anything else you need to put on?'

or

> *Parent:* 'How can you have brushed your hair when there's a big knot at the back. Let me do it.'
> with
> *Parent:* 'You've brushed the sides well. Show me how you can reach that difficult bit at the back.'

If children are to do things for themselves, they have to be allowed to learn how to do it. Learning involves making mistakes. They may take longer than you would and almost inevitably will not do it as well, but try to think of it as investment for the future.

Guide gently, help when requested or when your child seems over-whelmed by the task, and attempt to build regular activities, such as clearing up, into your daily routine. It makes sense to save rules and high expectations for things that really matter, and remember that you cannot expect a child to be helpful, co-operative and responsible only when you find it convenient.

> *'I always have to do the washing up again once he's gone to bed, but he's having a go and that's great.*
> Fiona P

Children may need some help clearing up their room, for instance. Sometimes it gets so bad that the child doesn't know where to start. You might say 'You do 10 minutes and I'll join you', or 'You do this bit and I'll do that bit', or help them put everything in a black bag from which they can take the things one by one and put them in their right place. Sometimes it just gets overwhelming for a six-year-old to do on their own. Sometimes it gets overwhelming for a 36-year-old!
Vivienne Gross, Clinical Director, The Institute of Family Therapy

Encouraging helpfulness and altruism

Professor Hugh Foot, specialist in child psychology
and social development

'Most children will respond very positively if given the opportunity to do something that is good for somebody else, especially their parents. The whole process of helping in the home, helping Mum, helping Dad, helping brothers and sisters and understanding it will be reciprocated is a good, constructive attitude to engender within families.

'The worst thing is children who have everything done for them and who never have to lift a finger, who have not had to strive for anything and who have not had the opportunity to learn the pleasure of doing things for other people. Little children love to help with cooking, even if it is just stirring flour and water together. So they make a mess in the process, so what? They have enjoyed it and the parent is paving the way for the child learning family obligations and responsibilities, which makes it a lot easier later on to get the child to help with routine housework such as washing up without having to be bullied, coerced or bribed into doing it.'

Humour

My son sat down in the park and refused to move saying 'My legs don't work any more. All my bones have gone'. I had his sister, too, and no buggy, and I couldn't carry them both so I just said 'Ooops, so have mine' and did a wobbly walk which made them laugh. He forgot his temper.

Deborah C

He was lying on the floor, moaning about not wanting to go to school and waving his feet in the air. So I asked him why his shoes were called Clark. It really made him laugh.

Rob N

Humour is a great tool for encouraging children to co-operate. Most children laugh easily and if you can help your child laugh, smile or simply enjoy himself, tension is released. As fun is contagious, you will both feel better. Your child will have also learned an important lesson in using humour to diffuse difficult situations. You could try a race to the bathroom when your child refuses to go, or a race to clear up the toys, or try a big bottom lip competition to see who can stick theirs out furthest if your child's is just beginning to protrude in a minor temper. A happy, or at least happier, child is more likely to do as you would like, so it is worth a try.

Wishing is another silly diversion that may help diffuse potential conflict, as in:

> *Child*, faced with walk home from a much enjoyed playground: 'I wish we'd never come. I hate walking.'
>
> *Parent:* '*I* wish I had a rocket on the back of my jumper and I could fly us all home.'

Your child may come back with more wishes, and so can you, until you make it to the front door. Even if he doesn't, his mind will, hopefully, be taken off his own temper by his parent's bizarre imaginings.

Aim not to direct humour at your child in ways that might make him feel laughed at, but rather use it to distract attention elsewhere. Also pick your moment. If your child is genuinely distressed, cracking jokes would be not only insensitive but also likely to backfire. You will know when the time is right – and that will be surprisingly often. When it is, making your child laugh can turn even a bad situation into a good time.

> *They would not go upstairs for their bath without a battle, so I'd say*
> *'How do you want to get up the stairs, like frogs or rabbits or monkeys?'*
> *Whichever they'd choose, we'd hop or jump up the stairs and they'd go quite*
> *happily. Listen, if you're desperate, dignity goes out the window.*
>
> Paula A

Choices

At its simplest, this is a trick – giving your child two options, both of which you are happy with. As in 'Would you like a bath with bubbles or soap?' The option your child is not offered is no bath at all. This is useful in areas where you have clashed in the past, as the child feels he has some say in his life but you set the parameters. 'Would you like your hair washed tonight or tomorrow?' will probably result in a day's delay but at least you may have some agreement that it happens at all, and it is usually easier with forewarning.

At a deeper level, giving choices helps children become aware of the consequences of their actions and find their own solutions, both crucial if they are to grow to be self-reliant and self-disciplined.

Even choices such as 'Would you like carrots or broccoli with your tea?' or 'Would you like Helen or Christopher to come to lunch tomorrow?' can show a child that his opinion is valued and that life isn't something that only happens to or for him but rather requires him to play some part in its outcomes.

At their most effective and educative, choices inform your child of the natural consequences of his actions, for example:

> 'If you stay in the bath there won't be time for stories. Are you staying in or getting out?'
> 'It's up to you. Clear up quickly and there'll be time to go to the park. If you don't, there won't.'
>
> or
>
> 'You decide. If you eat your grapes now, there'll be none for your packed lunch tomorrow.'

A threat, on the other hand, is a sanction imposed by the parent that has no natural link to the act: 'If you don't pick up your toys you won't go to the party tomorrow.' These teach a child what is not allowed but don't explain why, so tend to be much less effective in the long-term (see Consequences, p.179). Most parents resort to threats in times of desperation, but beware. If your child gets used to bribes and threats, they could be used against you. Natural consequences are more educative and much less likely to rebound.

> *My six-year-old started saying 'If I can't watch the end of this,*
> *I won't eat my tea', or 'If I can't play football I'm not going to bed'.*
> *I'd been threatening him, not by hurting him but by trying to control his*
> *behaviour by taking things away, and he'd learned it from me.*
>
> Sasha D

Deciding their next step

Remember to listen from your child's point of view. Our opinions, knowledge and judgements can be useful in some situations but this is the time to listen and we can easily overpower both the exchange and your child's ability to find their own way simply from our own desire to fix things quickly.

Camila Batmanghelidjha, psychotherapist and Director of Kid's Company

If children are allowed to work out for themselves how best to proceed in a new or tricky situation:

1 They are more likely to put their conclusion into practice. They have thought the matter through and understood it more fully than if solutions were imposed by their parents.

2 It is habit-forming. Once children realise they can work their way through a situation without their parents telling them what to do, they are in a far stronger position to face the next tricky situation thrown their way.

Your role is to support the decision-making process and not impose your own opinions and judgements (see Reflective listening, p.84). A good first step is to let your child know you think he is capable of working it out for himself:

'It seems to me that you need to find another way to do that.
  Can you think of anything?'
or simply:
'That's a problem. What do you think you could do about it?'

If your child can't think of an answer, you can help. Some problems begin to untangle just by talking them through. If this doesn't work, you could offer suggestions or provide the missing bit of information he needs. Even if your child asks directly for your help or advice – 'What can I do?' – it is more helpful to provide possibilities and leave the final decision to him.

Child (desperate): 'I can't find it anywhere and I've got to wear it tomorrow. What am I going to do?'
Parent: 'How about asking Tom if you can borrow his for a day?'
Child: 'Or Christopher's. He's got two.'

Parent: 'Good thinking. Let's give him a ring.'

or

Child: 'I just can't do it. You do it for me.'
Parent: 'Well how about trying this way? Or this?'
Child: 'I want to do it this way.'
Parent: 'OK.'

Sometimes there are no solutions, simply situations and emotions that have to be dealt with. If your child can describe and express how he feels, he will be better able to cope without crumpling or exploding (see Communication, p.70 and Dealing with feelings, p.94).

Who has the problem?

You want your child to co-operate but you're not sure how to help him. What next? Standing back from a problem and working out who is affected by it often makes it easier to choose an effective solution.

If it is your problem. You will need to say what the problem is, why it bothers you and what you want done about it. Simply telling your child to pick up the school bag from the hall, for example, doesn't indicate why doing this is important. It doesn't bother him, after all. Instead, try: 'Your bag's in the hall. It could trip someone up, which worries me, and it looks untidy. Put it away now, please.'

If it is your child's problem. Let him work out how best to proceed, with your help (see Deciding their next step, p.165). If, for example, he hasn't been invited to a friend's party, encourage him to talk about how he feels and what, if anything, he would like to do about it (see Dealing with feelings, p.94 and Reflective listening, p.84). Resist the temptation to make it your problem, too – ringing up the mother and asking why your son wasn't on the guest list won't solve the situation.

If it is a problem for both of you. You need to negotiate. If the morning mayhem makes you late for work and your child late for school, you both need to consider ways to ease the situation. Maybe you could lay your child's clothes out if he would agree to try to dress himself.

Learning that life isn't perfect

*I hate this notion of always, always responding to your child every
minute of every day of every week. Some advice to parents about this – that
you should respond immediately to your child's every need – is quite persecuting
and can make your own self-esteem low because you know you can't be like
that all the time. You are a human being and children need to know that
you have your limits. You are not going to prevent them from ever feeling
neglected or misunderstood and they have to be able to cope with that.
As your child grows older, you have to counterbalance being responsive
and listening to their unique needs as an individual, with letting
them experience age-appropriate frustrations and postponing
gratification, in other words, letting them wait for their needs
to be met. This is socialisation.*

Vivienne Gross, Clinical Director, The Institute of Family Therapy

Want some good news? Being imperfect is good for your child. This is
nothing to do with being harsh on your child and everything to do with
not being harsh on yourself when you occasionally fly off the handle,
do not act as well as you wished or cannot do immediately all that your
child desires or requires of you.

Being honest, human and fallible helps your child understand that
life doesn't always go as we want it to and helps him learn to cope when
it doesn't. This is crucial to his ability to know how to behave in difficult
or frustrating situations without feeling swamped by his own anger, upset
or outrage. He has to learn how to cope with adversity and it is much
safer for him to learn this from a person he loves and who loves him.

Learning that other people have needs that may have to take
priority is essential if the child is to progress successfully and happily
from the infant's sense of omnipotence (see Pre-toddler mood swings,
p.122 and Tantrums, p.124). Learning to wait for non-material and
material pleasures also increases their value as they become invested
with the pleasure of anticipation.

If a child's parents and his own experience tell him that he will
always get what he wants and that he influences everything, he may
blame himself when things go wrong that are outside his control. This
notion can blight a child's life. Even a child brought up to believe that
good always overcomes bad, that the truth will always be told and that
the guys with the white hats always win, can be deeply shocked when

real life gets in the way and it doesn't happen like that. Those with a more balanced experience better understand that this is not a reflection on themselves.

It is my observation that many well-meaning parents bring up
their children badly. If a child is brought up to believe that the world is

---

The problem with 'perfect' parents

Christine Puckering, psychologist and Co-founder of Mellow Parenting

'Life will present us with many frustrations, and learning to deal with frustration and disappointment in small ways is a very good stress innoculator for later. Children who have never experienced any frustration don't know how to handle it; they have not learned to negotiate.

'Respecting a child is not the same as giving in to their wishes all the time. In fact it is not good for a child to have what they want all the time, so I have no problem with telling a child "I know you want two biscuits but one is enough". They need these useful lessons. It is important to acknowledge and validate their feelings and wishes, but not necessarily to grant them.

'We followed a group of women who had depression when their children were two years and some of those mothers were being "the perfect mother". They got up at 5 o'clock in the morning and did all the housework so when the child got up at 7.30 they could spend the whole day with the child. They had very warm, very intense relationships with their children. Observing them at two, I thought, "Gosh this child is the happiest child, what a wonderful childhood." When we saw them again at entry to playgroup these same children had absolutely no idea how to deal with frustration.

'There was a group of bigger boys who were playing a bit rough and I remember vividly one of these children who had had this wonderful relationship with his mother going up to these kids and expecting to just get what he wanted. They hit him and he did not know how to handle not getting what he wanted. He just kept going back for more.

'It is forgiving for parents to know that having the odd bad day and their children surviving it is actually quite useful. If they haven't learned to cope with people in bad moods they won't know when to stand up and be assertive and when to let this one go, when it is best to stay clear. This little boy standing up to four bigger boys when starting school hadn't really learned it. It is a huge social and survival skill and you do not learn this if you get all your needs met instantaneously.'

a fair and just place to be as an adult, he or she will be disappointed. Some adults can never really get over this. Just think about how unpleasant the business world is. You need to be prepared for that. We need to stop pretending the world is a perfectly fair place but rather an interesting one in which we can encourage children to take on challenges and face problems with as much courage as possible. It is important to educate children on what helps them survive life.

Dr Dorothy Rowe, psychologist and writer

CHAPTER NINE

EFFECTIVE DISCIPLINE

It's like starting again, beginning again, both having another chance.
Jacqui C

*You feel so isolated. You feel it is just you and this kid
you're having trouble with.*
Melanie M

*I like to talk about soft love and firm love and the need for both.
Soft love is the very patient sort of love, the kind you ideally have
around little babies. Firm love is the capacity to really hold the line with
your child. It is done in a loving way but it is firm – 'It is not OK to hit
your sister', 'You cannot have the ice cream until after your tea'.
This is a tricky area for most people, particularly those who
grew up with very harsh parenting.*
Steve Biddulph, psychologist and author

This chapter is about troubleshooting, about what to do when your child behaves in ways you want or need to stop. Books that concentrate solely on preventing problematic behaviour miss the point that life isn't always that neat. No matter what you do and how hard you try, there may be times when your child behaves appallingly.

Managing these times so your child's behaviour improves can be difficult and stressful, but nowhere near as difficult and stressful as leaving the behaviour unchallenged. Only by showing your child where you draw the line can she ever know which side of it she should be on (see Rules and boundaries, p.145).

To do this constructively, in ways that bring the results you both need without terrifying or crushing your child in the process, you will sometimes need to be gentle, sometimes tough, often both, and always strong enough to stand your ground. This has nothing to do with being harsh and everything to do with being caring, responsible and responsive enough to want to help your child.

Thinking ahead and considering your options will make it easier to deal calmly with your child's worst moments. Choosing which discipline strategies, if any, best suit your circumstances is also easier if you:

Know the difference between discipline and punishment

1   Discipline is an investment. It teaches children what they have done wrong, the consequences of their behaviour and how they could modify it. It thus increases their understanding of what is expected of them and why. It encourages self-discipline and motivates them to do better. It is not a soft option (it often requires much parental effort, thought and time) and can be astonishingly effective in turning around problematic behaviour.

2   Punishment involves making children suffer for misbehaviour in an attempt to control it. It aims to shame, frighten or otherwise force children into compliance without them necessarily understanding why. It therefore risks teaching children to modify their behaviour for the wrong reasons, such as the risk of being caught.

The distinction between the two is not always clear-cut and some strategies may involve an element of both, but your ability to recognise the type and likely outcome of each approach will help you decide how best to proceed.

Invest effort up front Encouraging positive behaviour and helping children communicate, cope with emotions and feel good about themselves will all help reduce outbursts of mind-numbing misbehaviour. Focusing on prevention as well as problem-solving will save you both much time and emotional energy.

Put yourself in your child's shoes Imagining what your child is feeling and why can help you gauge how best to respond. Is she tired? Poorly? Upset? Too young to know better? Or simply indulging in anti-social antics that have to be stopped for her own good and your sanity? Sometimes the most constructive response is a very definite 'No'; sometimes a gentle explanation or cuddle.

When you are backed into a corner what comes out is usually what you are familiar with, how your parents treated you. You end up saying the things your mother said after swearing that you never would. Once you are able to put yourself in your child's shoes, you can learn to do things differently. Different approaches would suit different situations and parents need the choices and skills to work out their own solutions, but first they need to be able to imagine how their child feels and to do this the child has to be respected and related to as an individual.

Christine Puckering, psychologist and Co-founder of Mellow Parenting

Know your role You are your child's parent, not her friend. Sometimes your child will object to you guiding her behaviour but she will get over it and so will you (see Horribly normal: Saying they hate you, p.141).

Check your responses Is your child's behaviour unreasonable or are you so tired or stressed you are over-reacting? If you know it is the latter, try explaining how you feel to your child in a calm, non-confrontational way she can understand: 'I am not able to do that at the moment because I'm too tired. We'll do it later' or 'I know it's not your fault but I can't bear the noise right now. Can you keep it down a bit?' (see Dealing with feelings, p.94).

Take one step at a time Tackling every behaviour issue at once, or even one issue with each of your children, could confuse them and exhaust you. Focus on the behaviour that concerns you most and attempt the achievable, in small steps rather than great leaps.

*I'm a single parent with two children and a full-time job, so there's
not a lot of time. The best way, I find, is to focus on the biggest problem
at any one time and put the others to one side until that's sorted out.
Too much at once and I'd end up giving up. Sometimes I sit down
and write a list of what needs tackling next. It's just a way of
checking whether something's hanging around, something that
keeps getting pushed to the bottom of the pile but still needs
sorting out. That may make it a priority.*

John M

Use your power sparingly This requires you to pick your moment,
your issue and your strategy with care. Inappropriately tough
approaches can shock a child into surliness or silence and also increase
the chances of you cracking under the strain of your own unreason-
ableness. Standing firm for 30 minutes only to cave in after another five
will confuse and/or delight your child and could mean it will take twice
as long to stand your ground next time.

The discipline strategies below are for use when the going gets
tough. Over-use them and they will lose their impact. Picking up every
little problem with your child's conduct can also crush her confidence
or willingness to listen. This is obvious with, for example, a baby's messy
attempts at spoonfeeding, but is often forgotten as the child grows.
Effective discipline is as much about parents managing their own anger
as it is about children managing their behaviour.

*I'd heard he'd been rotten to a girl at school, calling her names
and pulling her hair, and I came down on him like a ton of bricks.
I really grilled him about what happened. I was very angry, very stern.
He just grunted 'I dunno' to everything I asked, so I sent him to his room.
My brother was bullied so I was determined no child of mine would
ever do that. Weeks later I found out it hadn't been my son at all.
I was so incensed, I had lectured him without stopping to try
to talk about it. He'd not even been able to
tell me it wasn't him.*

Anna C

Know you'll sometimes get it wrong

*Some parents say you should never apologise or make up with
your children. Wouldn't you like your children to know what to do when
they have made a mistake? How are they going to learn that except by example?
To hear you say 'I am sorry, I am having a bad day and am very uptight
but this is not your fault' is hugely helpful for children. It is an opportunity
for them to know we have limits, we are not perfect and to
see how to repair mistakes.*

Christine Puckering, psychologist and Co-founder of Mellow Parenting

Comfortable with discipline?

Steve Biddulph, psychologist and author

'We have lots of trouble with discipline in our society, because this is a generation that has emerged from some pretty terrible and oppressive discipline – of hitting, shaming and blaming. This has been a violent and stressed century and we are keen to find more loving ways. But when our children are difficult, it still presses all our buttons. Without discipline methods and listening skills, we tend to back down at first, let the child get really out of hand, rely too much on reasoning, which has limited effect on someone as self-centred as a two-year-old child. Then we tend to finally lash out, getting angry and quite scary. So there is a volcanic quality to a lot of 'enlightened' parents.

'If we get comfortable with discipline as a regular, on-going teaching need, it is less of a worry. The most miserable children I know are the children of well-meaning, over-permissive parents who condition the child to think they deserve everything they want, that their feelings rule the world.

'People mistake discipline for punishment, but discipline actually means teaching. The big lesson for the two-to-six age group is learning that they are not the centre of the universe – learning that other people matter, too, and learning how to get along with others. It's natural that a child should need lots of teaching and make mistakes; discipline is just helping a child figure out how to proceed. It acknowledges what they are feeling, what they need, and shows them how to get it effectively. It needs lots of repetition; you need to be good-natured and have a sense of humour.'

In a warm, supportive home, it may be better for a parent to get very cross with an errant child and later apologise than do nothing at all. However, in families low on warmth and high on criticism, negative incidents accumulate as if to remind a child that he or she is unloved.

From: Child Protection (1995), Messages From Research[1]

I apologise to my kids and I need to. Sometimes I am horrible.

Anne P

All parents occasionally explode when they shouldn't, over-react, pick the wrong issue to tackle or the wrong time to tackle it. Saying sorry can relieve you of some of the guilt cranking up your stress levels and also teach your children how to cope when they have done something they regret. If your relationship is usually warm, loving and supportive, it will be resilient enough to cope with a smattering of parental mistakes.

In most relationships there are arguments and children need to learn what happens next. Far from seeing this as a weakness, most children gain great strength from it and learn to admit their own mistakes calmly. For some children, this can be key to them overcoming what would otherwise be a debilitating fear of failure.

Try to remember that every day is a new opportunity. Each new day that something good happens between you and your child is another layer of their life experience. If you have a period of problems, hopefully you will move on and put down more layers of the kinds of experiences you would like your child to have.

Vivienne Gross, Clinical Director, The Institute of Family Therapy

Effective discipline strategies

As ever, only consider those approaches that feel right for you and appropriate to your child's age, understanding and temperament (see Comfortable with discipline?, opposite). If any strategy does not work as you hoped or loses its effectiveness, change it. These are tools for you to choose between, and different ones will suit different situations.

Learning to challenge

A lot of destructive situations happen when people are confrontational and don't use assertive, positive skills. Assertive discipline, as opposed to hostile or pleading discipline, is calm, measured and fair. It involves you modelling the behaviour that you want the child to use and giving them the information they need to put things right.

Anne Cowling, teacher

This changed how I do things as well as how he does things. It's helped us both turn a corner.

Leslie C

Challenging unacceptable behaviour

Adapted, with kind permission, from Challenging, part of the Parent-Link course from Parent Network (see Contacts, p.355)

To do this we need to be firm, disclose how we feel and keep in mind four important aims:

— We want to change the unwanted behaviour
— We want to avoid bad feelings with our children
— We want them to feel good about themselves
— We want them to learn to take our needs into account in future

To achieve these aims, we need to get into the habit of describing what we see and how we feel about it when challenging our children about their behaviour. The easiest and most effective way to do this is to remember to use 'I' when speaking to the child – 'I feel . . . ' rather than 'You make me feel . . . ' Ideally, this can be done in four steps, though these can be in any order:

1   **Describe the offending behaviour** Stick to the facts of what you see and don't label the behaviour or the child: 'Your clothes are on the floor' rather than 'You are so messy'.

2   **Tell the child how it makes you feel** Perhaps you feel used and resentful. If you are really upset, show them! If it is only a minor problem,

Challenging is a key skill for turning around a child's behaviour. It takes practice. To those who have never tried it, it may sound too 'reasonable' to work in the heat of the moment, but both parents and professionals vouch for its ability to stop children in their tracks and praise its simplicity and effectiveness in bringing about long-term improvements.

It works on the principle that most children will stop behaving unacceptably if they are told in no uncertain terms how it is affecting others and are given the opportunity to change course without loss of face.

It makes children face up to their behaviour and its consequences and decide for themselves how best to proceed, and it helps parents to be assertive, not aggressive. As such, it involves everything that effective discipline requires – information, education and respect, both for the

react in an appropriate way. If you are not 'straight' with children they will either mistrust you or not take you seriously.

3 **State the effect the behaviour has on you** For example, it is creating extra work.

4 **Ask the child to help you solve the problem** Say something like: 'I don't like what is happening and need your help' or 'I have a problem with this. Will you help me?'

A simple way to remember this in practice is to say:
'When you . . . ' (describe behaviour)
'I feel . . . ' (state feelings)
'Because . . . ' (state the effect)
'How can you help me?' or 'How can we help each other?'

Examples:
'When you leave your clothes around the house I feel resentful because it makes extra work. What can we do differently so that it doesn't happen any more?'

Or

'When you splash your paints around it gets on the furniture. Then I feel angry because it's difficult to clean up. What could you do instead?'

child's need not to be crushed by criticism and negativity and the parent's need for the unacceptable behaviour to stop.

If delivered in a firm and loving way, it is far less likely to provoke a defensive, knee-jerk reaction from your child than more confrontational approaches. You be the judge.

Saying no and meaning it

Children do know when you really mean it. You have to be willing to put a lot of effort into seeing it through.
Brigid Treacy, Parent Network co-ordinator

If you mean it, really mean it, your child is much more likely to get the message. If you don't really mean it your child will pick this up in your expression and body language and either ignore you or provoke you until you do. This knowledge may at least save wasted effort – half-hearted 'nos' are rarely worth the effort.

If you do mean 'No', say it in a way that increases its effectiveness. Sometimes you may need to be sharp and stern – perhaps your child is hurting another or putting herself in danger. Sometimes your child's safety may depend on you shouting it at the top of your voice. On other occasions, a firm but quietly spoken 'No' can be formidable.

To help your child know you mean business, try getting down to her level so you at least have a chance of eye contact (see Communication, p.70).

Try to stay relaxed and say, calmly but firmly, 'No. You are to stop that now – no more.' This stops you getting drawn into negotiations and keeps you on very certain ground. Children often echo their parents emotions; staying in control in an otherwise fiery situation may help her follow suit.

Removing the victim, not the culprit

If two children are fighting, rather than removing the child that is doing the attacking, as is often advised, try removing the victim from the scene.

If you remove the aggressor, that child wins the attention of the moment, which may encourage him or her to demand further attention in this way. If you calmly remove the victim, explain why you are doing so and walk away from the aggressor – perhaps even leave the room – then it is the victim who receives the attention. Many parents of battling siblings have reported success with this approach.

Dr Elizabeth Bryan, consultant paediatrician and
Director of the Multiple Births Foundation

Removing the victim is especially useful in educating very young children not to hurt others. It denies the aggressor the attention that may fuel her behaviour and also makes the victim feel safer with you than being left alone.

If your child is hurting another, always explain why you do not like that behaviour and how you would like her to behave instead. Even if she is too young to understand the words, she will understand the basic message by your tone of voice.

Consequences

It always surprises me that little kids sometimes don't realise what's going to happen next, but they don't. It might feel like stating the obvious to us, but to my two it can come as something of a revelation. You can almost see them thinking 'Oh yeah, maybe that's not such a good idea'.

Sarah P

My husband is always saying things like, 'Right, that's it. Any more of that and you're not going to Grandma's tomorrow,' or 'One more time and I'm putting all your Easter eggs in the bin'. What's the point? They know he won't do it. To my knowledge, it has never stopped them doing anything. It drives me nuts.

Helen P

Helping children understand the *natural* consequences of their actions is crucial to them improving their behaviour and learning self-control (see Encouraging positive behaviour: choices, p.163). This approach can also be used when your child is displaying behaviour you need to stop. For example:

Parent (firmly and calmly): 'Joe, if you throw your toys someone
will get hurt and you don't want that to happen. Play without
throwing or put it down.'

This is often all that is needed to help a child think through the
consequences of an action – and stop. But what happens when you
have told your child the *natural* consequences of an action and she
carries on doing it? Or when you have reminded her of a family rule
and she still breaks it? To make it very clear where you draw the
line, you may have to impose an *artificial* consequence for crossing it. For
example:

The weapons rule: You may have a family rule that no toys are to
be used as weapons to hurt or frighten other children. This can apply
equally to a stick, a pile of bricks, a doll or a paint brush. As with all
family rules, you explain it to your child so she understands what the
rule is and why you need it (see Encouraging positive behaviour,
p.143). Whenever necessary, you remind her of it and tell her the natural consequence of breaking it (ie. 'You will hurt'). You may even
challenge her behaviour (see p.177). But two minutes later she hits her
brother on the head with a drumstick. What next?

The consequences: Three strikes and it's out.
1   Any toy used as a weapon (ie to hurt or frighten others) is immediately
    removed (for an hour, for the afternoon, for the rest of the day – the
    older the child the longer the time can be).
2   If it happens again, it is removed again, for longer.
3   If it happens a third time, it is put in the bin.

In general, imposed, artificial consequences do not educate a child
about the effects of behaviour as well as natural consequences, so it
makes sense to try to make your child aware of these first. But let's be
realistic. Sanctions are sometimes necessary. To use them most effectively it helps to remember that:
—   Artificial consequences can be unwanted or even unpleasant but
    should not harm in any way
—   They aren't intended for use before you have tried to help your child
    co-operate, but rather if you have and she hasn't taken any notice

— Children need praise more than they need criticism (see Encouraging positive behaviour, p.143). Remember to notice if she turns her behaviour around

— Discussing and agreeing these consequences in advance with your child makes it easier for her to understand, accept and stick to them. It may even help to write them down together. If this isn't possible, at least inform your child of what will happen if she continues to misbehave. For example:

> 'Stop poking him or you will have to leave the room. Which is it to be?'
>
> or
>
> 'If you throw sand one more time, we will have to go home. Think about it, because I mean it.'

— Punishments imposed out of the blue, with no prior warning ('Right, that's it. I'm taking you home'), give a child no chance to behave better

— Say it only when you mean it, because you may have to carry consequences through (unless you know your sanction is unreasonable and it would be cruel to impose it)

— Artificial consequences should be in proportion to the misdemeanour. Overly severe sanctions are not only unkind and often counter-productive, but also run a higher risk of you not carrying them out

— The younger the child, the sooner the consequence should follow the misbehaviour. A sanction imposed tomorrow may not impress a three-year-old for whom tomorrow is too far away to worry over

— The closer the link between action and artificial consequence, the easier it is for the child to learn from it. For example 'If you use a toy as a weapon it will be taken away' is more likely to be understood and accepted than 'If you use a toy as a weapon you won't go to Grandma's for tea.'

— Artificial consequences make it clear that problem behaviour has to stop, but not necessarily why. When the situation is calmer, it is important to work out with your child why and how such clashes should be avoided in the future (see The follow-up, p.196)

The steps and consequences, making it clear what will happen if you carry on, that's what's worked for me. It's an attitude thing. I'm not going to get mad or rise to it any more because I know exactly what I'm

going to do and he knows it, too. Six months ago, his behaviour was
off the scale. But we handle it now. We're doing all right.
Melanie M

Keeping on track

This has stopped me shouting. Almost.
Pauline F

This technique is for use when your child is arguing back and not taking the slightest notice of what you are saying. It involves you repeating your instruction over and over until she does, ignoring any other ghastly behaviour along the way.

Avoid getting into a dispute – your child may prefer that to doing what she is told. If there are matters to be discussed, this can be done after her behaviour has improved. For now, focus on your demand and repeat it, however much your child argues, whines or prevaricates. Most children soon get the message that you mean what you say.

Staying calm shows you are in control of the situation. Acknowledging how she feels shows you have listened but still mean business. Using her name simply helps to catch her attention and emphasise your point.

> *Parent:* Alice, I've told you to come in. It's time for tea.
> *Child:* But I haven't finished playing . . .
> *Parent:* That must be annoying, but I need you to come in now.
>   You can play again later.
> *Child:* It won't take long . . .
> *Parent:* Alice, I need you to come in now.
> *Child:* It's not fair. I'm never allowed to play outside [not true].
>   I hate you [very true at that moment].
> *Parent:* Alice. In now.
> *Child* (grumpily): Oh, all right.

For similar reasons, try not to be side-tracked by any ghastly behaviour your child may display when being reprimanded or given an instruction. Favourite 'secondary' behaviours include pouts, mutters,

A six-step plan for co-operation

This approach may prove useful when your child is not listening to your requests or when you are in a hurry and need your child's co-operation quickly.

Noel Janis-Norton, Director, New Learning Centre

'The six steps are for parents to do, not the child. They are:

1   The parent needs to stop what they are doing and look at their child. This immediately rules out shouting at a child who is upset.
2   Wait until your child stops what they are doing and looks at you. You literally wait – nothing else. These first steps are respectful so by the time you get to step three the child is much more likely to be listening because they are not being told off or feeling invaded. The steps are calming. They allow you to collect your thoughts and ask clearly and calmly without shouting or nagging.
3   Tell the child what you want them to do: clearly, simply and only once. Parents find it hard to believe but the child or teenager will most often do what is asked. Parents are so used to leaving out steps 1 and 2 and starting on step 3, which is much less likely to work.
4   If steps 1–3 have not worked – and this will be for a small minority of children – ask the child to tell you in their own words what it is you have asked them to do. Somehow saying what needs to be done seems to make it much easier for them emotionally to just get up and do it. It is almost that they have a moral obligation to do it once the words have come out of their mouth. What often happens is the child won't actually repeat it, they will just get up and do it. Steps 5 and 6 are for the very tiny amount of resistance that is left.
5   Stand and wait until your child has done what you want them to do. Most parents feel far too busy to do this. But if we do, the child knows we are serious and that what he is experiencing is not scolding and nagging but calm and reasonable.
6   Notice and praise everything the child does in the right direction.

'The six-step plan is an investment in time. It pays off much more rapidly than parents expect. Be realistic about how much energy and time you already spend nagging and repeating and reminding, justifying and bribing, which is putting in the time after something has gone wrong. This is never as valuable as putting in the effort before, where you have the benefit of prevention or early intervention, 'nipping something in the bud' rather than waiting for a crisis and then somehow finding a way to manage it.'

stomps, grimaces, shrugs and dismissive 'So what's. If you rise to the bait, your child is setting the agenda. If you ignore her antics, you are.

If secondary behaviour is driving you to such distraction that you must show disapproval, be quick and try hard not to stray into arguments or confrontations about issues that are not your main concern.

Standing back

Sometimes the very best thing a parent can do is to do nothing. If your aim is to educate your child about the consequences of her behaviour, often the best lesson is leaving her to sort things out herself (also see Assertion v. aggression, p.314).

If you try to referee every minor dispute between children you may fuel an argument that would have fizzled out of its own accord. You are also quite likely to blame the wrong child and end up in the dog house. If you react to every misdemeanour you could spend most of your time reining in your child's behaviour which, by the law of diminishing returns, means she will take less notice and you will become increasingly frustrated and angry.

Liberate yourself by choosing times not to react immediately. At the very least, this will allow you time to assess what you want your child to do and how important it is that they do it, or whether you can let it go. If it is behaviour you feel you must challenge, a considered response is generally much more effective than a knee-jerk one.

My two were hitting each other over the head with plastic spades and both came running to me, blaming each other and shouting. I'd had enough and I told them so. I said I was going to the kitchen to have a cup of tea and I didn't want to see or hear them until they could tell me what they were going to do instead of hurting each other. Honest to God, they came back a few minutes later, best of friends, and said they'd decided to play golf with the spades instead. I always try to remember now – if they can sort it out, let them.
Fiona W

Making them think

I asked one girl how she was doing and she said 'Oh I'm in trouble because they can't control me'. I said, 'What do you mean? You're the only person who can control you.' They used to think it was the parent's job and the teacher's job to control them and now they know it's up to themselves. They make their choices.

Jenny Oberon, Leeds Attendance and Behaviour Project

This is best held in reserve for when the going gets very tough. It is a forceful and extremely effective form of discipline that requires the child to not only reflect on sorting out the immediate problem but also work out different and acceptable ways of behaving in future. Crucially, its structure can also act as 'Time Out' for you and your child, which both of you may need.

It can be used sparingly in times of relative calm but really comes into its own when your child has behaved appallingly and needs to think through the cause and effects of her actions, and you are close to explosion. It usually requires parents to be very firm to keep it on course.

Some children never need to be disciplined in this way, but most do, sometimes.

The approach has four main ingredients:

1   Identify the problem ('You hit him')
2   Show you understand how your child feels ('I know you are angry' – ie. the child has made her point)
3   Draw the line ('. . . but hitting is not OK')
4   Make your child think it through – 'I want you to tell me':
    . . . what you did wrong (ie. the child agrees it was a problem and admits to having done it)
    . . . what you could do to make things better now (apologise, give back anything she took that wasn't hers, replace broken items, etc)
    . . . how you could do things differently next time (proof that she has learned from what has happened).

Expressing your confidence in your child's ability to respond (a simple 'I know you can do it' may be enough) will encourage you both to look on this as a constructive, if tough, procedure rather than an exercise in 'shaming and blaming'.

If your child is calm, you may leave her to do her thinking or stay nearby. If not, stay with her and repeat the steps once you know she is calm enough to listen, and follow them through to the end.

Keeping your expectations appropriate to your child's age is crucial. A young child may not be able to manage much more than telling you what she did wrong and saying she won't do it next time. If it is her decision it is still a huge step forward.

Knowing when to stop

Any approach can be abusive if you use it too much or use it in particular ways. You do have to be honest about your motivation – any discipline should be to help a child learn, not to humiliate them. It is so important to know when to stop. Once you have discussed it and sorted it out, that is the end of it. You should not keep going on and on or keep standing over children when things have moved on.

Sarah Darton, health visitor

If you have made your point and the message has got home, try not to use this success as a platform to comment on every aspect of your child's behaviour that annoys you. It is this 'and another thing' syndrome, the urge to remind her of what she did last Tuesday, which can stop children listening to their parents. Best avoided.

Once the issue is over, move on. Try to show confidence in your child's ability to act better next time and allow her to start each day afresh unless the misdemeanour is extremely serious.

As important is the ability to know when you are on a hiding to nothing. Most parents get locked into a downward spiral of argument and upset with their children at some time. The trick is to recognise this and break the pattern. Your child is too young to do it so it has to be your responsibility to say, 'This is getting out of hand. We should stop and talk about it later when we're all calmer.'

Speech bubbles

This technique helps children who are 'stuck' in patterns of bad behaviour. It is a very clear and accessible method of helping them think of better ways to manage difficult situations, emotions or thoughts (see also Assertion v. aggression, p.314). If your child can't yet write, she may want to talk through her answers, ask you to write them down for her or to draw pictures instead. The nature of the approach makes it most suitable for school-age children.

Jenny Oberon, of the Leeds Attendance and Behaviour Project, explains: 'We've been doing a lot of work on speech bubbles with the kids. We have drawings of people feeling different things – stressed, frustrated, angry, withdrawn. With each there are two bubbles – a "think bubble" for the children to write in what the person may be thinking at that particular moment, and a "speech bubble" for them to write down what that person has to say to:

1   get the help they need
2   not hurt anyone
3   not get themselves into trouble.

They can put what they want in the "think bubble" and you can't tell them off for that, just as in life you can't tell a child off for their thoughts. They might be thinking that they'd like to hit, shout, swear. But it's how they deal with their thoughts that's so important. By filling in the "speech bubble" they can see clearly the difference between what they think and what's acceptable to do.

'Working through these exercises shows children the problems that can arise if they say exactly what they think or do exactly what they are feeling all the time. It shows them there are better ways of getting their needs met.'

My daughter was in real trouble at school, on the point of being excluded. I felt I just couldn't cope with her. Since she's been shown things like the speech bubbles, they took a bit of a while to get through to her, but since they did, she's been able to work out the consequences of doing things her old way and come up with something different, something that will work better. It's shown her that you can still be angry without shouting and screaming. She's decided now that she's making a turnabout, not for anybody else but for herself, and this has shown her how to do it.

Jacqui C

Short cuts, tricks and quick fixes

We are not perfect, our children are not perfect and we have many constraints on our time, energies and patience. For all these reasons, it helps to have a few quick fixes up our sleeves for those moments when we need to turn around a child's behaviour but really haven't the time or energy to invest in longer-term approaches.

'Quick fix' methods usually involve 'training' a child to behave in acceptable ways. They can be useful for breaking a pattern of negative behaviour but, in the longer-term, it is much more effective to help children understand why they should behave that way, as such understanding is the root of self-discipline.

So these approaches are not the whole story, and are best retained for emergency use only and followed up with one of the more constructive, educative strategies detailed above (see Effective discipline strategies, p.175). But everybody needs short cuts sometimes.

Rewards

The best rewards are the non-material ones. The most rewarding thing children receive is descriptive praise. You need to start noticing and mentioning all the things a child does well.

Noel Janis-Norton, Director, New Learning Centre

I don't want to knock the government and schools when they are finally taking seriously the need to build in some kind of emotional relationship to children. Using a star chart system, for example, may help children feel rewarded. But we need to go deeper than that in order that children begin to internalise their own values.

Susie Orbach, psychotherapist

Many parents and teachers have used reward systems to help children break patterns of difficult behaviour. They are often cited as an effective means of modifying children's conduct and they can work well in the short-term.

However, they are not a long-term solution because they lose their potency over time and offer such limited scope for a child to learn – is a child complying because she understands why she should, or because she wants the reward?

On their own, therefore, they are not enough to encourage self-discipline. Yet if they help you both feel good enough to take a next, more constructive step, they may be useful.

There are four basic types of reward for behaviour:

1 **Material rewards** For example, a toy, a sweet, a fun day out. These are bribes. If you need to resort to them out of desperation, use them sparingly. They are a high-risk option because the child who is bribed soon becomes the child who demands, the child who ups the stakes or, even worse, the child who loses self-motivation.

2 **Tokens** For example, a star, a sticker, a home-made Superstar certificate for behaviour or achievement. These are sometimes used as tangible evidence of parental appreciation, but it is the appreciation that counts most.

3 **Positive effects** If a child's behaviour results in adult praise and acknowledgement, the child has a powerful incentive to behave that way again. Being told the positive effects of their actions on others (eg. 'Thanks for sharing your toy, that made Joe feel very welcome and happy') and themselves ('Because you put your toys away so quickly, we've got time to go to the park. Well done.') rewards them with positive feedback as well as teaching them about consequences (see p.179).

4 **Internal** This is the reward of doing something for its own sake, because the child knows it to be the right thing to do and feels good about doing it (see The value of values, p.333). It is the core of self-discipline.

As a useful rule of thumb, if your use of rewards is near the top of the list (and most reward schemes are), aim to move it towards the bottom. If you need to use either type **1** or **2**:

— Avoid mixing rewards and sanctions (ie don't put crosses on star charts, make targets unattainable or withdraw rewards once won).

Reward systems aim to shift the focus on to the positive, not remind the child of 'failures' or misdemeanours.

— Remember these are short-term options with limited value. Even if they succeed in breaking a behaviour pattern, you should look to other, more educative methods of building on your relationship with your child and equipping her for the future.

Some parents pay their children to do routine, everyday tasks like the washing up or even setting the table. I think that is appalling. What sort of partners are they going to make? The trouble is they will come to hate those kinds of activities because they will associate them with that which they are paid to do. If you are paid to do something then intrinsically you view it as not a normal thing to do because you know you have to be bribed to do it.

Professor Hugh Foot, specialist in children and social development

Warning: rewards can backfire

Elizabeth Newson, Emeritus Professor of Developmental Psychology, University of Nottingham, researcher and author

'I am always looking for ways to make *the action* itself rewarding, which is the key thing; in other words to look for intrinsic rather than extrinsic rewards. I don't like the use of rewards for doing well at school, for example. I think there are all sorts of good reasons for doing well or not so well at school, which cannot be related to rewards.

'I feel that if you reward a child with something that has nothing to do with the key issue it's a complete waste of time because they get so hooked on the reward they stop even thinking. I remember doing some research years ago which involved doing a task with four-year-olds and someone suggested I rewarded them with Smarties, which sounded like a good idea. I took Smarties along and these poor little kids got so focused on the sweets that they just simply stopped thinking about my task and certainly stopped enjoying it. I gave it up after one trial because it took their minds off what they were doing. I thought it was a very negative thing.'

Counting

It works for reasons I don't understand because I never say what's going
to happen when I get to ten. Maybe it just shows that the mood has switched,
I'm serious now. Having said that, it only works for two of them.
My daughter counts with me then blows a raspberry at the end.
She's never taken any notice of it at all.

Jenny T

Counting – as in 'You have until I count to three/ten/whatever to stop that, do this' – can work well, especially as a way of getting your child to focus on what she is required to do and to communicate the fact that you are serious and reaching the end of your patience. But its success depends largely on the temperament, mood and age of the child involved.

As a way of helping parents keep their cool, however, counting can be invaluable (also see Time out, below). Whether you count aloud or to yourself, it imposes a pause for thought and can make all the difference between managing your child's anti-social behaviour and saying something you later regret, or otherwise flying off the handle.

Even counting to 10 can give parents the chance to avoid the automatic response
which might be to lash out in frustration. Most parents say, 'I don't hit my child
because I think it's a good thing. It's because I've run out of other strategies.'

Christine Puckering, psychologist and Co-founder of Mellow Parenting

Time out

There is not a neat solution to this. I have heard of children who have started
pulling the wallpaper off when they are kept in their room because they are so
angry and then the parents get even angrier with them and so it goes on. There are
downsides to every strategy. But if you need to separate children, creating space
between them even for a short while can be helpful as it helps you collect your
thoughts and think about what you want to do next. You have to keep control of
the situation. Actually locking a child in a room to teach them a lesson, however,
can feel like abandonment to that child. To my mind, it is too extreme.

Vivienne Gross, Clinical Director, The Institute of Family Therapy

If everyone is getting upset, the most important thing is to separate
everyone and then talk to each of them on their own, starting with the person
whose need I think is greater, which is usually the one who's most upset.
They will need to be in separate rooms and then they have to think about
it and say their piece when they come back. They have to bring back
an understanding of what they have done wrong and a way to put this right.
It works. They always do come back and make up. Sometimes one
will stay away for ages, but they will come round.

Emma P

Some children have a great time if sent to their room, others find it intolerable. As ever, how this works and whether it is appropriate will depend on the situation, your child and you. Sending a child to her room can be a vital safety measure if you are extremely angry (see Coping in hard times, p.229). It can also be a useful means of separating sparring siblings or showing a child that you will not tolerate her behaviour any longer.

A child could be told to stay in her room until she has calmed down (remember that young children may need your presence to do this. They are not going to calm down quickly if 'Time Out' makes them frightened or hysterical, or they simply don't understand what's required of them. See Tantrums, p.124). A school-age child could be told to go to her room and come down when she is ready to co-operate and apologise. Never lock the door – this can terrify a child – and, if the child is to decide when she is ready to come out, be prepared to wait!

The risks of Time Out are greatly reduced if the chosen spot is not a bedroom but a quiet, boring place not so far removed from the rest of the family. The bottom stair will do.

Do the unexpected

This can help if you and your child are stuck in a pattern of repeated behaviour – the familiar routine of 'You do this then I react and we end up having the same old argument'. Try to stand back from the situation and observe at what point the annoying and repeated behaviour begins. Then try to think of what you can do to stop that point arriving.

A man who I'm working with just now says, 'My son drives me crazy. He won't give me any space. For example, when I come home at night I just want to read my newspaper and he always takes the paper from under my arm and runs off with it.' I suggested he hid the newspaper and, if his son did find it, to playfully hit him over the head with it. It works because it interrupts the daily routine and the argument that by now is on automatic pilot and the humour interrupts the emotional tone of the interaction between father and son.

Jim Wilson, family therapist, Cardiff Institute of Family Therapy

Shouting

Once you are behaving on their level it just goes downhill. Don't get me wrong, sometimes I need to shout at mine. I can't go nicey nicey when he's trying to put a brick in his brother's head. There's no point going all 'Oh daaarling, don't do that.' But this shouting, bawling and screaming at the kids, like we've all done sometimes, doesn't do any good.

Julie M

I realised we all had to calm down a bit when my 16-month-old started shouting in the morning like everyone else. Not anything in particular, just 'aaaarrrrgggghhh'.

Judy O

It is OK to shout at them sometimes. There are obvious boundaries and shouting in itself need not be abusive. Rather it can show the child that you can get angry, show that anger and still love them.

John Bristow, psychologist and psychotherapist

In a perfect world parents would never need to shout, the sun would always shine and the birds would always sing in the trees. In real life shouting is sometimes necessary and can be a very effective means of attention-grabbing if saved for rare occasions where your sanity or your child's safety demands it.

If you do raise your voice, try to drop back to a quieter voice as soon as possible. If you keep shouting you increase the risk of your child shouting back or switching off. Worse, if it goes too far, shouting can leave a child feeling frightened or crushed. If you quickly revert to your normal level or quieter, you show you are angry and in control of the situation. If your child is shouting, the shock of you talking quietly in response may make her listen.

Many people reading this will see yelling as a very negative thing as it was for them with their parents. Often, when they were yelled at, it bore no relation to what they were doing but more to what their parents were struggling with – their marriage, their money etc. As a result, the yelling was not to get the child's attention and went on far longer than its first impact on the child. But sometimes it is OK to yell at a child to get their attention. The difference is you are watching them for their response and respond to that, you are only yelling to get through.
Steve Biddulph, psychologist and author

The yellow card

This approach, and any variant of it that suits your child, works on the principle of warning. It provides the child with physical, tangible evidence of your intention to act if she does not improve her behaviour. Once its significance is understood, it should save you having to tell your child in detail what will happen next because she will know. It will also help the child feel she is taking control of her own conduct.

In football, the referee gives a yellow card to a player as a first warning. If the player misbehaves again he is given the red card and sent off. It may be a way of getting through to your children. If they are pushing the limit you say, 'Right, I'm getting the yellow card out. Any further behaviour of that type and you will be sent to your room.' I know a boy who used to get into terrible fist fights in the playground. He and his family developed this yellow card system and eventually he was able to take the yellow card with him in his pocket to school and when he felt himself getting riled he would feel the card to help remind him not to get involved. It reminded him that he would be suspended from school if he got into any further trouble. Sometimes a simple, physical thing like a bit of yellow cardboard can help get the message across very clearly.
Vivienne Gross, Clinical Director, The Institute of Family Therapy

Clear, strong and calm

Vivienne Gross, Clinical Director, The Institute of Family Therapy

'I think it is very helpful to be as clear as you can about what you want. I sometimes see parents who appear to say "Oh don't do that Johnny" in such a lame way or with such ambivalence that the child is bound to pick up that there is a big gap they could slide through.

'I think when you are saying very firmly "I am absolutely not going to have this", being clear and showing that you are really at your last ebb with this one lets the child know where they stand.

'Part of the problem with children who are out of control can be that they feel nobody can manage them, so they can't manage themselves and it becomes a vicious circle. Drawing the line, keeping the child in one spot and saying "No, you have to stay there until you calm down because I cannot trust you to be with your sister at this minute. You are too upset and agitated and I am going to keep you here until you calm down" is seeing through what you have decided needs to happen. As far as physical safety is concerned you might have to interpose yourself between two children and that is part of your duty to protect each of them.'

Using physical restraint is the hardest thing for me. I hated it but I don't think I could have done anything different – he was much too angry to let loose on his brother. But that whole thing of using all your strength to hold back your own child is incredibly disturbing. I try to balance it out – if I've had to be a human barrier I make sure we all have a hug later on.

Jane P

This is just a tip, really, but I found it easier to hold my child from behind. I could then fold his arms over each other and hold him firmly without having to grapple with him. It also reduced the chances of me getting hit.

Pauline T

Holding

This means using your physical superiority to control a situation – something many parents feel uneasy about. It should be saved for urgent situations when drastic measures are needed.

The intention should never be to hurt but rather to hold, reassure and not let go until the child's rage has subsided. Some children do respond well to being held like this while others simply get more angry (see Tantrums, p.124) and only you can judge whether and when it will help your child through a temper. There may be other times when, like it or not, your child will need to be held for her safety or the safety of others. This is basic protection and a fundamental parental duty.

The follow-up

Your child has complied with your wishes. What next?

Once the immediate situation has calmed down, you need to work out ways to avoid such clashes in the future (see Encouraging positive behaviour, p.143 and Effective discipline strategies, p.175). At the very least, both you and your child will need to talk and to listen (see Communication, p.70). Try to untangle the causes of any problem behaviour and discuss between you:

— What happened
— How your child felt about it
— How you felt about it
— What your child could do differently in future

Smacking isn't the solution

Research on huge numbers of children shows that those who were hit grow up with all sorts of negative outcomes, for example they grow up to hit their parents.[2] New research even suggests children who were hit decrease in cognitive ability, ie. their IQ goes down.[3]

Dr Dorothy Rowe, psychologist and writer

Very substantial research evidence highlights negative, violent and humiliating forms of discipline are significant in the development of violent attitudes and actions from a very early age.

The Commission on Children and Violence[4]

*No baby should be smacked ever, under any circumstances, and yet it
is not at all unusual that people smack their babies.*
Ann Herreboudt, midwife and family therapist

*There is now a large and growing body of research evidence on the effects
of physical punishment and the message is clear: while it might stop misbehaviour
in the short-term, we can be almost certain that physical punishment does not
improve behaviour in the longer term. Indeed, it now seems very likely that
physical punishment leads to an increase in misbehaviour. In particular,
children who are physically punished tend to be more aggressive. Some researchers
have recently suggested that physical punishment increases the chances of
depression and even reduces intelligence. And it seems that even moderate
levels of physical punishment − the occasional smack that is typically
used by most parents − can have these effects.*
Gavin Nobes, lecturer in psychology

This book is unashamedly anti-smacking for the simple reasons that
smacking is:

— counterproductive
— unnecessary
— potentially damaging
— an abuse of power

This is a highly contentious issue so, as the nation's hackles rise
once more in indignation and defence of parents' rights to do as they
damn well please, it may help to look calmly at the facts.

1 Being anti-hitting does not mean being anti-discipline or that anything
   goes. Discipline is essential for a child's healthy development, so it is
   extremely important that a parent's chosen method of discipline works
   effectively.
2 Smacking does not work.

A huge amount of research worldwide[5] shows that physical punishment
may produce obedience in the short-term, but it does not inform or
educate children in a way that enables them to improve and control
their own behaviour in the future.

They may stop what they are doing and so the method may seem
instantly successful, but the children may not understand why their
behaviour was wrong or how or why they should improve it; it therefore

does not promote self-discipline. Many parents who use physical punishment admit it is not an effective or enduring means of control.[6]

Worse than that, over time it tends to backfire by increasing the probability of aggressive and violent behaviour inside and outside the family, during childhood and adulthood.[7] Put bluntly, children who are hit learn to hit others.

As a parent you are powerful. To a very large degree, you control your child's routines, what she eats, the clothes she wears, her activities, her toys, how good she feels about herself. You can use your power responsibly and effectively to guide and challenge your child's behav-

Parents' voices, parents' choices

'I have never hit any of my three boys, who are now in their late teens and twenties. They've turned out fine, but I'm astonished at the number of colleagues and friends who simply do not believe me. They don't believe it is possible to have boys, especially, and never had occasion to hit or slap them. We've had almighty arguments, but they have never been hit. What's the point?'

Bill S

'I feel strongly about not hitting children. I have hit my eldest three or four times and my younger daughter a lot more. I have flung her across the room, I have dragged her across the floor. It is horrible, it really upsets me. I have also had to face the fact that having a routine of conflict just doesn't work. It is insecurity on my part. You feel the child is going to have one up on you, that they have one over on you, you have lost and they have won. But if I don't make it a battle quite often it won't become one. If you let it go or wait until things have calmed down, you can work on the goodwill that is created because you have broken the pattern.'

Pete L

'As a smacked child I hated it. For me it is not on. It does not work, it can make children deceitful, defiant and really angry. I remember looking at my mother and thinking you can hit me all you want and I will not please you, I will not cry. I have managed never to hit my children. They are grown up now and are very disciplined within themselves.'

Bridget T

'Six months ago I was feeling really violent towards him. I was so angry with him, I

iour without resorting to physical or emotional threat. You do not need to hit her so why do so when there are other, more effective means of discipline?

If physical punishment is so ineffective and potentially harmful, why do so many people do it? The answer is partly cultural (see A very English vice, p.200). It also has much more to do with the parent's mood and stress levels than the child's behaviour.

Research[8] has now confirmed what most parents already know – that children get punished or chastised most when their parents are

---

hated him because he was doing stuff to get me going all the time. I felt he was like my enemy and I'm telling you he'd have been in care, he'd have gone. But we've both learned different ways of handling it. Now we both know what will happen if he starts up, and I just don't need to smack him one like I used to.'

Melanie M

'My parents never hit. Physically, they were very gentle and kind. But my father could lash us with his tongue, just tear us apart, slowly and precisely, when he was angry. I think sometimes the smacking/not smacking debate can be too simply put. I am passionate about not smacking, but I am passionate about not terrorising and humiliating children in any way, and I think that can include what you say to a child as much as what you do to them.'

Helen F

'I'm sure I could get my toddler to stop throwing his food much quicker if I slapped his hand every time he did it. It's almost Pavlovian – do that and something you don't like happens, so you learn to stop doing it. But I don't want to go down that road. If it takes a bit longer for him to get the message, that's OK. We'll get there in the end. I just don't want to start slapping for this and smacking for that.'

Mandy N

'I believe there is a difference between a tap on the hand and a beating but the stages in between are blurred. I've never hit at all because for me it's a very clear line to draw and stick to. If you allow yourself to tap your child, what happens when you're really mad? Does that little tap become a harder one? And what happens when a slap doesn't work? I think it can crank up and I'd rather not get into it in the first place.'

Graham P

A very English vice
Francis Wheen, journalist and broadcaster

'Spanking is known throughout the world as "The English vice". It was entirely predictable that Britain should be the last country in Europe to ban corporal punishment in state schools, in 1987 – and then only because the European Court of Human Rights gave us no choice.

'The Archbishop of Canterbury, George Carey, advised his flock in 1996 that: "You say 'Don't do this', 'You mustn't do that' and you gently slap them if they transgress and there is nothing wrong with that as long as it is done with love and firm discipline within the family set-up." He went on, "We older people must practise what we preach . . . We actually live the kind of discipline we are wanting a future generation of people to grow up with." Oh really?

'I find it inconceivable that George Carey would take a swipe at an Archdeacon who had been "misbehaving". Why, then, do we believe we are setting children an example and preparing them for adult life, by administering "loving slaps" every time they stray from the path of righteousness?

'The other distinction, some may say, is that the smacking of children is administered in a "private, loving family context". Following that logic, we might as well legalise wife slapping and granny bashing.'

tired, angry or stressed, not when the child's behaviour is at its worst. Physical punishment is thus more a response to the parent's inability to manage their emotions than a response to what the child has done.

I think most parents smack their children and they will justify their actions by referring to something that their child did. But overall, the surprise of the research [see Physical punishment in the UK, opposite] was the dominance of the parents' mood in affecting whether a child would be hit as opposed to hitting being something that was thought about and considered the right thing to do in certain situations (ie. the parents did it for themselves rather than the child).

Marjorie Smith, psychologist, Deputy Director of the Thomas Coram Research Unit, Institute of Education, University of London, reader in the Psychology of the Family, Institute of Education

Understanding what provokes physical punishment is a first step towards finding more effective, more respectful, more consistent and

Physical punishment in the UK

Recent studies have detailed the frequency and type of punishment administered to children. The shocking findings should be required reading for anyone who still believes attitudes towards physical punishment of children do not need to change.

Marjorie Smith and colleagues at the Thomas Coram Research Unit studied 400 families in research sponsored by the Department of Health[9] and found:

— 91% of children had been hit
— 77% of them in the last year
— 75% of one-year-olds had been smacked in the year preceding the interviews
— Punishments parents admitted administering included 'physical restraint' (including 'wipe face with cold flannel, physically restrain child, cold bath/shower, hand/object over mouth, place head under water, shake, push/shove, throw') and 'punishment by example' (including 'pulling hair, scratch, pinch, bite/nip/chew, Chinese burn, burn/scald, put in cold water). Over 40% of the children had experienced 'physical restraint' and 'punishment by example'. 'Ingestion' was experienced by 12% of the children (including 'forced to eat food, make eat something nasty eg mustard sandwiches,

forced to drink salt water. wash mouth out with soap and water').
— Almost a quarter of seven-year-olds had received 'severe' physical punishment from their mothers. (Severe punishment was defined as the 'intention or potential to cause injury or psychological damage, use of implements, repeated actions or over a long period'.)
— Children who were frequently aggressive with their siblings were four times as likely to have been 'severely' punished at some time as those who were rarely aggressive with their siblings.
— About 10% of children in the study had been hit by an implement.

Marjorie Smith explains how the smacks administered tended to get more severe as the children grew: 'In the youngest age group (one-year-olds) parents were describing it as a tap, for example fingers on the hand, and they were saying they were not hurting the child in the main. At age four it has moved to the leg or the bottom using the whole hand and the parent is more likely to report she has possibly or definitely hurt the child.

'My feeling on this is that once you start hitting, be it tapping in a controlled way, it escalates to be the same action but with more anger and force.'

less traumatic ways to manage your child's behaviour. This requires parents to stand back and observe their children, to examine their own actions, stresses and flashpoints and to recognise those situations that often give rise to conflict and do something about them. All these require humility, courage and honesty.

I smacked my son once when he was little and I remember feeling so ashamed. It was my problem that had led to me doing it and I was very aware it would have been enough to tell him. I made a promise never to hit a child again. I have managed this by recognising risky times and taking action. For example, I am most prone to lose it in a very hot car. If I feel this happening I pull the car over and get out of the car with the child until we sort it out.

Steve Biddulph, psychologist and author

Attitudes about the physical punishment of children are changing. A detailed study of childrearing in the 1960s[10] found that 95% of parents hit their children and that 80% of them thought it was the right thing to do. By the mid-1990s, the percentage of parents hitting their children had dropped only slightly, to 91%, but most parents said it was not something they wanted to do (see Physical punishment in the UK, p.201). The use of implements had halved since the earlier study and there was no longer a marked gender difference in how girls and boys were punished by their parents.

These are small but significant steps. If more parents were able to recognise how their own moods influence their child's chance of being hit, the number of children being physically punished would drop further still. This does not mean we should deny our frustrations and anger – it can be important for children to know when they have pushed too far – but rather that we learn to express those feelings in ways that are effective and not potentially harmful to our children (see Effective discipline strategies, p.175 and Dealing with feelings, p.94).

CHAPTER TEN

IMPORTANT RELATIONSHIPS

Caring for your child means also looking beyond your relationship with him. The important relationships in his life are so inter-connected that none can be properly addressed in isolation. What happens between siblings, parents, parents and grandparents and with other carers will all influence how your child views himself and his world. Identifying potential pressure points and considering how best to manage them will benefit you all.

You and your partner

We must not minimise the demands on a couple. We romanticise it and we need to be more honest. Children are dependent and demanding, requiring of our time, our thought, our love, our money. They raise issues constantly: what school, what bedtime, how to discipline? Every issue requires the couple to come to some working agreement and this touches daily on the differences and sensibilities of the partnership. It does not surprise me that without a lot of back-up, many families just cannot hold it together.
Peter Wilson, child psychotherapist and Director of Young Minds

I think it is so important to focus on the family rather than just the woman after the birth of a child. The whole family is in a period of transition.
Yehudi Gordon, consultant gynaecologist and obstetrician, specialising in holistic health

How you manage the parental relationship matters to your child. His view of accepted behaviour and the potential of human relationships will all be influenced greatly by what he sees at home.

If you are raising a child within a happy relationship, be aware of its value. It is perfectly possible to raise children successfully and happily as a lone parent, but it is incredibly demanding. Also be realistic. Creating, nurturing and raising a child together as a couple is a powerful and profound bond. Great intimacy can grow out of needing each other, trusting each other, experiencing pleasures and sharing love and tenderness towards the child. Yet the gap between imagined familial bliss and reality can be shocking.

You now have your child's needs to consider and these can be great and sometimes overwhelming. As parents, you and your partner will have very different experiences and therefore very different and often conflicting needs. Recognising this will help the transition from couple to family, and so help you all.

Ensuring you are both involved in or at least informed of the day-to-day decisions of a child's care is the simplest way of feeling like a couple in a working partnership rather than isolated individuals or even opponents pulling in different directions. Try also to look after your needs as individuals and as a couple. Try to have time together, preferably away from the child, to talk and relate to each other as adults again rather than simply as parents. This can be astonishingly hard to achieve and requires commitment, planning and support, but think of it as a family investment and book that babysitter.

By looking after your needs you are providing your children with a positive role model – of how to get their own needs met in a way that respects others but also respects themselves. The life our children are surrounded by has the strongest impact on them, it is not just a matter of the time you give.

Stella Ward, nurse and Parent Network co-ordinator

Taking it out on the children?

Research into levels of physical violence to children in their homes in the UK, sponsored by the Department of Health,[1] found that overcrowding, low income and single-parent status did not significantly increase the risks. But a third of children living with parents who had a poor marital relationship experienced severe physical punishment, compared with 7% of those whose marriage was good.

Sex

*After being pulled and tugged this way and that by the children,
especially when I was still feeding, sometimes the last thing I wanted was
physical stimulation, someone else wanting my body. What I needed
was more like sensory shutdown – moments when I could have my body
back for me and do absolutely nothing with it. But it's hard to explain
without being hurtful. We never did discuss it.*

Lisa D

*After our first baby, sex completely disappeared for months.
We both lost interest. It was the last thing on our minds.*

John C

Parenthood combined with broken nights and an upturned sex-life can strain the best of relationships. Most couple's sex life goes on hold for a short while after a baby is born and recognition of this is extremely important. As your baby grows, sex drive may increase but opportunities for sex may still be few and far between. And when they arise, you'll just be getting it together when a child will cry, wet the bed, come in for a cuddle or decide now's the time to tell you the name of the school caretaker's cat. A sense of humour is important, as is considering ways to negotiate these huge shifts in your relationship. Having no sex can be habit-forming and you may need to act to break the pattern.

*Sex in the first few months is intermittent, possibly absent, and tends
to come back to normal in the latter part of the first year, six months onwards.
Normal being not as before but to an acceptable pattern in the couple. In my
experience it never goes back to exactly how it was before the baby, there just
isn't the time, there isn't the energy. Particularly for women, with
breastfeeding and the hormonal changes, the sex drive lessens.
Also, having the baby so close means she doesn't have the
same need for physical contact.*

Ann Herreboudt, midwife and family therapist

Sex after children

José von Bühler, sexual and relationship
psychotherapist

'There are three main psychological stresses
that affect a couple's sex life after the birth of
a baby:

1   The couple have to adapt to a change
     in roles and identity. A woman has
     changed from lover/wife/partner to
     also being a mother. For the man, too,
     this may be a difficult adjustment.
2   From the moment of birth the male
     has to cope with the woman's
     attention being divided between him
     and the new baby.
3   The woman's body has been through
     an enormous upheaval and this is
     anti-sexual. Her body may feel sore
     and tender while production of

prolactin (the hormone related to
breastfeeding) further reduces libido. At
the same time, men usually feel in great
need of sex and the reassurance they
get from it. It takes time for the woman
to start wanting sex again. So you have
a shocked man and a shocked woman
and no sex – it is this combination that
can really add to the strain.

Practical Solutions

1   **Education.** We need education for
     the father before a baby arrives
     about what the woman will go through
     and what his potential feelings are
     following the birth. We also need
     information about what is normal
     sexually following the birth. We are all
     different so there can be no guide as to
     the number of times you have sex, etc.

Reviewing the role of fathers

*Men have major life changes after a baby is born. Their partner gets a lot
of positive attention in the pregnancy and the birth and is now focusing on
someone else. Men can feel very left out and, importantly, often have even fewer
places to go and talk things through. As the bond between mother and baby develops,
the father can feel a sense of increasing separation from his partner, particularly
if the parents had a very close relationship before the baby was born.*

Ann Herreboudt, midwife and family therapist

*The biological and physiological differences between mothers and fathers
often means the way in which they bond with their baby differs. This can be
exaggerated by the additional time the mother spends with the baby in the
early weeks. One way of dealing with this difference positively is for the
father to take care of the mother while she takes care of the baby. This is*

But it needs to be understood that normal means possible change and that there will be temporary loss of libido in the woman. It is helpful not to be surprised by this or take it personally.

2 **Communication.** The woman needs to explain what has happened to her, and the man needs to listen. The man also needs to explain how he is feeling and ask questions about what he does not understand. This is intimacy. If this vital reciprocal communication happens the woman can say for example: "At the moment I feel like this. I do love you and I just need some time without sex. I am not rejecting you."

3 **Intimacy of Touch.** A couple can use this if there are sexual difficulties.

It involves a shift away from sexual touching and towards intimate touching. After the birth the couple need to start touching each other but non-genitally, rediscovering the healing power of touch and the togetherness it brings.

Later, touch can become genital but it is important to go gently, in stages negotiated between you. Some women will not want to be even touched for a while and even when the process of touch begins again, it is essential to feel OK about not having sex until both partners are ready. The worst thing is for the man to put pressure on the woman for sex.

Both verbally and physically this process is reassuring for the couple until such time as the woman is ready to come back to full sexuality.'

where his input is invaluable and he may also bond with the baby
in the process of taking care of the mother.
Yehudi Gordon, consultant gynaecologist and obstetrician, specialising in holistic health

The level of support, understanding and care a father brings to his family may be crucial to its happiness and to the parental relationship. Every family dynamic is different and couples' expectations will vary, but for most families the same truth holds – the more the father can be involved in the raising of his children, the more everyone will benefit.

Studies suggest that both fathers and mothers now spend more time caring for their children than previous generations, and that the greatest shift has been in the time spent by fathers.[2] For many, this has been a considered and conscious effort to take a greater part in raising their children – no mean feat in a culture still constrained by the longest working hours in Europe.

Father and child

Steve Biddulph, psychologist and author

'Fathers have three big contributions they need to make:

1   The first is time. You cannot be a good dad if you work a 60-hour week. Kids need you for several hours a day – not just playing with them, but cooking, working, doing things together. They need time to download your qualities and feel close to you in many moods. A workaholic father will harm his daughters, but he will cripple his sons. This is the big lesson of recent years. Dads are irreplaceable.

2   The second is to be a real equal parent – not be a lightweight dad. Some dads just do the fun stuff, and leave discipline to their partners. Be sure to help with the discipline – supervise homework, organise tidying up or laundry.

3   The third thing is the opposite of the second – to loosen up. Some dads are never any fun. Often if our dads were stiff and remote we find it hard to get down on the rug and play. Even to give a hug or a kiss is hard for some dads. So take a few risks and loosen up. You'll find it wins your children's hearts.

'So it's a balance. There is great fun to be had from parenthood and great pride from discovering that you can really change the course of your child's life.

'What is so helpful for building all relationships is to ensure there are opportunities for one-to-one relationships between all family members. For example, dad and daughter could go off for the weekend together, basically so every pair relationship can find its own rhythm. Traditionally there has been a tendency for the mother to be the relationship fixer. This can mean the father always relates to the children through the mother. We recommend that the mother takes off for a weekend with her friends once in a while so that the father can find his own footing.'

In the early months of parenthood, at least, many fathers feel on the periphery of the action while some other being they've only just met has first call on their partner's heart, mind and body. Yet fathers do have a crucial role in the early months of their child's life. This cannot duplicate the role of the mother because of the intensity of the mother/infant relationship and the physical dependency of the baby if breastfeeding, but the involvement of the father and the support he provides is invaluable.

Support can involve everything from cooking meals to taking the baby when the mother needs to rest, from helping with the baby's physical care to taking every chance to be with, get to know and understand his new child. With the break-up of extended family networks and support systems, the father may be the only person around to provide the support both mother and baby require.

As they grow, most children have moments when they still need their mother most, especially when they are poorly, frightened or tired. This can be hard for fathers, but may be easier to accept and understand if seen not as a rejection but as an affirmation of the powerful mother/child bond they have supported and helped develop.

The father's sense of exclusion usually diminishes as his own relationship with the baby develops. In a recent Canadian study[3] all fathers, from those who expressed an immediate love for their child to others who said their love grew over time, said an important factor in the development of their relationship was when the baby smiled and 'spoke' back to them. An understanding of how very young babies communicate would obviously help here (see Communicating with your baby, p.9).

As the child becomes less dependent on the mother, so the father's role in his day-to-day care and upbringing can increase. How the bond between father and child intensifies and develops will depend on his time and involvement, and these depend largely on circumstance and partly on choice (see Fathers under pressure, p.210). But any caring father knows that the more involved he can be in his children's upbringing, the greater difference they will make to his life and he will make to their present and future.

In the beginning it felt like I was watching my former life disappear and I had no idea what was going to replace it. But then an incredibly powerful love develops. There's much talk of a mother's instinctive, natural bond with the child but men have one, too. It may not be the same, but that's surely the point. It's the difference that makes another parent/child relationship worth having. I think some men have always been greatly involved in raising their children and have got great enjoyment from it. The difference now is that more men are going public about it and admitting not only their role but also the fun and intense pleasure of having children.

Russell C

Fathers under pressure

UK fathers work the longest hours in the EU, with more than a third of men with young children working 50 hours a week or more. Those who do are less involved in family activities.[4] In a recent poll for the NSPCC,[5] almost one in five of the children living with their father could not recall doing anything with him in the previous week.

The extent to which fathers share in the care and socialisation of children is a key factor in mothers' marital happiness and satisfaction in life.[6]

In the 1950s, just over a third (38%) of mothers said the father helped with the practical care of their babies; among mothers in the 1990s the figure had risen to over three-quarters (82%) – which still leaves another 18% who give no practical help at all.[7]

In a recent survey 95% of fathers felt paid paternity leave was essential yet almost half had none and only 4% had more than a week's paid leave. They were involved and wanted to be involved much more but working patterns did not allow it.[8]

Following the birth of their child, 80% of fathers in a recent study said they felt worried, 60% said they had felt lonely; 12% had felt depressed and 6% said they felt jealous.[9]

Most mothers are still chiefly responsible for looking after their children, organising their children's care and doing most household chores, even in those households in which both parents work full-time.[10]

Qualities children say they require of good mothers and fathers are remarkably similar and suggest children think in terms of good 'parents' rather than differentiating on the basis of sex.[11]

If yours is a family without a father or without a mother, you and your child may benefit hugely if a trusted friend or relative whom your child knows well could drop by from time to time, offering another role model, another voice and the support of another caring adult in your lives.

I have been a single parent and looked after my children for the past 10 years. It has brought home to me just how important it is for both parents to have a relationship of trust with their child because anything can happen.

Peter Walker, yoga teacher and physical therapist

You and your parents

If you think your upbringing wasn't that bad you'll do something similar yourself. Some people with unhappy memories will be fairly determined to make it different for their children. Others repeat the things that were painful to them as children and say things like 'I got hit and it didn't do me any harm'. I find the most useful thing to do in these situations is ask the parent how they actually feel when they smack their child now. Nine times out of ten they will be honest and say they feel wretched and then they begin to see there is little to gain from repeating it.

Carol Ann Hally, health visitor, clinical practice teacher

Children learn from example and as far as parenting is concerned you become a parent from the dysfunctional family you grew up in.

Cheryl Walters, Head of Research and Policy, National Stepfamily Association

Your parents now have another key role in your life – as the grandparents of your child. This relationship matters to children – in an NSPCC survey, 78% of children said their grandparents were important to them[12] – and can be supportive of you all, offering time, patience and love.

Yet a much more fundamental process is also taking place which is likely to have an even greater influence on your child's life. Having children, especially your first child, throws your relationship with your own parents into sharp relief. Suddenly you can see life from a parent's perspective and how that affects you will depend on your own experience of childhood. Many people find their understanding and respect for their parents increases dramatically. For others it is a disturbing time, when old wounds are opened and memories revisited. For many more it is a mixture of both.

Whatever your experience, you can use your heightened awareness of your own parents' strengths and weaknesses to consider how you would like to raise your child. What was it that you enjoyed or benefited from in your childhood, and how could you give the same gift to your child? If there was a problem, how could you avoid the same mistakes?

It helps to be aware that the areas of people's upbringing they found most difficult are often also the areas they find difficult to negotiate with their own children. If you were disciplined harshly, for example, you may repeat this instinctively or avoid even necessary firmness. Addressing this balance and breaking away from old patterns and reactions may demand honesty, courage and strength. At the very least, it may require you to learn some new skills to enable you to raise your child as you wish.

I think most of the problems do come from an adult's own parenting as a child. So when you are faced with a tricky situation you will often say exactly what your mother would have said to you, for better or worse. It can be quite a shock. In the absence of parent education what else do people have to base their parenting on?
Eileen Hayes, Parenting Advisor to the NSPCC

Siblings

The world is packed with siblings who resented each other's existence then developed a strong, loving bond over time. Occasional feelings of anger, threat, jealousy and resentment are very common and very understandable. No parent can eliminate them, but there are ways to help your children manage them better.

A new baby

You have to do more for the baby because he needs more doing, but in the other children's eyes you aren't being fair. However hard you try, in their eyes it's one-sided.
Dan L

I was completely unprepared for the anger being directed at me. I had thought so much about how my son needed help when the twins arrived, and how they would need protecting. I hadn't realised that it was me who would need protecting!
Kate K

I thought there would be no fallout because he was so much younger and because they obviously adored him, but it comes out in other ways. They have never taken it out on him but my younger daughter became much more clingy, desperate to be a baby, even saying she wanted her arms and legs cut off to make her small. My eldest daughter became a manic tidier, quite obsessive.

Marina C

The arrival of a new baby may turn a child's life upside down. Periods of transition and change can be very disturbing for children (see Helping your child cope, p.233) and if ever there was a time of transition, this is it.

How this is displayed depends to a large degree on the child's age and temperament but, as a crude rule of thumb, very young children may take their frustrations out on the baby, hence all the pokes, pinches and hair tweaking. Older children who realise hurting the baby is wrong may turn their anger on their parents, other siblings and, sometimes, themselves. They also may find it hard to resist the loving hug that turns into over-tight squeeze. Sleep problems, stroppiness at mealtimes and regression back into toilet training and tantrums are all common and almost all fade over time.

Preparing your child well for life with a new baby will help to lessen the shock for him and the fallout for you all.

Prepare well

All I remember was my mother holding this thing in her arms that was lying in my place. I was the youngest of seven and known as 'Baby Maloney'. My mother said 'Come here, you can hold her', and I really didn't want to and said so. That morning the shopkeeper greeted me with 'And you're not Baby Maloney any more!' I felt so confused. I thought who am I? I am Baby Maloney, I haven't changed.

Brigid Treacy, Parent Network co-ordinator

Talk to your child about what life may be like when the baby is born, the ups and the downs, and how he may feel. Allow him to air anxieties and ask questions. Crucially, try to explain the nature of love – that your love for him will not diminish when the baby arrives. Many young children think of love as finite, almost like a cake cut into pieces. If a baby comes along, whose slice is it going to take? Assure him that your love for him grows every day and no one could ever take any of it away.

Allow time for adjustment The emotional turmoil caused by the birth of a sibling rarely peaks at birth. Most families find it increases in later babyhood, when the novelty has worn off and the reality dawned that this baby is not going back.

Accept it is not possible to plan away your child's feelings, just to make the situation more manageable and less painful.

If you find it hard to understand your child's negativity, consider this tale, told to many parents in many versions: 'A man comes home to his beloved wife and says, "Darling, I love you so much and life with you is so good that I've decided to have a second wife. She's arriving soon, she'll be sleeping where you used to and we'll be one big happy family. Won't it be fun!"' Accepting a new and unrequested family member can be tough.

Telling your child off for resenting the baby will not stop him resenting but rather fuel the resentment. Instead, put a stop to any behaviour that could harm the baby, shower praise on positive behaviour (see Encouraging positive behaviour, p.143) and show you understand how he feels (see Dealing with feelings, p.94). Also look beyond the obvious. Older children, in particular, may not be behaving in ways you find hard but may still be struggling to make sense of it all.

Use whatever methods you can muster to make your child feel loved Tips suggested by parents include:

1   Avoid holding the baby when your child sees you both for the first time after the birth.
2   Ask friends not to go straight to the baby when they visit, but to first acknowledge and play with the child.
3   Nudge close friends to bring a little gift for the child as well as or instead

of one for the baby. Young children, especially, may accept a gift 'from the baby'.

4   Involve the child in the day-to-day care as much as age, ability and inclination allow. Carrying nappies and pushing the buggy can make a child swell with pride one day and feel taken for granted the next.

5   Share jokes about the baby – how little it can do, the funny faces it makes. It's harder to feel threatened by something you can laugh about.

6   Make a scrapbook of photographs and mementoes of when the child was a baby. Tell him lots of tales of what he did and how you felt, how you first held him, when he first smiled – so he realises he had this special time, too.

7   Go easy on the 'big brother', 'big sister' routines. Children sometimes resent their identity being interwoven and dependent upon the new baby. They are still who they always were, thank you very much.

8   Think of things that your child likes doing and that you can do together when you are feeding the baby, so he doesn't feel pushed away. Perhaps a special book to look at, a special video or a favourite treat.

9   Keep to old routines and habits as much as possible. Insisting a child now dry himself because you've got your hands full may be perfectly reasonable to you but may feel like rejection to him.

10 Have times, even short times, together without the baby so your child can be heard, feel special, loved and know that he is not being replaced.

Sibling rivalry

Rivalry is normal. Many children fight and grow up perfectly OK.
It is only really a problem if one is being particularly dominant because this could go on for a long while through life. But let's not forget that having a sibling can be hugely beneficial to a child. They have their friends and they have their moments but they have each other.
Carol Ann Hally, health visitor, clinical practice teacher

Adults [should] not make attempts to stop conflict between children; such attempts are useless because conflicts exist. Instead, conflicts are accepted and children are shown how to resolve them without violence.
The Commission on Children and Violence[13]

Children, especially siblings, are often horrible to each other. A certain amount of conflict is a perfectly normal and healthy part of sibling relationships so don't overburden yourself with guilt and blame if your children argue and fight. Nevertheless, reducing the frequency and intensity of the arguments and helping your children resolve their disputes (see Effective discipline, p.170 and Assertion v. aggression, p.314) could improve every family member's quality of life.

Make special time for each child on their own This is hard given the demands on your time, but is a very effective way of keeping in touch with each child's needs and experiences and helping each child feel respected and treasured. Perhaps you could read together while another child sleeps, go shopping together – anything to give you a chance to talk one-to-one or simply enjoy each other's company.

Accept children's feelings about each other but work on how those feelings are expressed Encourage them to express their anger or jealousy rather than act them out with their fists or other anti-social behaviour (see Dealing with feelings, p.94).

> *It's so easy to think of sibling rivalry as abnormal behaviour.*
> *It might be maddening but it's perfectly normal. I'm 32 and a mother myself,*
> *yet my 35-year-old brother has the ability to annoy me to a greater*
> *extent and in a shorter time than anyone else I know. And I think*
> *we both still watch the amount of concern, time and attention*
> *our parents give us, just to check we're not missing out.*
> Lucy D

As far as possible, leave siblings to sort disputes out between themselves (see Encouraging positive behaviour, p.143 and Effective discipline, p.170). Intervening or, even worse, taking sides when children could sort matters out between them robs them of the chance to learn how to resolve arguments and may encourage the battle for your favour.

Enforcing co-operation by expecting them to share all belongings all the time can also create feelings of hostility that actually hinder

Brothers and sisters

A study of the calls to ChildLine showed that 14% of children ringing about their family relationship problems discussed anxieties about siblings.

Some 6% of those calling about family problems believed their parents favoured a sister or brother.

development of a co-operative relationship (see Refusing to share, p.134). In the long-term, setting rules for everything between siblings can result in them relating primarily through their parents rather than with each other, even into adulthood.

There are so many positives to sibling rivalry. It is a good way for a child to find his own strength and learn how to be with others in terms of sharing, taking and giving. You cannot hide from the harsh bits of sibling rivalry but that is the reality of the world. The problem comes when we don't let children feel these negatives or experience fully what is going on. It is often the suppression of the feeling that is damaging and actually causes a lot of the conflict.

Pat Elliot, psychotherapist and bereavement counsellor

Be alert to patterns of behaviour Disputes are normal and healthy. One child habitually dominating or even bullying the other is not. If you see such patterns emerging, try to help each child work out ways to behave differently (see Assertion v. aggression, p.314 and Bullying, p.318).

Parents are not always effective at sorting out the envy and jealousy between siblings. Yet if you do not recognise, say, that your third child is being bullied by an older sibling, or do nothing about it, you are being deficient as parents. The basic message must always be that everyone in the family is valuable and treated with respect. Children will often not complain about being bullied in the family because they know they will not be heard or they are aware that the parents have favourites. As a parent you do need to look at

what you are doing and be honest about that. We have to work
at getting along with each other and accepting our differences.
Dr Dorothy Rowe, psychologist and writer

Be realistic Recognise that it is very easy to expect behaviour way beyond the years of older children. Unrealistic parental expectations are unfair and sometimes cruel if the child is criticised for failing to meet them.

Respect each child's individuality Try very hard to avoid comparisons.

I've got twins and in one school assembly my daughter was a star turn,
reading the story and sitting centre-stage. Her twin brother's job was to bang
a chime. Once. I could have cried for him. But when I met them both afterwards
he was brimming with pride saying 'Did you see me? Did you see me? I banged it!'
He knew his sister could read when he couldn't but he was more concerned with
what he'd done right. The worrying thing was that if he hadn't said it I
might have been full of sympathy and said 'Never mind, darling'.
He didn't want that, he wanted praise for what he had achieved,
not attention and sympathy for what he hadn't.
Jane P

Trying to help children cope with their differences by treating them all identically often backfires. It is not humanly possible to give children the same amount of attention all the time, nor should you. Their needs will be different in different circumstances and at different stages of their development and you cannot respond to them as you should if you attempt to divide everything, always, in exact equal measure.

I learnt from experience that 'the same' is not necessarily fair or helpful.
I used to treat my children identically and it never worked – only the one whose
needs I happened to meet was happy. I'm amazed I did this for so long because
as a child I remember wanting to be treated differently from my sister but I forgot
completely when I became a parent. House rules are applied equally to all, but
beyond that I love them all differently but equally and consistently.
Brigid Treacy, Parent Network co-ordinator

Presume affection as well as conflict and plan accordingly
Allowing physical space for each child to play without interruption or disruption from siblings may help. Perhaps one child could play in one room and one in another, or each have their own corner. Equally, allow them the opportunity to be together, to play, fight, resolve issues and find pleasure in each other's company.

Choosing childcare

It's easy to underestimate the difficulties of getting childcare right.
Some parents find looking after children quite easy and don't realise that
not everybody does, so they will leave their child with someone who
is too young to cope on a full-time basis.
Some others are just scared. A lot of first-time mothers put off doing anything
about childcare until not long before they are due back to work. They are scared
of handing their child over at all, so end up doing something at the last minute.
Choosing childcare is a very difficult process and the sooner you start it the
better for you and your child because you will increase your options.
Sue Monk, Chief Executive, Parents At Work

One morning I heard my daughter absentmindedly call the childminder 'Mummy'.
It hurt, but at least she felt relaxed and secure.
Claire T

Childcare is the big one. Tears, frantic nights, anxiety. And that's just you. Choosing someone to care for your child in your absence is nerve-wracking because it is one of the most important decisions you will ever make, yet the right care can be hard to find, and even harder to finance.

If you don't go back to paid employment when your child is young, let no one say you have 'given up work' – raising children is one of the most important and valuable jobs any person could undertake. If you do need to return – and that need could be for financial or personal reasons; both are valid and important to recognise – your task is to find the best deputy your finances and circumstances allow.

No one route is the only right one, and no way is easy. Each has great advantages and significant drawbacks and which you choose depends on your needs and those of your child and family, where you live, how much support you have from others and how much you can afford to spend. But remember that money is not the only determinant of quality – much reasonable-cost care is excellent, some high-cost care is no good at all.

All young children need to feel they are truly 'cared' for in their parents' absence, so search for a caregiver who recognises your child's emotional as well as physical needs. This is your child's most important relationship outside the family in his early years, and it is the responsibility of every parent to give it their very best shot.

One of the most important things is that care is sensitive and responsive to a child's needs. Children need to know that the person looking after them cares about them, is interested in them and respects them as an individual. This can be done in so many ways, for example sharing their pleasure by smiling and laughing with them; talking to them about what they

---

 ## *Childcare and child development*

Surprise, surprise. Research shows that children require sensitive care, appropriate to their age and needs, from a small number of people.

'The idea that very young children can only develop healthily if they have one and only one caretaker, the mother, throughout the day, has now been clearly rejected by research,' explain Peter Elfer and Dorothy Selleck, senior development officers at the National Children's Bureau's Early Childhood Unit. 'However, the importance of reliable, responsible and responsive adults

is still strongly supported by research as well as clinical evidence.'

This view is echoed in the recent review of relevant research over 40 years, by the Institute of Education.[14] The key, the review states, is not whether it is the mother or another who cares for the child but rather the quality of the care. 'Family life,' it adds, 'continues to be the most important influence on young children's development, even when they receive substantial amounts of non-parental care.'

Choice and circumstance

At least 54% of women with a child under five now work full- or part-time (in 1986 the figure was 40%)[15] yet the cost of good quality, safe childcare in Britain remains among the highest in Europe. The traditional model of the family, comprising two parents, only one of whom works, now accounts for only a quarter of all UK families with dependent children.[16]

Two out of three working mothers in one recent study relied on family and friends to look after their children. Only 4 out of 10 of those with children under 5 used formal provision, and just 1 per cent of those with older children did so. Less than 2% of working mothers had childcare provided by their employers.[17]

or you are doing; not forcing them to eat when they don't want to; showing them how to button their coat; recognising when they are feeling a little under the weather and would probably prefer a quiet time looking at books rather than a trip to the playground. Children need a range of experiences to meet their needs, but their needs will vary with their age, ability, interests and mood.

Ann Mooney, researcher at the Thomas Coram Research Unit, Institute of Education, University of London, author of *Choosing Childcare*

One-to-one or nursery care?

I work in a relatively affluent area, where many parents seem to view childminders as a poorer choice of childcare than a nursery. Yet the nature of the relationship with a childminder, where they build up a one-to-one relationship in a family environment however different from yours, is still usually more natural for a young child.

Carol Ann Hally, health visitor, clinical practice teacher

Would your child fare better in a home environment or at a nursery? With one-to-one care or in a group setting? Different children respond differently to the same surroundings and your child's age, character,

Options and questions

*The lessons from recent high-profile cases are that no amount of
protection is a 100% guarantee of safety. Parents have to be aware that
choosing childcare is one of the most important things they will do
in their lives. This requires them to get well-informed, to allow
as much time and to ask as many questions as possible.*

Sue Monk, Chief Executive, Parents At Work

*If your childcare falls apart, everything else falls apart.
It's as simple as that. If I know anything now it is that it is essential
to ask all the questions up front, to see as many people and places as you can.
Because if it does break down, or if it's just not good enough,
it can be damned hard to pick up the pieces.*

Diane T

Your basic childcare options are:

— **A childminder.** Usually a mother herself. Care based in her own home and may look after other children. By law, must be police-checked, registered and vetted by social services staff.

— **A nursery.** Quality, availability and fees vary hugely. Most are not suited to the needs of very young children (see One-to-one or nursery care?, p.221).

— **A nanny.** Care based in your home. Most have childcare experience and/or qualification. Expensive, although nanny shares are often possible. Don't rely on nanny agencies to check references. You must do this yourself.

— **Au pairs and mother's helps.** Generally young, untrained and inexperienced. Not recommended for sole charge, particularly of pre-school children.

— **After-school clubs.** Quality is very patchy, ranging from excellent to poor. Visit and judge for yourself.

— **Relatives.** Will this be as reliable as you need? Do you share similar views on caring for children?

Issues to raise when questioning potential carers

— Relevant training and experience
— Their attitudes to childcare (discipline; comforting distressed children; food; play; safety etc)
— The structure of your child's day

— Continuity of care. This is very important for young children. How long do carers expect to remain in post? If you are considering a nursery, how long has it been open? What is its staff turnover rate?

— Availability of/access to facilities

— Age and number of other children in their care

— How will any questions and concerns you have be respected and addressed?

Questions to ask yourself:

— How did the care environment look? Feel? Sound? Atmosphere is important. Did children there seem happy? Did it appear to be child-centred, relaxed and friendly? Did the carer(s) seem happy, approachable and sensitive to children's needs?

— Do they welcome discussion of your child's development, needs and care?

— Will your child be given the care and affection he requires? How will the carer respond to his particular needs and habits? Will your child be read to? Cuddled? Taken to the park? Allowed to draw and paint and enjoy messy play?

— Respect your instincts. Do you like her? Trust her? Feel confident your child will be fine in her care?

References:

You must personally contact the parents of children cared for by your prospective carer, preferably over the last three to five years. Be wary of any gaps in CVs.

Have you seen all relevant certificates and checked registration details, including terms of registration (ie numbers and ages of children permitted and, for nurseries, staff/child ratios)? Your local Social Services department should be able to supply these.

Information:

Full details of options, questions and the latest regulations can be obtained from support groups such as Parents At Work (see Contacts, p.355).

The under-8s officer at your local social services department can provide advice and information on childcare options in your area. Talk to other parents, staff, carers.

Let your child meet his potential carer and watch how they behave together before you make any final decision – you will know much from their responses to each other.

Ask as many questions as you need to be reassured. This can feel strange, even rude – but it is very important that you do. No childcarer worth the name would take offence at what is only evidence of parental concern and care.

particular needs and ability to interact with other children will all influence your final decision.

If you are considering a nursery, it is very important to establish its ability to care adequately for your child's age group. Some take babies from as young as six weeks, but to fulfil a very young child's needs, each child needs be looked after by one, or at the very most two key carers throughout the day. This 'key person' system should in effect offer your child a parent substitute – someone who has the time, concern and dedication to get to know your child well, to monitor any changes in your child's mood and thus to understand and meet your child's needs. They must also have sufficient contact time to play with your child as well as attend to her physical care (see Building relationships, opposite). This is especially important for babies and children who are too young to ask for what they want or make their requirements clear in a group setting.

Preparing the way

He had to be pulled off me, limb by limb. He found it traumatic and so did I, but this was the only nursery in our area and it was this or nothing. It had to work because I had to work and, I think especially with your first child, you feel powerless to do things differently.
Fiona M

Those initial few weeks are probably the most important period in building the childcare relationship. For everyone's sake, especially the child's, parents must try to manage them as well as they possibly can.
Sue Monk, Chief Executive, Parents At Work

Your child will be disturbed by you going back to work and will show it. View the situation from his perspective and you will understand his upset and anger – he is having to adjust to times without you. Yet also understand that his distress does not mean he will suffer lasting damage. Separation anxiety is a perfectly normal reaction and can usually be negotiated successfully and sympathetically (see Separation anxiety, p.116). If you and the carer are patient, loving and understanding, he will settle into his new routine.

Building relationships

Peter Elfer and Dorothy Selleck, senior development officers,
Early Childhood Unit, National Children's Bureau

'Most nurseries will have a key-person system, but the important issue is whether the nursery has really thought through what this means in terms of the relationship between that person and your child. Some staff view it as an entirely administrative system while, at the other end of the scale, some nurseries take it to mean somebody who is key in your child's life.

'As parents you may have mixed feelings about this, due to the difficulty for you of your child becoming very attached to another. But this is desperately needed by a young child or baby. They need someone reliable who they are familiar with and who they can count on, who will make a relationship with them.

'So look closely – is there someone who will spend most of their time with your child, who will receive your child in the mornings, manage most of his physical needs through-out the day and build a relationship with him? Times when your child is anxious or in need of emotional reassurance will be frequent throughout the day, and the ability of the key person to "tune in" and be emotionally available most of the time is very important.

'It would be quite inappropriate for nurseries to make close relationships with children unless parents are very much part of that triangle, otherwise it may lead to all sorts of feelings of envy, jealousy and exclusion on the parents' part.

'Parents need to be involved and they have a right to a regular flow of information about what is happening while they are at work. If your child is cared for by many people in the day, it is more difficult for any one member of staff to give you proper feedback, and this is no good for you or your child.'

If you have any choice about when you go back to work, it is worth remembering that children tend to become more wary of strangers and new situations at around one year old. This can begin as early as nine months, and can last until the child is about three. Even if working around this timescale isn't possible, there is much a parent can do to help minimise their child's distress:

Prepare well Minimise the distress for you both by spending as much time as you can with your chosen carer, at the place where your child will be cared for, before you leave him. If possible, first leave him for only a short while and increase it gradually, over time. Good individual carers and nurseries should allow this, even though you may have to be prepared to pay for their time. If they won't allow it, ask why not.

Give the carer as much information as possible about your child's routine and likes and dislikes, medical information, emergency numbers etc. It often helps to write these down in a notebook. Try to get into the habit of exchanging information about what your child has been doing, how he has responded and how he appears to be feeling and try to build time for this into your routines.

Information exchange is vital with children of any age, but especially so if the child is too young to speak for himself. It is also a fundamental step to establishing the triangle of trust and communication between parent, child and carer that is so crucial to a healthy and happy relationship.

Try to separate your anxieties from your child's Your child will be OK if his care is good and he is supported through these early stages. He needs to know that you have confidence in the new care arrangements and that you believe you are entrusting his care to safe hands, so do your best not to crumple.

In the morning, after settling and reassuring your child, it may be best to say goodbye gently and go. Returning on a piece of elastic for yet more hugs and kisses could make him more anxious if he thinks you are unsure about leaving him. Let him know you understand how he feels and that you know his carer will help comfort him after you have gone.

> *Your response as a parent needs to be sensitive and accepting that your child feels like that, to let them cry and to not try to shut them up or to get angry. Ensure the carer is sympathetic to the child's feelings, too. Those feelings are not going to damage the child. What may be damaging is the response of the parent or carer to those feelings. To be cross, unkind, dismissive or cold is going to do the damage.*
> Linda Connell, trainer in communication skills for parents
> and health professionals

Be honest It may seem easier in the short-term to sneak out on occasions without saying goodbye to your child, but this is likely to create insecurity and backfire in the long-term.

Reassure yourself No carer worth the name could object to you phoning during the day to check your child's progress. Arrive a little early to pick him up sometimes; wait where you can hear or watch him unseen. Don't feel embarrassed about checking that all is going as it should – your child's happiness and safety depend on your vigilance.

While it is true that a small child who separates reluctantly may seem 'fine as soon as you've left' nobody should assume that it will be, or was so. Someone who knows the child well should, ideally, look in after a few minutes, without being seen by him. And however happy he seems, the childcare worker or teacher should stay in close contact and try to ensure that the child's private experience does not belie his public armour.
The Commission on Children and Violence[18]

He always cried when I left, which was turning me inside out. So my childminder suggested I waited outside the front door, where he couldn't see me but I could hear him. It didn't stop immediately, it took a minute or so for him to settle, but at least I went to work knowing he was OK. After that, I'd phone from work. I would hear him in the background, jabbering away quite happily. It made me feel much better about the whole thing.
Laura B

Establish routines and rituals Adherence to familiar routines and set times for arrival and picking up will help your child feel more secure – and this may require home routines adapting slightly if the caregiver's ability to adapt is limited. Very young children may find comfort in having something of their mother's with them, especially to sleep with (a T-shirt or a pyjama top that smells of you is perfect!). With older children, try to explain clearly what is going to happen to them and when you will be back, and stick to that.

Some children respond well to rituals such as waving out of the window – it helps them feel they are part of a process rather than powerless.

Watch and listen to your child If she doesn't seem to be settling, talk to the carer about why this may be. Distress is normal, but if you know that the chemistry between carer and child does not feel right, it is time to look at other care arrangements. Also be aware that you may need different sorts of care as your child grows or your circumstances change. Respect your instinct as well as your intellect to tell you when arrangements need to change – what 'feels' right is as important as what is right in theory.

> *Parents mustn't let their feelings be crowded out by all the anxieties of going back to work and being professional to the extent that they become insensitive to the signals coming from the child. If you know in your heart of hearts that it is not right and your child is unhappy, there is no magic solution but you do need to get out as quickly as possible before it escalates. If the childcarer herself doesn't seem to be handling it, it probably isn't going to work either. That's the time to put your energy into looking for alternatives.*
>
> Sue Monk, Chief Executive, Parents At Work

When you find childcare you are pleased with, don't forget to tell the carer. Happiness is infectious and a happy, appreciated carer is a very great asset. Treat her with all the admiration due someone who is looking after your child as you wish and as your child needs. You will still need to keep her informed about how you like things to be done for your child, but if she is helping make your life work and your child feel loved, she deserves your praise and respect.

CHAPTER ELEVEN

COPING IN HARD TIMES

W̶e cannot eradicate all upset and pain from our children's lives or sidestep all difficult situations. But we can help ourselves and our children manage and negotiate hard times more effectively and minimise their potential for damage.

Helping yourself
so you can help your child

Wherever you live or whatever your situation, being a parent is not easy.
Many parents feel exhausted and overwhelmed by the stresses of family life.
It is even more difficult if family or friends are unable to offer you support
and a breathing space when you most need them. Some parents lose confidence
in their ability to cope and most can remember days when they would
have liked someone to turn to. Everyone needs a hand sometime.

Brian Waller, Director of Home-Start, a charity offering support, friendship
and practical help to families with children under five (see Contacts, p.355)

My daughter had to learn to stay in her bed, but the reason I slapped
her was not because I thought that was the right way to teach her but because
I was so stressed out. I needed to talk things through, sort things out, and
I needed more help and support at home than I was getting.

Anne P

Children are extremely sensitive to parental stress and too often the butt of our moods. If a problem is overwhelming us, they suffer. The pressures on parents can be huge, but there may be ways to reduce the risk of us snapping under the strain.

Feeling miserable, tired, washed-out, tearful, being bad-tempered, snappy or unresponsive are all possible indicators of high stress and a warning sign for parents to take action. It may help to identify those everyday situations we find most difficult to handle. They may be unrelated to the root cause of our anxiety, and this will need to be addressed, but these 'triggers' or 'flash points' also need to be recognised and dealt with for our and our children's sake. Bathtime, the school run, mealtimes, bedtimes, Friday afternoons, Monday mornings – every

If you hurt your child or fear you may

He was still pretty helpless, about 15 months. It was the middle of the night, I was so tired. His cry really irritated me, it got to me at irritation levels you couldn't believe. I just wanted him to leave me alone. I lost it, I leaned over him on the nappy changing table, I yelled at him and shook him at which point my husband came into the room.

I sat on the tube next morning thinking they're going to take him away, or take me away. I can still remember the look of fear on his face, when it was happening it was almost as if I was watching myself doing it. You imagine you will be endlessly patient because they are your kids, but it is scary how close to the edge you can get, how that point is not far away.

It didn't happen again. It scared me so much, I knew it was an isolated incident. Thank God for my support systems, my family and friends. How people cope who haven't got that kind of support I'll never know.

Laura C

Shaking a baby or hitting a child can terrify and confuse. They can cause physical harm, sometimes brain damage or even fatal injury.

If you ever feel close to hurting your child, first deal with the immediate crisis:

1 STOP
2 Remove yourself from the situation. Put your baby in her cot. Leave your child in a room and take time out. The child may scream but do not go back until you are calm.
3 Wait. Are you calm enough to return? It might help to call an adviceline (see Contacts, p.355) or a friend. Perhaps you could get someone to take over for a short while? Try to remember a time when your child made you laugh or smile or melted

family will have a different list of difficult situations which compound other problems or bubble away to boiling point unless they are managed differently.

Is there anything you know might help? It might be sleep, a night off, a talk with a friend or tackling an aspect of your child's behaviour. It might be a relative to help with the bathtime/bedtime routine for a night or two. It might be reducing what you expect to achieve in a day or asking for advice or specific support. Whatever you do, try to carve

---

If the choice is between you hurting the baby or child or leaving him to scream until someone can come and help or you can calm yourself, it is better to leave the child to scream. In that extreme instant, mother or father need to look after themselves first in order that they can then look after their child.

Linda Connell, trainer in communication and group work skills
for parents and health professionals

---

your heart. You are the same people.

4   When you return, your child may still be screaming or behaving in a way that annoys or upsets you. Be prepared for that – you have reached a state of self-control, she may not have. Think of some ways you might help her cope with her distress (see Dealing with feelings, p.94 and Tantrums, p.124).

The next step is to consider what you must do in the longer term:

1   What help and support do you need? Make getting this a priority.

2   Is there anything you can change about what you do and how you live to reduce stress?

3   If you haven't contacted your health visitor, GP or a helpline for support and advice, try to do so now.

We are talking about very complex factors, here. Perhaps a parent has inadequate support or too many demands on them. There might be other factors that push them to the edge. Circumstances can weave themselves together in a way that isn't helping and you need someone outside the situation to help untangle it. It could be a neighbour, a friend, a professional person. If you feel at the pitch where you have shaken a baby or hit a child, or you fear you may, don't try to do it on your own. Ask for help, get the support you need.

Vivienne Gross, Clinical Director, The Institute of Family Therapy

out some time to relax, think and have a break from your routine (see Your needs, p.23). You and your family will benefit.

Without taking care of ourselves and our needs we can easily become resentful. This inhibits our ability to hear our children or be with them without feeling so over-demanded. We begin simply to see how our children are behaving, not why.

Stella Ward, nurse and Parent Network co-ordinator

If you ever feel stressed to the point of explosion, recognise this and act. Even counting to 10 or leaving the room for a few minutes may help you calm down enough not to snap (see If you hurt your child, p.230).

There are times when I just need five minutes to recharge, to get to grips with the situation. I will tell them I need five minutes on my own and go in my bedroom, shut the door and read a magazine.

Ros L

There is a popular view that people who physically or emotionally abuse their children are other people, at the 'psycho' end of society. But most are parents like you and me who have snapped under stress and done something they really didn't want to do. You have to recognise you are stressed and do something about it. One of the best ways is to recognise your flash points and walk away from those situations or, better still, make positive changes in your life to help you avoid those spirals that lead you to behave in a particular way. Whatever you need, the important thing is to act.

Eileen Hayes, Parenting Advisor to the NSPCC

Helping your child cope

*Whatever a child's circumstance, what matters most to a child's view
of themselves and the world is the relationship they have with their parent.
We have questioned 4,500 young people[1] and, while differences in background,
family structure, poverty or education levels affected 'can-do' attitudes,
the most significant difference related to their family's parenting style.
Parents who 'listen to my problems and views' were the most
likely to be associated with high self-esteem in children.*
Adrienne Katz, author and research associate
(Department of Applied Social Studies, Oxford University)

*Although they differ in the detail of their results . . .
researchers agree that long-term problems occur when the parenting style
fails to compensate for the inevitable deficiencies that become manifest in
the course of the 20 years or so it takes to bring up a child.*
from Child Protection, Messages from Research[2]

How our children respond to hard times and problems in their lives will
depend on their individual circumstances and experiences, their temperament and how we as parents equip them to cope. This requires us
to recognise situations they may find hard to handle and to understand
our pivotal role in helping them through.

The pressures many children experience on top of the 'normal'
demands of growing up are huge, from family crises to chronic social
and economic deprivation, and no one should underestimate their
impact. Yet young people themselves have identified a positive relationship with their parent(s) as a very significant factor affecting their self-
esteem and positive view of the world.[3]

Supporting children with this positive relationship is much more
within the reach of most families than a life free of problem times.
Whatever our children have to face in life, from the extreme to the
everyday, we can provide them with the support and skills they need to
increase their resilience and ability to cope.

Knowing the times and the signs Times of change and transition
can be particularly unsettling for children, as what they have come

to recognise as familiar and safe disappears and their future feels uncertain.

All children need adult help to negotiate major changes and crises, such as divorce, bereavement or becoming part of a stepfamily (these relatively common childhood experiences are dealt with in detail later in this chapter), yet most will also need support through changes that are simply part of life and growing up. Situations many children find disturbing and stressful include:

— moving house
— starting nursery or school
— falling out with friends
— the birth of a sibling
— moving from one developmental stage to another, experiencing new feelings, abilities and freedoms (see Tantrums, p.124)

Knowing how your child's stress may be reflected in her behaviour and even her health (see Stress points, opposite) will help you spot times when she may need more support than you are already giving.

Growing up is an anxious business because by definition you don't know what is going to happen next. Children can quickly find themselves in trouble or out of their depth, or in pain in new situations. This is all part of finding their own way, trying to establish their own identity. As parents we should be constantly vigilant but you do have to let them make mistakes. You don't need to be hovering around your kids but you do need to be available and to be responsive when they need you. They must know you are there, almost like a backstop.
Peter Wilson, child psychotherapist and Director of Young Minds

Keeping communication channels open If your child knows she can talk to you about her problems and emotions, you will be able to guide her much more effectively (see Communication, p.70 and Dealing with feelings, p.94).

Try to build in times just to be with each other. This is easily forgotten in the whirl of conflicting demands, especially in periods of family stress, but better communication and understanding often springs from simply being relaxed and happy in each other's company (see Helping them through, p.236).

Stress points

The potential effects of high stress on children include:

Behaviour problems Children's social and learning skills are often dented if they feel stressed and their confidence is low. This can result in 'testing' behaviour they know to be wrong. They may have difficulty in making or keeping friends or in concentrating and reaching their potential at school

Physical problems Stress can be a factor in headaches, migraine, asthma, eczema and other conditions. It may even affect children's growth[4]

Mental health problems, including depression

How can parents spot when their child is stressed? 'There are obvious signs, like children being more fretful or more clingy, not wanting to go to school, bed-wetting and nightmares,' says Peter Wilson, child psychotherapist and director of Young Minds. 'I think their persistence is key. We all have bad days, bad weeks, but a month or more of that and I would be worried.

'Listlessness also shows you something is wrong. Children who are well are happy and curious and alert. I would watch children who are really not interested or unable to really lose themselves in what they are doing. They do need to be absorbed at times, say when they are playing with their dolls or building something. When children can't do that I think it is a sign that they are stressed.

'Finally, parents need to look for changes in a child's behaviour. If he's been playing with lots of children and suddenly he's at home alone all the time, beginning to wake at night or becoming extremely fretful of going to sleep, all these things should alert a parent.'

Helping your child understand There is fear in the unknown. Much avoidable stress and anxiety is caused by children not understanding what is going on in their lives. Why are they feeling as they do? Why are they in this situation? Where will it lead? Confusion can bewilder, frighten and crush a child's ability to find her own way through a situation or problem.

Talking with your child about any significant and imminent change in her life will help her negotiate it more successfully. Try not to inflate it beyond its reasonable significance or to tell her what she will or should feel about it, but rather give her the information she needs to understand what is happening.

Helping them through

Mary MacLeod, Director of Policy and Research, ChildLine

'A child can cope so much better when things go wrong temporarily, including bad times in their own relationship with a parent and bad times in the relationship between the parents, if they feel a parent loves them and is on their side.

What they cannot survive so well are stresses from the outside world, not having enough food, clothing etc. Not meeting those basic needs overshadows almost everything else. Some families do manage very well but we should never underestimate the stresses they create.

Generally, it helps if parents acknowledge the bad times and don't pretend that everything is always good and wonderful for their children or for themselves.

1   **Say that in some way it has happened to you.** This can be really important, especially between fathers and sons. It is very hard for boys to admit to being bullied, for example, and this really helps.

2   **Say sorry and mean it when we get it wrong.** 'I screwed up there' or 'I absolutely shouldn't have done that' etc. This is terribly important in families, however we do it.

3   **Talk and listen.** Parents have to be alert to when it is the right time to listen. So often the really important stuff gets said indirectly and sideways and you do need to recognise these times and keep spaces for them, whether that is lying on their bed at bedtime, taking the dog for a walk, cuddling in front of the TV, or whatever.

We are getting a higher proportion of calls on family problems and family stress in the London and South East service, a highly urbanised area. I do think this is due to the rushing. We need to seize the moment when our children need to talk to us, to give them that time.'

Talk to the child about the situation in advance, talk about it while it is happening, and check back after a few days.
Vivienne Gross, Clinical Director, The Institute of Family Therapy

Story-telling may help communicate difficult concepts such as loss and separation (see Dealing with feelings, p.94) while role-playing or replaying scenes may help your child clarify a difficult situation and her place in it (see Setting out situations, p.238). Through these, she may see how she could handle a problem differently next time or, equally important, see that she was not its cause.

Self-blame can blight a child's life. Liberating your child from it is sometimes simply a matter of helping her see how she could not have influenced the outcome of events. Her parents' divorce or grandparent's death, for example, would still have happened whatever she did and however she behaved.

Children often receive an implicit message that they cause problems and can often blame themselves for what happens. By running through a story, you can help them see where responsibility lies. You can offer the child other perspectives and nudge them towards a more expanded, less critical, less blameworthy view.
Jim Wilson, family therapist, Cardiff Institute of Family Therapy

Other children can also provide important support and reassurance, particularly if they have had similar experiences. This need not be on a formal basis. Opportunities to mix, talk or simply play with other children, without a parent always listening in, can be hugely helpful.

Adults experience this feeling of 'Why me?' This feeling that you are the only one in the world to whom this has happened. Children are no different. Linking up with other children who can share experiences can help them come to terms with situations.
Professor Hugh Foot, specialist in child psychology and social development

Showing the way You are your child's most powerful role model and she will cope much better in difficult situations if she sees you coping. Try to show her the benefits of asking for support from others when necessary, of relaxation and of finding pleasure in life by finding time for these yourself (see Helping yourself, p.229).

Where a child in a distressing family situation sees that the parent remains able to cope and that the structure of their daily world, though changed, hasn't actually fragmented and broken down, that child is much better able to cope. Where children are told their parents have found a way of sorting out a dispute, even if the children don't directly see them doing it, that still helps them cope much better.
Gill Gorell Barnes, Honorary Senior Lecturer, Tavistock Clinic, family therapist, researcher, co-author of *Growing Up in Stepfamilies*[5]

Setting out situations

Dolls and other playthings can be used to act out scenes and help a child better understand new or confusing situations.

If your child does not initiate the game herself, you could set out the scene and its key players – perhaps a first day at school or a child visiting newly separated parents in different homes – then step back. The point of the exercise is to understand your child's version of events, not to impose your own.

Initially she may find it easier to talk about her feelings in role – 'This little girl is very sad because her daddy has gone away' – and we need to respect this. We can respond to what she says and make it clear we are listening and that we understand – 'Oh she does look sad.' We can also answer any questions without taking over or putting ideas in her head.

Once she has created and described her 'scene' she may go on to talk about how she feels directly, especially if she has your full attention and feels heard. There is no need to push her to do this – you can continue to acknowledge how the 'little girl' feels (or your child directly if she is ready/willing/able), even use the playthings yourself if it helps. You can also show her different possible ways of handling a problem or show her that a situation is not her fault or responsibility.

'It is important to follow the child and reflect the child but not to join in or take too much initiative yourself,' explains Pat Elliot, a bereavement counsellor and psychotherapist. 'It is like reflective listening [see Communication, p.70], but reflective playing. Rather than saying, "I'll be this and you do that," just let her do it for herself and observe and feed back what you see. This helps her know she has been understood, and this will help her move on.'

Jim Wilson, a family therapist at the Cardiff Family Institute, explains: 'It is for the parent to respond to the child's questions in a particular situation, not the parent to tell the story of how it should be.

'The core idea is to help children quite literally to look down upon themselves and see themselves as part of the overall situation. It allows children to begin to reflect on their own experiences.

'A child needing to develop social skills, for instance, could talk about a situation they have experienced recently and what was difficult for them – eg. being left out of games in the playground – and what they could have done differently to help themselves. The child choreographs the scene, and the role of the adult is to encourage the child to do that for themselves.'

Get help if you need it If you think your child is depressed or upset in a way neither of you can manage, seek help. It is not a sign of failure or defeat but of a parent who cares enough to want to help their child through a difficult time. Many organisations can provide emotional and practical support (see Contacts, p.355). Your GP may be able to advise you on which kind of support may best suit your particular situation.

We need to be our child's advocate, who else is going to be?
We know as parents when something is not right, we need to act on this as soon
as is possible and access the services our child may need if help is needed.
Lisa Blakemore-Brown, chartered educational psychologist

Coping with bereavement

I lost my dad when I was seven years old. I remember it all,
I was so aware of the loss, the big gap. I had a fantasy of how life should
be and I really felt it when there were other fathers around, on holidays and things.
I don't think I coped very well. I felt very sad and angry and I couldn't put
it into any perspective. When my mother told me Dad had died she said
'You are not going to see your Daddy any more,' and I remember thinking
'Has he gone to prison?' I couldn't work out where he had gone.
As it was I could still see him walking down the road.
Linda H

My wife died when our children were seven and four. I made them each
a memory box of things that were hers, photographs of them together, letters
that she wrote. They look at them every so often. It prompts questions and
stories and memories, and I think that's helped.
Philip D

As a parent of a grieving child, be prepared for the range of emotions she may display, from apathy and withdrawal to rage and anger. Rather than 'protecting' your child from grief or steering her away from it, give her permission to express her negative thoughts, emotions and fears and be as supportive as you can.

When a child feels overwhelmed by grief, anger or confusion, that positive bond between you can feel like a lifeline. Tell her you love her very much. She needs to know. You can also help by:

Preparing your child Preparing children for bereavement can begin years before you foresee them ever having to experience it. The more questions they can ask before if affects them directly, the better they may be able to cope when it does.

> *The idea that death is for ever is often in conflict with what children see in the media. We really do need to prepare them better for bereavement and one way is to challenge these media images of the hero never dying, or being killed and then coming back to life. Around three and four years, we can also introduce awareness by using the natural world. It provides many different examples to show how death is different to absence – the death of flowers, insects, leaves falling in autumn. Another way, however macabre it sounds, is having and losing pets. This can be a huge preparation. We need to introduce understanding of death in a gentle way.*
>
> Pat Elliot, bereavement counsellor and psychotherapist

Being honest Children need to know what has happened and what you believe happens next. It may also help them to know that people have many different ideas and beliefs.

> *What any one child will need to know about what happens after death will vary enormously, largely depending on culture and religion. Manage the conversation as honestly as you can based on what you believe, but in the context that others believe differently, so that the child can find their own place. A little boy I was very close to was three and a half when his father was killed in a climbing accident. A year later we were in a church in front of a painting of the Resurrection and he said to me: 'Do you think people come back from the dead, Mary?' I said to him: 'To be honest Christopher, lots of people do, but I don't,' and he said, 'I do,' and I said, 'That's great.'*
>
> Mary MacLeod, Director of Policy and Research, ChildLine

Using clear language and concrete information Young children may take euphemisms literally, if they understand them at all. 'Taken by the angels', 'gone to sleep', 'slipped away', 'resting' and so on can at best confuse and at worst terrify, because the child may fear the same will happen to them. Children may hold themselves responsible for the loss of someone close so, for all ages, it helps to state explicitly that no one is to blame.

Children aged five and under often have difficulty accepting the finality of death and that the person won't one day come back. It helps to keep explanations very simple and clear. Explain that when a person dies they stop breathing, eating, walking, also feeling pain or hunger or worry. Be prepared for them to ask the same questions, over and over again, until the issue is clear in their own minds.

Slightly older children may understand more but this may trigger a fear of their own death or of losing others close to them, and they may need your help to put this in perspective. They may also tie themselves in knots trying to see the reason or purpose behind the death. If you have no religious views to draw on, it often helps to state simply that death, like many things in life, is not fair.

With little children you need to be as concrete as possible because that is how they understand things. Not until 10, 11, 12 can they really think in abstract terms, which is why discussion of heaven and the spirit is so difficult. But let's face it, do any of us really get it? Humankind has grappled with it but we each fill the gap with our own faith.

Pat Elliot, bereavement counsellor and psychotherapist

Encouraging your child to talk Children can find it very hard to talk about what has happened and how they are feeling. It is important that your child only talks when she wants to, that you do not push her before she is ready or attempt to impose your own emotions. She may feel very differently from you, and she needs to be able to express this.

You can help by example, raising the subject and talking about the person who has died and how you feel, in a way that respects your child's age and vulnerability. Ask her if she would like you to tell her friends, or whether she would like to do this herself (you should inform her school, nursery, etc). Remember, your child is not there to provide you with support. Talk to her to help her express emotion, but do not burden her with the responsibility of making you feel better.

It is important to show some grief in front of the children but also to find adult support for yourself. I have seen quite a young child become the carer of a grieving parent. That is really sad and not really fair.

Pat Elliot, bereavement counsellor and psychotherapist

If you find it too painful to talk and listen to your child as she needs, ask another close and caring adult to do this. Bereavement counselling may help you both come to terms with your loss (see Contacts, p.355, or contact your GP).

Helping your child talk about death

Mary MacLeod, Director of Policy and Research, ChildLine

'Children do not seem to be encouraged to talk directly about death. We need to work with parents on this, to reassure them that children do not need huge protection from feelings of sadness. They are feeling anyway.

'Indirect means of exploring the realities of loss, through films and stories, can be very helpful. *The Snowman* by Raymond Briggs[6] is a good story to help children understand and revisit loss. Singing sad songs with our children is another way to allow sadness and tension to get expression and evaporate.

'Talking about the person keeps them real, not in terms of only blame or only praise, but talking about them as a real person with all their lovely parts and all the bits that made us fed up. All this can help a child talk about death and the dead.'

Answering questions A basic rule of thumb is that if a child asks the question, she needs to know the answer. The stream of questions may seem endless but encourage children to keep on asking, especially as their concerns and understanding will change as they grow.

It is important to make it clear they can ask any questions they like. The child may ask for a lot of details, sometimes in quite a gruesome or even macabre way, and it is important to give them these. Children also want to know details about illness and whether it is likely to affect them. Even in suicide it is very important to be honest because they will find out the truth over time and that is far worse. You do not have to tell them everything all at once; give them a little bit a time and respond to their questions.

Pat Elliot, bereavement counsellor and psychotherapist

Providing physical comfort Most children will need extra physical comfort at this time – cuddles, hugs, being physically close. Some may also regress and need more physical care than previously. Observe and respond to what your child is showing you she needs at this time.

Staying true to life The urge to talk only good of the dead is very understandable but idolising them can cause problems. Children may feel angry at the deceased for leaving them, but feel unable to express that about a person now considered perfect. An idolised dead sibling may be an impossible act for a surviving child to follow; an idolised parent may not tally with the child's own memories. All can cause hurt, guilt and a sense of failure.

How can you not always compete and fail against an ideal child who has died? How can you separate and become independent of a mother who is not there any more and who was perfect? It is so helpful to remain realistic.
Pat Elliot, bereavement counsellor and psychotherapist

Keeping to familiar routines As far as possible, keep to usual family routines, mealtimes, bedtimes and so on. These may seem trivial in the circumstances but can help children feel that, though they have experienced great loss, their entire life isn't in free fall.

Letting your child grieve This may not be as you would like her to grieve or even as you think appropriate, but it is what she needs to do.

Children can often go one of two ways: very withdrawn or almost frenetic. I think you need to be as natural as possible with your feelings and this allows children to be the same. Their grief may show itself in a different way. Children often go in and out of grief more quickly, so to be upset one minute and playing the next does not make the grief any less real and valid. You have to go with their flow as much as you can.
Pat Elliot, bereavement counsellor and psychotherapist

Allowing your child to be happy Children can feel very guilty at feeling happy or laughing when those around them are sad. It is important that they know that grieving does not mean having fun has to stop or that you have to feel miserable all the time.

Should children attend funerals?

Pat Elliot, bereavement counsellor and psychotherapist

'Attending funerals gives children an opportunity to be part of the public grief, valuing the person who has died and grieving as part of a community. The ritual is also sometimes a way things can be expressed that cannot be said. It can be an emotional release.

'It is a delicate balance, though, between allowing children to show their feelings and being faced with a formal ritual which by definition involves things that you do in a certain order and a certain amount of holding yourself together. It is ideal that children be given some choice, they may prefer to have a ritual on a smaller scale at home with loved ones for example; they could make their own ceremony of saying goodbye then later visit the grave. It does always help to say goodbye.

'If a child is to attend the funeral of a very special person, for example a parent, and the parent who is left is barely able to cope with his or her own pain, it can be very helpful to have a chosen adult at the funeral who knows the child well to be there particularly to support that child. In my experience children are far more often upset and hold it against their parents when they haven't been allowed to go. So if it is difficult, specific support at the funeral may be key.'

Divorce and separation

I think it is a very positive thing when children see parents handle a difficult situation, that they see a parent grasp the problem and deal with it. It must help them know the parent is a protector and it also shows them how to deal with their own problems when they encounter them.

Cherry H

We're the generation that grew up with divorced parents. We know what it's like and it's up to us to use that knowledge. We can deny that it hurt, say it never did me any harm. Or we can admit that it did and try to think of ways to lessen that hurt for our children. We do know, in a way perhaps our parents never did, and I think it's our responsibility to act on that.

John M

Parental separation and divorce can have a devastating effect on a child's view of themselves, their relationships and their world in general. Yet they can also be managed without causing major long-term damage. As a parent, you can help by letting your child know she is and always will be loved, cared for and respected. The following points will also help you both negotiate potential problems. You may not be able to achieve all of them all of the time, especially in times of crisis, yet even having them as goals will make a difference.

Reducing your child's exposure to conflict The level of distress a child experiences through and following parental separation and divorce depends in part on the amount of parental conflict she has been exposed to. If you are going through a bitter separation, be as careful as you can about what your child sees and hears.

> *Certainly research indicates that if separation takes place without too much high emotional conflict or, when there is conflict, it happens behind closed doors and the child isn't exposed to it, the child can get through it without too much distress. And it does seem that after about two years the range of disturbance among children of divorce is average rather than it being higher than the rest of the population. We have to accept that children are distressed when their parents break up, but that does not mean they are necessarily psychologically disturbed by it and it does seem to be quite a small minority of children who are.*
> Gill Gorell Barnes, Honorary Senior Lecturer Tavistock Clinic,
> family therapist, researcher

Distress following separation or divorce may be reflected in a child's behaviour and/or schooling. Some children seem to find school and school work a sanctuary from the stresses of home life; others find it hard to concentrate when their thoughts are elsewhere. It is important that teachers and others involved with the child's care are informed of what is happening so they can respond with understanding.

Looking at things from your child's perspective Your child may feel confused, guilty, anxious, scared, rejected, angry, desperate. Try to help her express her emotions (see Dealing with feelings, p.94) and take them into account when you tackle any inappropriate behaviour.

If a child is behaving badly or doing something to attract attention,
it is very important to say that you understand this is difficult for them and
that if they want to talk about it you are happy to listen, but how they are behaving
isn't acceptable. This allows the child to know the parent does understand and
that the parent is also holding the boundary on behaviour. It encourages the
child to communicate their feelings as opposed to acting them out.
Cheryl Walters, Head of Research and Policy, National Stepfamily Association

Keeping daily life as normal as possible If parents, siblings, grandparents, manage to maintain a 'business as usual' approach to daily routines, children feel safer. Their whole world is not crumbling around them and they are less likely to panic about their new situation and their future.

Distinguishing between your child's feelings and your own This is central to how well a child survives major family problems. You feel one thing and your child may feel another entirely. You may hate your ex and your child will still love him or her; you may feel liberated at the prospect of separation and your child may feel devastated. Allow your child her own emotions and try never to impose your own feelings or use her to 'get at' your ex. Being very clear that you are separate individuals with valid but different views and emotions will also help her see that she is not 'part of the problem'; she is not to blame.

As adults we must accept that children love both parents and that
they need to be able to feel good about each parent in order to develop and
mature naturally and feel positive about themselves.
Cheryl Walters, Head of Research and Policy, National Stepfamily Association

Planning what you will say How can you tell your child about the separation or divorce in a way that would help her most? Try to use simple words and explanations and, if possible, arrange for both parents to tell the child together. At least try to agree on the wording between you or have access to the other's version. If you are moving into a stepfamily, it is best for a child's natural parent to tell the child without the prospective step-parent present.

Be clear and up front with information your child needs to know – that she is loved, that she is not to blame, that you know it must feel strange for her, that certain changes are going to happen. Also give her

Family facts

— By 2010, the Policy Studies Institute predicts that more than half of UK marriages will result in divorce and remarriage.

— Every day around 640 children and young people see their parents divorce or separate.

— Lone parent families now make up 19% of all families with children.

— Official statistics do not count how many co-habiting parents separate although according to the National Stepfamily Association the rate is higher than for married couples.

— One in eight children is likely to grow up in a stepfamily.

— One in two of these stepfamilies will have a new child of the step-couple.

— At least 50% of remarriages which form a stepfamily also end in divorce.

— 25% of stepfamilies break down in the first year.

— One in six fathers lives apart from some or all of his own biological children.[7]

as many details as you can about the practical aspects of her life. Tell her what is going to change and reassure her about what will stay the same – will she be staying in the same house, the same school, have the same friends, toys, pets? If one parent is moving out, where are they moving to and how can you get there? If you are moving to a new house, what does it look like? What are you taking with you? The child needs concrete information to plan her new existence.

Then be prepared to censor. Sometimes, with the very best of intentions, parents burden children with facts they do not need and do not want, often to do with the breakdown of the parental relationship. As a general guide, if the parent is open to questions and if the child wants and needs to know, the child will ask.

We must speak and act with children age-appropriately.
I always feel short and simple explanations are best, but with the option
for the child to come back and ask questions, so they know this isn't a one-off
chat but an ongoing process of understanding. Little children, up to about ten
years depending on the child, do not need details. They have a right to know
what is happening to them and it is important to keep them updated.
But think in terms of giving them the basics they need in order
not to be fearful of what is going to happen, and then
try to answer their questions as they arise.
Cheryl Walters, Head of Research and Policy, National Stepfamily Association

Encouraging questions Let your child know she can ask any question she wants, now or later, and understand that what she needs to know and how she deals with the information she is given will change as she grows.

Books, such as *Dinosaurs Divorce*,[8] may help her begin to think and talk about what is happening. Building in a special time for questions – perhaps before a bedtime book – may help her know that she can ask what she needs to rather than having to always respond to her parent's agenda.

One thing that was really helpful for my son, who was seven at the time and would not ask questions, was my devising a questionnaire by imagining the questions he might want answers to. I then answered the questions and wrote on the bottom that I was sure these weren't all the right questions but could he tell me what I had got wrong and any gaps he had found. The extraordinary thing was how well this worked. It offered a matter-of-fact focus at such an emotionally painful time.
Jim Wilson, family therapist, Cardiff Institute of Family Therapy

Showing it is OK not to have all the answers Better to say 'I don't know what's happening with that yet, so I can't answer now, but as soon as it's a bit clearer, I will' than get it very wrong or say nothing at all.

Negotiating problem times Some events are more stressful than others when you are in a separated, divorced or stepfamily. These 'problem peaks' may include marriage, death, Christmas or other religious festivals, birthdays and holidays. Advance warning may at least help you plan accordingly – doing something or going somewhere completely different may help avoid heartbreaking comparisons with happier times.

Working at making it work for your child Much of what your child experiences in her new family structure(s) will be down to you and your ex-partner. It is the responsibility of every parent to try to make the new way of life work for the child – and to keep on trying.

Divorce involves adults sitting down and saying, 'What piece of hard thinking do I have to do to make things go well for the kids, however much I am in emotional turmoil? How am I going to keep a structure going which doesn't upset their lives fundamentally?' It feels artificial but it has to be done to ensure the kids' lives don't end up in a mess. You don't stop being a parent and anything that helps parents think that way will help the children.

Gill Gorell Barnes, Honorary Senior Lecturer Tavistock Clinic, family therapist, researcher

Coping with a new stepfamily

Children in stepfamilies face particular problems and it is important to explore what works best for your new family group. You can also help by:

Being aware Joining a stepfamily is a huge transition. When a child becomes part of a stepfamily she is often joining a new and unfamiliar unit, each member of which will bring their own temperament, habits, experiences, values, jealousies, expectations and prejudices. She may dislike her stepsiblings. She may dislike the step-parent or, equally complicated, like them and feel disloyal to the natural parent she no longer lives with. She may share time between two new stepfamily units and feel she 'fits' in neither. She may be unfamiliar with the everyday routines of her new home. She may feel scared, jealous, angry, confused, ignored, rejected, replaced, betrayed, powerless.

The very fact of living with a person you don't know is difficult. All their habits are different, their expectations are different, their understanding of the child is limited, they smell different, they don't feel the same as the person who's gone. These things are tremendously important and powerful, especially for little children, and we have to recognise that. The child is very often outraged by this replacement and the early days of stepfamilies are often very difficult times. There is often a lot of envy and rivalry.

Gill Gorell Barnes, Honorary Senior Lecturer Tavistock Clinic, family therapist, researcher

Giving it time The National Stepfamily Association estimates it can take between two to ten years for relations in a stepfamily to stabilise. Do not blame yourself and especially do not blame the child if all is not sweetness and light – there is much to work out and work through first.

Understanding behaviour When a child becomes part of a step-family, her feelings are often reflected in her behaviour as both parent and step-parent are, quite literally, put to the test.

The child is saying, 'Are you going to leave like my mother or father left? Is it safe to care about you? Is it safe to rely on you? Are you going to be there or are you going to leave if I am bad?' It is also about the child, in its own way, trying to heal that part of themselves that says 'I must have been really bad for my parent to leave', because somewhere in a child there is that sense that if they had been better, kinder, if they'd have done their homework, whatever it might be, this wouldn't have happened.
Cheryl Walters, Head of Research and Policy, National Stepfamily Association

Getting together You can help your child feel she has a say in at least some aspects of her life by ensuring that the stepfamily as a group routinely reviews how its members feel about the everyday matters of household life (see Reviews, routines and rules, opposite). Even a very young child can be helped to say what she likes or doesn't like about breakfast time or the morning rush etc. These may seem trivial points to you, but are crucial to how she feels about her new environment.

Being tolerant Be open about the fact that your stepfamily is made up of people from different pasts but hopefully a shared future, that you will have many different ways, ideas, attitudes and loyalties. Emphasise that differences can co-exist if you all try to be tolerant and under-standing and talk matters through.

Knowing your role If you are a step-parent, you can be loving, sup-portive and caring but you are not a replacement parent, especially when the stepfamily is relatively new. This knowledge may save you and the children involved a great deal of heartache. You will have to work at establishing a relationship with each child, but until that is done, it is best to leave the tough parental duties such as discipline to the parents.

A step-parent can put themselves under such pressure to be a super-parent, yet a very big part of failure in stepfamilies is unrealistic expectations of oneself and of others. It helps to recognise that things change over time. As a step-parent you actively have to build a relationship with children. You can't, for example, just come in and discipline children who are quite right to say 'Who the hell are you?' Knowing where to draw the line involves putting yourself in the child's shoes, imagining how what you are doing or saying might feel to the child.

Cheryl Walters, Head of Research and Policy, National Stepfamily Association

In our study[9] we found it was much harder for stepmothers than stepfathers. Dads tend to be brought in more as mother's partner, to get to know over time. Stepmothers are expected to do much more in relation to the children and tend to be brought in to take on the kids and run the house. Children have much more direct exposure and stepmothers often have a much more difficult and resistant time. They can be treated with incredible hostility.

Gill Gorell Barnes, Honorary Senior Lecturer Tavistock Clinic, family therapist, researcher

Reviews, routines and rules

Gill Gorell Barnes, Honorary Senior Lecturer Tavistock Clinic, family therapist, researcher

'We're a stepfamily and my own parents divorced when I was in my teens so I know the feelings as well as the theory of the feelings, as it were. I think the Pandora's Box issue – the fear that everything will flood out uncontrollably when you lift the lid and begin to talk – is a very big one in stepfamilies. I do think it stops people talking.

'This is where discussion of house rules helps hugely – saying to children, "When you come here let's think about how it is going to be different from when you are at Mum's. Let's see how we can make it go as smoothly as possible for you."

'It helps to talk about "house" rather than "family" rules because it is often an easier concept to buy into. It gets away from the child objecting because "This isn't my family". It also helps if adults are aware they are setting up a new organisation, a new habitat, and to think about its principles and rules and how these could be established. Talk these through with the children.

'Think ahead – should you agree telephone rules between the natural parents, such as no phone calls between 7 or 8pm, or agree telephone times when the child is available to speak to the other parent? In families where everything can be more open, such rigid rules aren't needed, but in situations where everything is very suspicious and "hot" it is very useful.'

Staying positive If you and your children or stepchildren are beginning to tire of references to stepfamilies' potential problems, it may help
to remember that 'many of the most important and creative figures in
European culture were stepchildren: among them Isaac Newton, John
Donne, Descartes, Spinoza, Michelangelo and Leonardo da Vinci.'[10]

Everyone involved in a stepfamily has to work to make it a success,
but they can work incredibly well. When they do, stepfamily children
can journey into adulthood with a wider network of supportive relationships and with skills that will benefit them for the rest of their lives.

*When it is a successful stepfamily, children learn to compromise in a
way they often wouldn't have had to in a first-time family. They also learn
to negotiate and they learn about the concept of getting something of
what they want but perhaps not all, of things being good enough,
so they are not always striving for the impossible.*
Cheryl Walters, Head of Research and Policy, National Stepfamily Association

CHAPTER TWELVE

GENDER AND DEVELOPMENT

How you relate to your child as a boy or as a girl, and how your child views his or her own gender, will influence the rest of your child's life. That much is obvious. What's been far less clear over recent years, as parents have been bombarded with new information about gender differences and development, is how they can best use that information to help their kids.

Letting children be who they are

It's really important with all children to let them be who they are.
If we've learned one thing from 30 years of feminism, it's not to put kids in boxes according to gender. If a girl wants to play soccer, or a boy wants to write poetry and look after young children, then that is wonderful. At the same time, we have also been learning lately what all parents always knew — that most boys and most girls are different. Knowing the differences actually makes our parenting more individual and sensitive.

Steve Biddulph, psychologist and author

If you are reading this while your son is attacking a bush with a water pistol or your daughter plays schools, or if your daughter has announced she's called 'Pirate Pete' while your son is swathed in glitter and netting, you won't have much time to muse on the latest twists in the gender and genetics debate. So let's cut the political correctitude and get down to the basics of what the most recent research tells us — which is what most parents knew in the first place.

Boys and girls are born different Small genetic differences appear to influence how boys and girls think and behave. Other biological differences between the genders, including brain chemistry and even pre-natal hormonal influences, could also affect behaviour and development.

Biological differences should be recognised but kept in perspective Blaming genetics alone for children's behaviour is not only daft but also potentially damaging as it lets adults off the hook. 'It's all in the genes' or 'Girls will be girls' may make a headline but doesn't make for constructive social policy or successful parenting.

Differences in the ways parents and society in general treat boys and girls has a huge bearing on a child's self-image, expectations, aspirations and actions Whether 'masculine' and 'feminine' behaviour traits have their roots in nature or nurture, they are moulded by parental influence and cultural learning – how children are brought up and what they are exposed to.

Gender stereotypes are just that – sweeping generalisations. Some girls like frocks; others are happiest in leggings climbing trees. Some boys like football or to shrug rather than talk, others are great communicators or cringe at the thought of competitive games. Tying our children to our own expectations of gender-related behaviour helps no one. As our knowledge of common gender differences increases, parents have the chance to use this information sensitively, sensibly and constructively – to better understand children and thus better respond to their needs.

We know from research and experience that boys tend to be more physically active, more action-oriented, less reflective and less receptive than girls. It is not, however, the prerogative of boys to be active or girls to be reflective, but there are trends that way and these can be exaggerated by parents' expectations. There are also differences in the pace at which they grow up. But we should be careful to remember the huge similarities between the genders. Children of both sexes are growing up with common experiences and common anxieties and as human beings we share a lot more similarities than differences.

Peter Wilson, child psychotherapist and Director of Young Minds

Parental influence

It is hard to know where to draw the line. I was never allowed Barbies when I was a kid because my parents considered them sexist. Which they were. But that made me want them all the more. I've let my daughter have them and we've had lots of laughs about how if she was real her ridiculously big bosoms would make her fall over, but whether that's a sensible compromise or a cop-out I've no idea.

Megan T

I think I do treat them differently even though I would never do so on purpose and I try my hardest not to. If I'm honest, I'm tougher on him and I think my wife's stricter with our daughter.

Mark F

We are sending our children messages about what it is to be male and female all the time, whether we know it or like it or not. Some of these are glaringly obvious – the toys we buy, the clothes we choose, even the names we give our children all speak volumes about our own understandings of masculinity and femininity. Your child will also be acutely aware of the nature of your own gender role and how you relate to adults of the opposite sex, so be wary of those ironic throwaway remarks – 'Just like a man', 'Never trust a woman', etc. Young children, especially, can take them very seriously.

Other parental messages may be equally powerful but much harder to identify and evaluate (see Parental responses, p.256). Yet an awareness of them, along with an honest acknowledgement of our expectations and prejudices, will help us understand our influence on our children's self-image and behaviour and how we can use that most constructively.

Parents can teach children respect for the opposite sex and their own gender and abilities. The father who shows respect to the mother, for instance, is also teaching his child respect for women generally, and vice versa. This is important not only to help lessen the impact of gender rivalries but also to help children grow into healthy, happy adults.

Parental responses

Susie Orbach, psychotherapist

'Much of the modern genetics debate is just a way of not taking responsibility. In fact, we do have an enormous influence as parents on what kind of relationship is possible with our children. Our children are a set of possibilities with which we engage, bringing all of who we are to our parenting.

'Every way in which we bring ourselves to infants is imbued with a sense of our and their gender. Whether we realise it or not, most parents coo in a different pitch and tone depending whether the infant is male or female. We hold baby boys for longer periods of time than baby girls. We tend to breastfeed boys for longer, wean them later and each feeding period is longer than it is for girls. We potty train boys later.

'On the other hand, we have proto-conversations with girls earlier and for longer periods of time. We encourage boys' physicality while bringing a certain reticence to girls, still. Differences such as these are based on our internal sense of what masculinity and femininity mean, what they elicit in us and what we try to confirm about our own sense of gender through the unconscious imposition of nuanced behaviour towards baby girls and baby boys.'

Helping boys

Childhood can seem complicated enough without gender issues thrown in, but they exist and it is only commonsense to recognise and deal with them effectively. The first important step for parents is to keep these issues in perspective. Boys are not collapsing under the weight of social and personal confusion and most gender differences narrow as they grow older. But there are factors which may make boys' early years particularly tricky to negotiate and, for all parents, forewarned is forearmed.

Girls, once the object of boys' derision, are outstripping them academically in the early school years and seem more able than ever to take their place and state their case. At the same time, facets of 'masculine' behaviour once considered positive, such as physicality and emotional reserve, are increasingly viewed as problems to be negotiated or overcome. As adult men deliberate the latest media constructs of modern masculinity – are they New Man, New Lad, New Dad or Old

It's different for boys

Steve Biddulph, psychologist and author

'We are discovering some really important differences that can help us raise boys better. First and foremost has to be the difference in the rate at which boys' brains grow. In a word, they're slower. At birth most boys make less eye contact, smile less at their mum or dad, and we have to be really determined to chatter to them, be social with them, and help them learn to talk and communicate as they grow through to be toddlers. By the age of six, the average boy is still six to 12 months behind the average girl in fine motor skills – holding a pencil or scissors, sitting still to write or read, etc. Boys also develop in a different order to girls.

'Girls may need more help to run around, ride bikes, throw a ball and so on. Little boys need help to learn to love. That means chatting, cuddling and playing with them. Not leaving them in front of a TV set. Not putting them in a crèche for long periods if you can avoid it – they are much more prone to separation anxiety and depression than girls. Fathers playing with them, being present and teaching them things is a proven boost to their ability and confidence.

'Around the age of six fathers actually become the primary parent in a little boy's eyes. So doing things and going places with Dad really matters. A single mum can raise boys just fine, but trustworthy grandfathers, uncles or teachers taking an interest are very important.

'Always allow boys to have their feelings. Give them a hug, and tell them "Yes, it is very sad" when they are missing a friend who has left, or a pet dies. We want men who can feel, because then they will be more resilient and less lonely as men. Boys especially love to talk while doing some activity. Teach them housework and do it alongside them, so they can chat about their day. Girls will tend to talk more directly, but boys (and men!) prefer to talk sideways, while sharing a task. We like to do something with our hands while we get our sentences together.'

Confused? – boys are also bombarded with conflicting messages about what it is to be male. All these issues overlap and, if not managed properly, can combine to make boys uncertain of what is expected of them.

Social and learning skills Different speeds and patterns of development between the genders mean many young boys' social and learning skills lag behind girls' of a similar age. The heavy emphasis on literacy over numeracy in many nursery and primary classes can also create a sense of bias in girls' favour, leaving boys with a misplaced sense of underachievement (see Gender and schooling, p.264). How your son negotiates this will depend partly on the sensitivity and ability of his school and teachers, and partly on parental support (also see Play and learning, p.275 and Dealing with feelings, p.94).

Communication

The kind of man we want now is changing. We don't need men who can wrestle buffalo. They need to be able to talk!
Steve Biddulph, psychologist and author

Many boys find it difficult to talk about how they feel and even to ask for help when they need it. Helping them is one of the most important tasks any parent of a boy can undertake. Boys especially tend to recoil from intense, face-to-face 'How Do You Feel?' conversations and benefit most from 'sideways' talk – doing an activity together and feeling comfortable in each other's presence while talking, rather than always sitting down to chat (see Communication, p.70 and Dealing with feelings, p.94).

The expectations and images we transmit to our children in their earliest years are also crucial here – you can't expect your son to be emotionally literate if you believe that 'big boys don't cry' and that stoicism is always a virtue. A recent ChildLine report detailing a 71% rise in suicide by young men in ten years shows with chilling clarity the pressures on boys and how dangerous it can be for them to bottle up distress.[1]

Physicality Many boys need exercise in the same way that a Labrador needs a walk every day. Yet physical exuberance is now often seen as a problem to be contained rather than a childhood joy to be encouraged.

Fewer children of either gender are allowed to play out in the street or to roam and run until they come home tired for tea. Boys tend to enjoy team games more than girls, yet in some schools, understandable concerns about boys' physical domination of play spaces[2] have led to ball games such as football being banned or discouraged without the provision of necessary alternatives. Which all means that if your son

Boys' talk

Research into the calls made to ChildLine indicates that the feelings and problems boys and girls experience are similar, but that the way they respond to and talk about those problems are very different.

The study[3] found that:

1 Boys appear to find it hard to talk. They think people expect them to look after themselves.

2 All children find it difficult to ask for help but boys especially so. Some seem to see it as a sign of weakness and a failure of their masculinity – 'If I said what I feel, they would call me a wimp', 'I can't tell anyone about this, they'd laugh at me', 'If I told my Dad, he would just say, "You've got to stand up for yourself"'.

3 Boys were more likely to be self-critical about having a problem at all – as if a 'real' boy would have prevented or put a stop to the bullying, assault or domestic violence, or been able to handle loss or family difficulties without feeling overwhelmed. They view the very thing they need most to recover from childhood trauma – emotional support and the freedom to talk about their feelings – as yet another aspect of failure.

4 For many boys, confiding in friends is unthinkable.

5 On the whole, girls are encouraged to share their problems. Their concept of self-reliance includes asking for help, while boys' appears to exclude it.

'As boys begin to grow they get more and more affected by what it is to be a boy,' says Mary MacLeod, ChildLine's Director of Policy and Research. 'It is as if they consider asking for help and being a boy is a contradiction in terms. There is an expectation in themselves that they ought to handle problems that of course they cannot, for example physical abuse from their fathers.

'It is important not to generalise too much. Some boys, for example, just want the chance to say what they are feeling and both girls and boys need permission to have attention given to their feelings. Rather than waiting for children to tell you, you may have to look for other signs that they are not coping, such as not wanting to go to school, becoming short-tempered, nastier to a sibling or parent or simply being on a short fuse.

'When talking to boys about problems, you probably need to get into a more active discussion about options and manage the discussion about feelings in a different way than you would manage it with girls. "How does that feel?" will be far too direct for most boys. You have to give them permission for their feelings, saying for example, "I've heard from lots of other boy in your situation that . . ."'

does need action and exercise it may be up to you to organise it. Try to aim for a kick about in the playground or a walk instead of a car ride at least once a day.

Schools can be more or less boy-friendly – it's important to check when choosing a school. Check teachers are comfortable around boys and don't just want to squash them. Boys need firmness and rules, and also they need chances to get exercise and run about, have lessons that are practical and have outdoor sessions. A school we know has 15-minute exercise breaks in the morning before classes start, because so many kids come by bus or car. The boys love it, and it helps them to be calmer in class. The girls love it too.

Steve Biddulph, psychologist and author

Self-image

I was thrilled when he started loving football because I knew he was a gentle child who'd found a way to hold his own in any male peer group.

Madeleine M

While many parents are aware of the inherent dangers of expecting or encouraging 'macho' behaviour in young boys, many still feel ambivalent towards them showing any feminine side – it is still generally easier to be a 'tomboy' girl than a gentle, more 'feminine' boy. Parents tend to be overfearful of behaviours that are nothing more than a boy exploring, discovering and using his imagination (see Gender exploration, p.271). Many worry that their son will be teased and vulnerable. Yet boys who feel they should bury their more feminine side may also shut down their ability to express their feelings and fears, which will ultimately make them weaker and more lonely. Recognising your own attitudes and prejudices is the first step to accepting and appreciating your son for who he is rather than how you'd find it easier for him to be.

Boys are not helped by the paucity of effective role models in their early years – a working father may see little of his children during the week, most pre-school children mix mainly with women and most primary schools have few male teachers (some have none at all). Try to consider what masculine input your son has in his life and remember

that he will have to get his ideas of what it is to be male from somewhere. If it is not from trusted adult males at home or school, who
can show him how to use his strengths appropriately, it may be from
television or the big oik in Year Three.

If there's no good father figure to help the boy learn right from wrong,
he'll take his ideas of being male from watching videos and from the gangs he
hangs out with. So you can get this artificial sense of what is male.
Steve Biddulph, psychologist and author

Aggression

Violence is overwhelmingly a male problem, and the roots for this appear
to be primarily social rather than biological, highlighting the inadequacies of
current socialisation of male children, and the promotion of macho male attitudes
and models in society . . . Both men and women [should] take trouble to separate
ideas about masculinity from the concepts of personal 'toughness' that often
relate to violence . . . If boys are taught that they can't cry when their sisters
can, it's not surprising if they hit instead. 'Boys will be boys' only if
we permit, even encourage, macho attitudes and behaviour.
The Commission on Children and Violence[4]

The male sex hormone, testosterone, increases the tendency towards
violent behaviour, but that does not mean boys have to be violent. Boys
brought up in non-violent households and in non-violent environments
are no more violent than girls brought up in similar circumstances[5] –
parenting and experience count much more than gender.

A parent can help a boy be non-violent and more effective in
getting what he wants and needs by:

— Enabling him to express his feelings, so frustration, sadness,
apprehension, embarrassment and other emotions do not turn into
aggression because they festered without expression (see Dealing with
feelings, p.94).
— Building his self-esteem and ability to talk so he doesn't feel he has to
hit to have influence (see Communication, p.70).
— Helping him know the difference between assertion – expressing
opinions and needs effectively in ways that respect other people – and

aggression – expressing them in ways that intimidate and threaten, and are likely to backfire (see Assertion v. aggression, p.314).

— Help him to develop his social skills so he can interact with his peers and others sociably and effectively (see Growing independence, p.304).

— Role modelling non-violent behaviour. If he sees you being aggressive, he'll copy.

— Providing opportunities for exercise and physical release.

— Being tolerant of rough-and-tumble play. This can be a great way for boys to learn where to draw the line, ie. when boisterous behaviour is OK (when all participants are enjoying it) and when it is not OK (when someone is feeling threatened or hurt by it).

— Setting clear boundaries to leave him in no doubt about what is acceptable behaviour and what not (see Encouraging positive behaviour, p.143).

Most boys will pretend sticks are guns or swords and there is little you can do to stop this. Whether you let your son have actual toy weapons is very much a personal decision but it is worth remembering that:

Children will play up to what they have Young children especially will act out the role of the costume they are wearing or the toy they are playing with. Do not expect a boy in Action Man combat fatigues or with a plastic Kalashnikov to sit drawing for an hour. If you are happy to encourage army games, let him have army toys. If it bothers you, don't.

If you have toy weapons in the house, use them to confirm house rules Make it very clear that they are to be used for play and not to really hurt or threaten. Anything used as a real weapon (whether it is a toy gun used to hit a sibling or a ball thrown at a friend's head) should be removed immediately. Playing is fine, fighting is not (see Effective discipline, p.170).

Testosterone levels peak at various stages in a boy's development (one, inconveniently, appears to take place around four years, when many children start school in the UK) but the violence to which boys are exposed seems the greatest influence on whether those levels stay high.

Boys have one increase of testosterone at four and a half and again at 13-14. But again the environment we provide for them can make huge differences to what we see as their nature. Their testosterone level automatically rises during exposure to violence, and can stay elevated if the exposure continues. Studies in schools where there is a lot of bullying have shown the boys to have constantly higher levels of testosterone. If anti-bullying programmes were then effectively introduced, the testosterone levels throughout the school dropped. When you have situations of high stress, testosterone levels rise and this leads to more masculine behaviour and the whole thing feeds itself. If you have a safe environment, then boys are more like girls in their biochemical make-up.

Steve Biddulph, psychologist and author

Helping girls

There is an admirable 'We can do it', centre-stage feeling about girls' play which simply wasn't there 10 years ago.

Elizabeth Grugeon, senior lecturer in teacher education[6]

I think we do have clear expectations of our sons and daughters. We reward sociability in girls and I no longer think this is valid. From the research I have done I would suggest it is better for girls to be a bit rebellious and question what you tell them. The girls in our study[7] who took more initiative and answered back more were more resilient, whereas the girls who were very obedient and did everything parents said were also more likely to later on do what a boy said or what their peer group suggested.

Adrienne Katz, author, research associate

The recent shifts in how girls see themselves proves that changing our view of how boys and girls should be does bring about changes in their behaviour and outcome. After centuries of little girls being undervalued and limited by society's low expectations of their capabilities, female propensities are now considered important and valuable and, in very general terms, girls do seem to be having a better time than boys (whether women are having a better time than men is, of course, another issue entirely).

Gender and schooling

We are continually seeing in the media that girls are doing brilliantly and boys are doing hopelessly. This kind of reporting is one-sided and can often sound hysterical. There is an equally clear message from research that boys are ambitious and they hit the job market running and never look back. You need to break down the statistics further to make sense of them.

Bethan Marshall, lecturer in Education, Kings College, London

New and groundbreaking research offers fascinating insights into how boys and girls generally respond to schooling. Cutting through the hype to the core messages beneath will help us understand how best to encourage and support our children through their early school years.

The core messages:

— **There are identifiable differences in early years achievement between the genders.** 'Boys lag behind in early literacy skills when they first enter school.'[8] Girls tend to outperform boys in every subject in the early school years.[9]

— **The reasons lie in our children, our schools and our homes.** Boys' learning skills develop more slowly. This 'gap' is compounded by other factors, including:

1 *The lack of male role models*[10] (there are few male primary teachers; mothers tend to read with their children much more than fathers).

2 *The age at which formal education begins.* There is increasing evidence that starting schooling at four rather than six, as in many other European countries,

may disadvantage all children, but particularly boys.[11] There seems to be no advantage in terms of general academic achievement to starting so young, and it risks school seeming a struggle from the start. This can be a huge 'turn off'.

3 *Teaching and testing styles.* The ways our children are taught tend to favour girls. Influencing factors include teacher expectations, assessment techniques, curriculum bias and what and how teachers reward and discipline.[12]

— **The gap narrows as the children get older.** There is a difference in performance, but it is not huge[13] and it narrows to a few percentage points by A-level.[14] Boys go on to perform better in the job market.

— **Some boys seem particularly disadvantaged.** A minority of boys are very disaffected by their early learning experiences. They tend not to reach their potential at school and leave at the earliest opportunity.

These boys are falling by the wayside. What happens in this country is that we start education before most children are ready for it and they find it difficult. Some begin to feel a failure very young and this then creates a fear, a mental block about learning. This is where the problems start.

Bethan Marshall, lecturer in Education, King's College, London

What can parents do?

There is a huge amount parents can do to help both girls and boys.

— **Avoid pushing children too far too soon.** Respecting your child's capabilities is crucial, especially in the early years of schooling. No young child should be made to feel a failure. Aim to light the spark, not extinguish it by fanning too fiercely (see Play and learning, p.275).

— **Provide role models.** This is important for any child, but particularly boys. Fathers, uncles, grandads etc reading more to boys in the early school years will provide a tremendous boost to their literacy skills.

— **Let children experience success.** Praising what your child is good at is a powerful motivator. This may be counting, reading, drawing, telling jokes, caring for a pet, kicking a ball (see Play and learning, p.275).

— **Build children's sense of worth** (see Dealing with feelings, p.94). It is important that parents let children know they are loved for themselves and not because of the speed with which they pass a developmental milestone or achieve a certain grade. All children, but girls in particular (see Helping girls, p.263) may need to be reminded that life doesn't begin and end at academic achievement. This balance will boost their confidence to tackle new challenges and will help them cope better with schoolwork, especially when they are struggling.

— **Be observant, supportive and understanding.** Parental awareness of children's development and needs is crucial if they are to reach their potential happily and healthily.

Children are individuals but we need to be careful not to push them too young, boys especially. This can cause so many problems, including the feeling of failure which can set up a vicious circle that puts them off education and learning for life.

Clare Mills, co-author of Britain's Early Years Disaster[15]

One study[16] into the rising number of confident, motivated and optimistic young women in Britain highlighted various factors that had affected children's self-esteem, from material circumstances to health, education and even pop music and 'girlpower', but the key factor identified by girls themselves was supportive and understanding parents who 'listened' (see Communication, p.70).

Can-do girls

from *The Can-Do Girls – A Barometer of Change*[17]

'This study [into confidence, motivation and optimism in girls] suggests that what goes on within a family, even more than its structure, has a particular influence on a girl's confidence and belief that she can do things.

'Ways in which parents communicate with their daughters appear to be the key. Listening to their views, treating daughters fairly and encouraging initiative emerged as particularly important to girls. Many girls equate listening with fairness – if your voice is not heard your sense of self is lessened. Having a trusted adult providing emotional support is another vital element. When this family support is present and the school and community environment contributes, those girls living in a positive climate for women develop a 'Can-do' outlook that enables them to live life to the full.'

Girls generally have greater social skills and become conscientious earlier than boys, and develop cognitive and fine motor skills sooner. Yet it is important that these apparent 'advantages' do not blind parents to girls' needs. Just because girls commonly display less anti-social behaviour than boys[18] does not mean the problems they face affect them any less deeply or require less parental support.

Girls are self-motivated, conscientious and tend to set themselves high standards. This can spill into a stressful drive for perfection.

from *Understanding Our Daughters*[19]

Many young girls may be more good than is good for them. Their culture is changing, but the risk remains that many still value-judge themselves to too great an extent according to their school achievements and ability to please others. Blind obedience does not breed self-reliance, and success for the sake of others can have a short shelf-life. The effects of this are most obvious later in life but the roots often lie in a child's early years.

Because girls are more conformist and schools under more pressure to get results, girls are increasingly being pushed through exam hoops. This can disadvantage them when they leave school. In the real world and the job market they may need to be more risk-taking, original and creative. These are not the qualities that necessarily get you through exams.
Bethan Marshall, lecturer in Education, King's College, London

This desire to 'be good' may spill into communication between girls and their parents. While girls want parents to listen, the evidence is that girls tend to tell parents what they think they want to hear. Even very young girls often wish to protect parents or not disappoint them. At best this inhibits a parent's ability to parent; at worst, it is potentially dangerous.

You can help your daughter avoid the 'too good' trap by:

— Building up her self-esteem and showing that you love her unconditionally for who she is, not what she does (see Dealing with feelings, p.94)
— Let your child know she can tell you anything (see Communication, p.70). Listening to what girls have to say is very important, but so is an awareness that they may not be communicating all they need to tell

On the flip side of this, research indicates that increasing numbers of girls are now hit by their parents (see Smacking isn't the solution, p.196) and involved in physical bullying, while increasing numbers of young women are now being convicted of violent crime. As girls begin to shake off the passivity and vulnerability displayed by previous generations we should grab the chance to teach all children, girls and boys, the difference between aggression and assertion (see Growing independence, p.304). The sooner all children are shown more effective ways to state their case than physical intimidation, the better for us all.

Gender and aggression

Dr Michael Boulton, child psychologist, Keele University,
specialising in research into aggression, bullying and victimisation

'There is evidence that the type of bullying differs between the sexes. There is lots of evidence to challenge the view that males are more aggressive. What they do seem to differ on is the forms of aggression and it is exactly as you would predict – boys tend to be less subtle and more physical. They will kick and use action to victimise another peer. Girls will use more subtle psychological forms, such as social exclusion, manipulation of friendships, spreading nasty rumours, etc. There seems to be no difference in levels of aggression in verbal bullying by the two sexes.

'However, these are general trends. There is a wide degree of difference within any one sex. So any one boy may be less physically aggressive than any one girl. It is fair to emphasise that there is a wider range within each sex than between the sexes. It is dangerous to think only of male and female types of aggression because it blinds to the possibilities of girls being physically aggressive and boys being more subtle and psychological in their abuse.'

Discovering their own bodies

I was always laid back about what my children did with their own bodies and I never attempted to stop them, I'd just pretend not to notice. Then when my daughter was five she was reading on stage at her class assembly, in front of the school and parents, and halfway through thrust her hand down her knickers. There it remained for the next half an hour as she absentmindedly played with herself. Everyone pretended not to notice, but I realised that maybe I'd gone too far and a little awareness of appropriate public behaviour would be no bad thing!

Jenny P

Young children, from babyhood onward, fiddle with their genitals because it feels good. They are sensual beings who like touching themselves and it is important for their sense of self and gender that they be allowed to do so. A parent's aim should be to respect their child's right to enjoy and explore their own bodies and also to equip them with the knowledge of what is appropriate in public.

*The simple physical possibility of excitement is there from the beginning.
Children are discovering their own bodies and finding out what touch is nice
and what isn't and in what types of ways, and I think it is very easy for
adults to be intrusive of that process in a completely unnecessary way,
saying, for example 'Don't touch yourself'. It is much easier and more
sensible to say 'That feels nice but generally you do that on your own'.*

Mary MacLeod, Director of Policy and Research, ChildLine

Respect, respect, respect

José von Bühler, sexual and relationship psychotherapist

'Children are developing sexual beings and parents' attitudes towards this natural development should be one of total respect and absolutely no interference or abuse.

'It can be difficult for parents to see their child as a sexual being in his or her own right, so we can deny this exists. Children have a huge amount of sexual behaviour. It is not helpful to reject this or pretend it is not there. Parents should remain emotionally supportive whilst being very clear about boundaries.

'Any attitudes parents have towards sexuality are going to be noticed and used by the children. If parents feel in some way the body is indecent, for example, the children will pick this up pretty quickly.

'Adults in general need to respect that the child's process of sexual development is a strongly personal one. Hence, the role of the parent should simply be a nurturing one: to inform when asked, support when in pain, guide gently when appropriate. Parents have a responsibility to explain where the boundaries are. These may vary a bit between families and cultures but in our society, there are clearly defined social norms about sexuality the child must learn sooner or later. It is vital this is seen as a learning process, not a punishing, non-permission-giving process. Expressions that are invasive of a child's sexual self-discovery such as 'That's dirty', 'Don't do that', 'What's the matter with you?' – are to be avoided. Negative intrusions may not be seen as damaging now but they may possibly be later in life, when the child establishes their adult relationships.

'If your child asks questions about bodies or sexuality, be calm and gentle and do not overload them with too much information. Calmly teach, as you would in other areas of their life, what is acceptable. Avoid moralising and preaching or children getting the message that what they are feeling is wrong; such behaviour may have the opposite effect of what you intended. Remember, there are always specifically qualified professionals able and willing to help you if you are not certain.'

Children go through phases of more or less inhibition about their bodies but generally, over time, they like to take their clothes off less and less in front of people outside the family. This often occurs from around school-entry age. If your child shows no inhibitions and this concerns you, you could gently bring their awareness to what your boundaries are by showing where you enjoy and need privacy, for example, by shutting the bathroom door and explaining why. Also respect children's boundaries once they begin to emerge – bursting into your child's room announcing 'Don't be embarrassed' will not give a child necessary privacy. It is important for parents and children not to confuse privacy with secrecy – a child exploring his or her own body should not be a shameful or furtive act but rather private and personal.

By the age of six and seven, you can talk to your child about what is usual or expected behaviour. The emphasis should be on what is desirable where, not on there being anything wrong with what the child naturally enjoys doing, whether it is stripping off in the sunshine or playing with themselves.

> *You need to differentiate as a parent things that are done in private and things that are secret. They may look the same but they are not. You need to show the child that he can have a private life as we all do but it is not secret. This is key. It helps for a child to be free to talk about these things within the family and us as adults set a model which children can take in. So our communication as adults is important, both verbally and non-verbally.*
> Domenico di Ceglie, Consultant Child and Adolescent Psychiatrist, Tavistock Clinic, Director of The Gender Identity Development Unit, Portman Clinic, Honorary Senior Lecturer, Royal Free Hospital School of Medicine, London

> *With younger children it is hard to get the message across that we as adults need boundaries, for example when we go to the toilet, but children do learn it and it is essential to this process that we respect their need for privacy, too. This is a reciprocal thing.*
> Dr Dorothy Rowe, psychologist and writer

What and when you tell your child about his or her body and about sexual development and sex will vary between families and cultures, but it is important for the child's healthy development and safety that your child feels OK about asking you questions and telling you things you may rather not hear or deal with. Without true understanding children will lack the ability to know what is OK in their own behaviour and that of others.

Most professionals agree that it is best to take your lead from your child (if communication between you is good, your child will generally ask the question when he or she needs to know the answer) and to avoid giving unrequested and unnecessary details, as this can confuse. Be honest, and if you're not sure how to respond at that moment, say so: 'I'm not sure about that, let me think about it', or 'I need a bit of time to think how to explain it in ways you'll understand, but I will' are all positive responses leaving open the possibility of future communication. Ignoring your child or crushing curiosity do not.

In terms of sexual education, I think it would be helpful for the parent to take the lead from their child and be in some way responsive to verbal clues but also non-verbal clues from their child. So to respond to issues as they arise. You also need to make it clear to the child that they can express themselves and ask questions and these questions will be listened to. The child should never feel that they should not have asked the question.
Domenico di Ceglie, Consultant Child and Adolescent Psychiatrist, Tavistock Clinic

Gender exploration

The most important thing a parent can do is accept a child for how he or she is.
Dr Dorothy Rowe, psychologist and writer

Gender exploration is a very natural and normal part of children's development as they try to establish their identity and how they fit into the world. Very young children can be downright sexist as they try to impose order on their universe. Comments like 'Mummy, do that' or 'Daddy, fix it' may make you wince, but are only an indication of their increasing awareness of gender and roles and their desire for rules and predictability in an uncertain world.

Once a child begins imaginary play, they may begin to explore gender roles and behaviour for themselves. Whether a boy or girl plays out macho roles or more 'feminine' ones is irrelevant – some will be drawn to what is familiar (usually women), others to what seems exciting and

Tutus and swords

Parents have a huge influence on how their children feel about themselves and their bodies. Being relaxed and realistic about boys playing at girls and girls playing at boys helps children explore, develop happily and healthily and keep their self-esteem intact. For parents to do otherwise risks much more harm than good.

'By the age of 3, 4, 5 you can already have a sense of where a child feels he or she belongs as a boy or girl,' explains Domenico di Ceglie, Consultant Child and Adolescent Psychiatrist at the Tavistock Clinic. 'Parents should know that gender exploration is not the same as atypical gender development. The first is much more flexible, the latter is much more fixed, with the child insistent that he or she actually *belongs* to the other sex. This is uncommon.

'As parents you need to recognise your child's behaviour and accept it exists in a non-judgemental way. By denying the behaviour exists you are communicating to the child he shouldn't be feeling these things or behaving in this way. What normally happens then is that the child stops showing

From 2 years to 4 years Joe just loved dressing up in dresses.
Always Snow White, never the prince and he had a fabulous eye for
accessories. I remember him and Jack going to playgroup and both
coming out dressed in frocks. Jack looked like Eddie Izzard but
Joe looked stunning. I did in moments of madness wonder if
it meant he would be gay but generally it didn't bother me.
I chose not to encourage or discourage him.

Maggie T

different. The exploration is a form of learning, like any other, and it does not indicate your child's final sexual orientation. Some children will explore through role play, some through dressing up, some a little, some a lot, and the best thing to be is relaxed about it. What little evidence there is indicates that discouraging exploration or pressurising a child to hide such behaviour could itself have negative and long-term consequences.

these behaviours and pursues them in a secret way. The behaviour or interest does not disappear.

'The child then has to develop two aspects of himself or herself at a very young age – one for public consumption and one that is private. These problems remain and explode at adolescence. In the meantime, the child will continue to behave this way but secretively.

'There are two problems with this. Firstly, they will become worried about disapproval and being found out and could become quite isolated. Secondly, the secret can become quite exciting and this can sow the seeds of developmental problems. In a sense you start with an issue and then, depending on your behaviour as a parent, you can develop two or three problems as the child grows up.'

My eldest boy had a doll called Baby he would carry around everywhere. Over time we became more and more aware of other people's reactions. They would say it's unusual or ask me if it was good for him. As he got older he changed his favourite thing to a black and white bull and then a Fireman Sam hat. I feel pleased we were comfortable with his Baby. He is particularly kind with young children and I do sometimes wonder whether it is linked.

Claire S

I've always lived in jeans and trousers so it came as a shock to have a girl who loves pink and frills. But that's her. I could gag at some of the clothes she chooses, and at six she's got a greater range of lipsticks than me and wears them more often. But she thinks she's beautiful, and that's fine by me.

Debbi O

Children own their bodies

It is crucial for your children's healthy development and safety that they respect their bodies and learn that they are theirs and theirs alone (see Skills for safety, p.330). This will not happen easily unless respect is shown towards the child by the parent and adults in general.

This respect should go right across the board. It makes me tremble when
I hear comments like 'Let's dress you up to look pretty for Daddy' or 'Big boys
don't cry'. These may reflect how unthinking adults can be when commenting
on matters so fundamental to the balanced development of children.

José von Bühler, sexual and relationship psychotherapist

Try very hard to recognise and respect the boundaries children set themselves. Take notice when your child shows you the first signs of feeling embarrassed – comments like 'Don't be daft, you've got nothing to hide', however well-intentioned, can give a child the message that it is not for them to decide what feels OK for their own bodies. Let them know that they can tell you if you've failed to notice that they want things done differently. Parents can also role model respect for their own bodies and for others. Children learn by example and how you care for and consider yourself and where you set your own boundaries are powerful lessons.

CHAPTER THIRTEEN

PLAY AND LEARNING

P lay and learning are inextricably linked throughout childhood, and especially so in the earliest years.

PLAY

T his is how our children find out about themselves and their world. Through exploration and imagination, they begin to learn about their physical self and their emotions, develop their language, communication and social skills, their understanding of their physical environment and their relationships with others. All while having a good time.

Our society has become so obsessed with educational toys and accelerated learning that the whole point of play is sometimes lost in the rush for the flash cards. So it is worth stating the obvious. Play is meant to be fun. Childhood should be a time for having as much of it as possible. Through it comes increased self-esteem and resilience, an appreciation of life and even enhanced relationships. It is often our ability to find fun in life and humour in difficult situations that tips the balance between us having a good day or a bad.

Play is also an incredibly powerful tool for learning – a child having fun is absorbed and engaged and soaking up experiences from his very first infant games (see Communicating with your baby, p.9). But it is much, much more besides. Strip the fun out of play and its potency is lost, so try to back-pedal on well-intentioned worthiness and see fun for fun's sake as an end in itself.

Children enjoy humour from an early age. Very little ones will smile
when you pull a funny face. Slightly older ones will love pee-po games.
Many six-year-olds will have a fine set of puns and corny jokes. But you
don't have to look for signs of delight. A child looking very serious as they
stick their fist in and out of a plastic cup may be having a great time.
A seven-year-old with a construction toy is not going to whoop with
joy but is still having great fun. It's all important. There are many,
many studies which show that the richness of a child's early play
behaviour and early interactions does correlate with their social
and emotional adjustment later in life.

Professor Hugh Foot, specialist in child psychology and social development,
Department of Psychology, Strathclyde University

Encouraging play

We have to remember the world is very exciting for a child and we have
an important role in sharing that excitement with them. In the 1970s I was a
researcher for Sesame Street *and it struck me so strongly that a little girl enjoyed*
seeing Big Bird on the screen, but she took enormous pleasure from running and
telling her mum and sharing it with her. This ability to share with our child,
being available and responsive in a spontaneous way, is one of the most
important things we can do for our children's development.

Lisa Blakemore-Brown, chartered educational psychologist

One of my strongest memories of playing as a child is splatting about in
the mud in our back garden. I was a very happy squelcher.

Catherine F

Your responses to your child's play may be key to the amount of
pleasure he finds in it, from his first interaction games on. Just as
parents can give children the message that play is an irritant of little
value other than to entertain them elsewhere – 'Just go outside and
play' – so we can also show children that it is a pleasure by responding
to their enthusiasms.

Guiding principles

Young children may need to be shown the potential of a play material or how a toy works before they have much of an idea what to do with it. From dough to construction bricks, you can show your child the possibilities, spark his enthusiasm and imagination, then watch him take it from there.

'Take a rattle,' explains Professor Hugh Foot, specialist in child psychology and social development. 'While you and I know that a rattle is for shaking, a child who's never seen one doesn't. By shaking it and smiling the parent is telling the child what this object is for.

'The same applies until the child is old enough to read instructions or work out a game for themselves – you can't simply open the box and expect them to enjoy the contents, you first have to show them how.'

If you are losing the battle against the rising tide of primary coloured plastic in your home, it may help to know that most play specialists suggest parents provide more play materials rather than more toys. Toys with limited function have limited appeal and life span. Sand, water, paints, paper, dough, cake mixes and old clothes for dressing up are all potentially messy but provide far greater opportunities for imagination and discovery – and cost less.

Encouraging play also means knowing when to butt out as well as when to join in. Help your child get a game started but try not to impose your own idea of the best, quickest or only way of doing it. He will be much more proud of a misshapen biscuit or a rickety tower he made himself than a perfect one you made for him, and the experience will be a much greater spur for his future self-reliance and curiosity. Let him take the lead and show you when he wants your assistance, knowledge or companionship and also allow him to mess things up, make 'mistakes', imagine and do things his way.

If a child is absorbed in what they are doing I do not think it is right to interfere but wait until they do look up and want to share. The timing is important. A lot of parents try to explain what is going on when a child may not want or understand it. Verbal explanations can be more useful later if the child chooses to talk about it. There are different phases for children and it is not always helpful to strip the magic out of things with logical explanations.

Angela Gruber, psychotherapist

What your child may enjoy

	Big movement (gross motor)	Small movements (fine motor)
0-1 Year	Exploring safe environments. Being held to stand, push/pull toys.	Safe things to hold: rattle, bricks, our hands, etc (let the child explore objects with his/her hands).
1-2 Years	Slow walks, running on grass, climbing stairs with you, roly poly play – learning control of body, etc.	Increasing their control: building small tower blocks, basic tasks, eg. stirring. Opportunities to use play materials: paint, play dough, crayons.
2-4 Years	Pedalling and steering tricycle/riding bike with stabilisers. Simple ball games. Chasing games, rough-and-tumble, pillow/pretend fights. Climbing frames. Jumping, balancing games.	Using scissors, painting, crayons, play dough, basic cooking etc. Jigsaws, different size boxes to tower, bead-threading, turning pages of books.
5-7 Years	Vigorous exercise: eg. rhythmical dance, skipping, climbing, riding bike without stabilisers, skating, football, etc.	Sewing, dressing themselves. Yo-yos, tracing – more difficult drawing, cooking including measuring ingredients etc, computer games, junk modelling.

Relationships with people, environment, themselves.

Developing the senses (mothers holding them, talking, laughing, etc). Mobiles (close to infant's gaze), different light, colours, sounds. Interacting with faces; familiar routines; peek-a-boo (from a few months enjoys gentle teasing and begins to understand things appearing and disappearing).

Nursery rhymes and actions. Playing alongside friends. Rolling balls back and forth (interactive play). Naming/pointing to body parts, putting on hat and shoes. Exploring nature. Imitative play; watering plants, dusting etc. Hide and seek, piggy-back rides, etc.

Kicking balloons (big effects of small actions). Blowing bubbles, etc (how things appear/disappear). Children to play with (play co-operatively, 3/4 years), throwing/ catching ball (give and take). Visiting farms, etc (looking at the world around them). 'Helping'. Dressing-up games (make believe/role play). Doing what they can for themselves.

Choosing own friends and play: uninterrupted play to build dens, creating dance routines etc. Team sports, games with rules, clubs they enjoy (be led by your child). Creating own stories, shows, characters, etc. Funny poems, stories, simple jokes. Music.

Thinking and understanding

Looking at picture books/simple stories. Fascinated by toys or household objects.

'Reading' picture books together. Having time to absorb (going at their pace). Large construction bricks, pegs in holes, safe household items; kitchen cupboard to empty/fill, etc (working out how things fit together and come apart).

Ordering objects into size/colour order. Building a tower then knocking it down (small steps achieve big task). Discovering distance, measurement, time (fascinated by watches, height charts, tape measures, etc.) Stories about themselves, photographs etc (their place in the world). Large construction bricks/models. Filling a dolls' house, parking toy vehicles, etc (using spatial sense).

Drawing then making a model (talk with them about how they do it. What do they like about it? What might they do differently next time? ie. planning and problem-solving). Simple experiments eg. gravity with a feather and heavy ball, guessing weights, measuring siblings, etc (discovery). More complex models. Expressing opinion in games, making up games. Looking after a pet. Word games: scrabble, I-spy, etc.

I've a friend who is obsessively tidy and insists everything is put back in the box it came in before there is a suggestion of another toy even touching the floor. We take the mickey mercilessly because it's so uptight. Then I look at my place, ankle deep in bits that don't match, stray limbs from dolls and gunky old paint pots. There must be a happy medium but it's not in our house.

Bernadette M

Encouraging free and quiet times Getting the balance right between parental involvement and children's freedom also means allowing your child free time for quiet or unstructured play or for simply being bone idle.

Recent studies have confirmed the obvious – that children's outdoor play has changed radically in less than a generation, fuelled by fears of abduction and other harm (see Protection v. exposure, p.327), and is now heavily dependent on the availability of safe public spaces where children can play in view of their parents.[1] As our children's lives become increasingly timetabled, regulated and restricted, it becomes even more important to allow them some unstructured play outdoors. Inside the home, now perhaps more than ever, they need times away from adult gaze once they are old enough, and more opportunities to be in our presence but away from our interference to do as little or as much as they please.

The idea that every minute has to be gainfully occupied is the antithesis of childhood.

Adrienne Katz, author of *Teaching Your Child to Read*

We live in a very busy world and we need to create serenity rather than just 'doing'. I believe in silence as well as talking. Children need calm.

Christine Fahey, Montessori teacher

These free times allow children to develop self-awareness and the capacity for reflection, both crucial to their emotional development and learning. Even being bored on occasions and having to find something to do will build their resourcefulness and creativity. A baby, allowed to stare absent-mindedly into space for as long as he's happy or take gentle pleasure in the simple, sensorial things around him rather than constantly having rattles rattled and nerves jangled, has a good chance of growing into a child who can run round like a mad thing but also stare up at the clouds, fiddle with his belly button, relax and reflect. Which seems a healthy combination.

It is in free play that the children's culture takes over. It is hard to see they are playing sometimes. For example even quiet play in a line going in to school dinner can be intensely imaginative. Children really do make the most of the spare time, spare objects, spare corners and space left over from adult activities. I do not think they have lost their own play culture but I do think there is less opportunity for them to play unsupervised.

Dr Pat Petrie, senior research lecturer, Thomas Coram Unit, Institute of Education, University of London

---

Freedom in free time

Our unusually early start to formal education in the UK makes our children's opportunities for free play even more important.

'It is children's right to childhood,' says educational psychologist Corinne Abisgold. 'The progress children make in play is very hard to quantify and therefore we are losing sight of some of the benefits, in a culture in which teachers have to say exactly what they are doing with the children and why. It is easy to say they know 20 letters and x numbers and this approach can become like a disease. Even our leisure is becoming pressurised – how well can we do? How much can we do? It is really easy to destroy the joy in children's abilities to explore things for themselves. When I go to playgroups I have to bite my lip when parents talk about the need for tasks to be set for the children. I think we are becoming quite frightened of letting children play naturally.'

Encouraging play with other children

Through playing with other children a child learns how to negotiate and bargain, to make compromises, to control aggressiveness and assertiveness in others, to constrain and confine their own aggressiveness, when and how to be assertive, to caretake other children, to begin to handle rejection, bullying, loneliness, taking a lead, joining in games, seeking company and striking out on their own, when to lead and when to follow, to enjoy humour, and so many other social skills they couldn't possibly learn by playing with an adult who, by their very presence, is in the controlling, restraining or caretaking role.

Professor Hugh Foot, specialist in child psychology and social development

The sooner children begin to mix and play with others, the easier and more natural this will seem. Only-children will reap obvious rewards, but even children of large families can benefit hugely by being liberated from their role as 'the little one' or 'the responsible one' (see Ripping up labels, p.108).

Play will not always be positive between children and that, to some degree, is the point. It makes no sense to encourage a child to play with another who is continually aggressive and domineering, but disagreements and disputes will arise even among children who get on well. Learning to negotiate their way through small but sticky situations enables children to learn some of the basics of children's culture before they start nursery or school and to practise its finer points once they begin (see Growing independence, p.304).

We need to monitor how our children are doing and if we believe it is going too far, we do need to step in. But we shouldn't make their social environment so sterile and safe that they never fall out with one another because then, when they do come across the inevitable conflict, they would not be able to sort it out.
Dr Michael Boulton, child psychologist

Encouraging rough and tumble

You want your children to be joyful and exuberant creatures. If the child is going to make secure physical as well as emotional attachments then the more general physical play that isn't too boisterous, the better. Children get this from each other but they also need it from their parents. I often think that young adults who don't form sound interpersonal relationships themselves may come from homes in which they were not often touched by their parents. They were touched for dressing perhaps when younger, but not touched in a jovial and playful manner when they were small.
Professor Hugh Foot, specialist in child psychology and social development

Children's rough-and-tumble play may not do a lot for your mental and emotional well-being but, if it's any comfort, it is very healthy for theirs. Through it, children learn to be physically confident and know what they can cope with and what they can't. They test the limits of their bodies and their tempers, experience competing, winning and losing, and learn how to control their aggression and when to stop.

Whether it is rough and tumble with parents or friends, clear ground rules will help. In other words, it is fine, fun and can continue as long as no one is harmed or inflicting harm, all participants are enjoying it and there is no risk of damage.

Rough and ready?

Steve Biddulph, psychologist and author

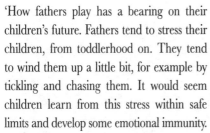

'How fathers play has a bearing on their children's future. Fathers tend to stress their children, from toddlerhood on. They tend to wind them up a little bit, for example by tickling and chasing them. It would seem children learn from this stress within safe limits and develop some emotional immunity.

'Girls, particularly, can become more physical and confident in their play. Later this positive role model seems to delay sexual relations and help the choice of healthy partners for girls. It may remove the high need for male approval.

Girls without this seem to get more confused when choosing a partner and if they muddle needing a father with a partner they may choose an authoritarian male who will tell them what to do.

'For boys, rough-and-tumble play can be the way they learn to control their temper. Playing with them like this can stop and teach them to calm down if they get out of control, teach them to stay safe, and not to hit or hurt. It's an important lesson.'

Encouraging imagination games Through fantasy play children can transform their world and their part in it (see The developing imagination, p.284). By four, they may enjoy acting out roles, dressing up and exploring what it would be like to be someone else. By six and seven, they may be constructing long and complex dramas, interweaving their roles with those of their toys. At any age, these games will help them develop communication skills, increase their understanding of others and explore and express their emotions. It may help to remember this next time your sofa is turned into a pirate ship.

A parent's role is to spark their child's imagination through stories, books, games, thoughts (see Stories and games for thinking, p.301), by providing props, joining in when requested and even initiating games occasionally. The key task, though, is simply to let children play.

The developing imagination
Professor Hugh Foot, specialist in child psychology and social development

'From about 12 months, a child moves on from purely object-driven play to using pretend objects, eg. 'drinking' from an imaginary cup. A little girl of, say, 15 months may hold an imaginary cup up to a doll's lips, ie. moves on from doing imaginary things to herself. These tasks become welded together in a sequence, for example, undressing, bathing, putting a doll to bed.

'The child may ask the parent to do something for her while she is washing the baby – turn on the tap, hold the towel and so on. It is healthy when parents participate in this way, when the child is in the driving seat. Children can be quite upset if you do things out of order, if you break the rules of the game. It is very ritualistic.

'Children close on two can have imaginary play friends. Something like a fifth to a quarter of children do, for a short time at least. It is more likely to happen to solitary children but of itself is not really anything to worry about. Playmates of this kind are usually "there" when the child is playing on their own but forgotten when the child is called by their mother.'

Screen time

All [adults should] make it their business to be familiar with the material to which children have access; to enforce all regulations designed to protect children from 'unsuitable' material; to discuss violent or otherwise disturbing stories and images with children, and to offer non-violent equivalents wherever they can. There are legitimate arguments against censorship, but there are none for leaving children to cope, unsupported, with whatever material comes their way.
The Commission on Children and Violence[2]

Parents know the power of example and exposure to TV – that's why my boys went World Cup crazy, that's why I watch Sesame Street with my little one. How can we know that, and at other times delude ourselves that they don't learn from what they see?
Simon P

The battle is still raging between those who believe viewing violent images may desensitise us all and increase violent behaviour in children, and those who challenge them to come up with the proof. This is still the most contentious issue surrounding the use of TV, videos and computers by children, yet it may be diverting attention from two simple points:

1 A heavy diet of violence does a child no good. How much harm it does, in what way and to whom, is still in dispute, but while the academics argue, why take the risk?

2 Heavy screen use cuts into the time children have for activities essential to their healthy development – such as talking and playing and running around. While the focus has been on what influence screen images have on what children do, a much bigger problem for most children may be what screen time stops them doing.

Too much screen time is anti-social. It will limit your child's opportunities for socialisation, free time and exercise and present him with a very restricted view of the fun to be had in the world. 'Lack of contact with other people', fuelled by the increase in TV watching, has been pinpointed as the main cause of an apparent increase in shyness among people in general and adolescents in particular since the early 1980s.[3] Delays in the development of selective attention and an increase in language problems in very young children has also been linked to overuse of television and videos (see Communication, p.70).

Children's small-screen entertainment can be inspiring, educational, great fun and a very positive part of their lives. But let's be realistic. Most parents use it for their own purposes, to keep children quiet while they get on with other things. A timely burst of *Robin Hood* may turn a fractious child into a silent one long enough to get his tea ready. But use the screen as a babysitter too often or for too long and children are likely to become restless, fizz pop round the house like a demented puppy or explode in frustration or temper. Alternatively, they may turn into human blobs, too lethargic to raise themselves from the sofa while they whinge about being bored. Neither will make life easier.

It does seem that the happiest children watch the least TV. Favourite, repeated videos, chosen for their beauty and excitement and appropriate to the kids' ages, are better than the randomness of TV. And I suggest never more than an hour a day unless it's a special situation.

Steve Biddulph, psychologist and author

The same dilemmas and contradictions surround children's use of computers. Interactive teaching software has been shown to boost development of literacy and numeracy skills – as long as computers are properly used, supported and limited. One recent study into the effective use of information and communications technology in schools recommended that on-screen time be limited to 15 to 20 minutes, three times a week.[4]

We should also be aware that children have access to more negative and potentially damaging images than we would care to admit. It is, of course, easier to blame television and videos for violence among children than to look closer to home. Research worldwide has confirmed that the greatest influence on a child's behaviour is his family and his own direct experiences – what he comes to recognise as norms of behaviour.[5] But it would be naive to suggest that part of that caring and supportive home environment does not include parental monitoring of what children view.

Unrestricted view?

One survey[6] of primary pupils aged 9 to 11 found that two-thirds had watched violent 18-rated videos such as *Pulp Fiction*, *The Terminator* and *The Silence of the Lambs*, suggesting that many have few restrictions imposed on their viewing and that some films were likely to have been seen by much younger children. Four in ten said they had watched the films with their parents' permission.

The average US child is estimated to have seen 32,000 murders, 40,000 attempted murders and 250,000 acts of violence on television before the age of 18 (UK figures are not available).[7]

Not to monitor risks us relying too strongly on children's ability to separate fiction from fact at an age when they are still trying to make sense of their world. It may also allow academic arguments about causality (direct links between screen images and behaviour) blind us to what common sense tells us – that a diet of violent images and repeated exposure to scenes of negative and anti-social behaviour may, in real but subtle ways, make aggression seem 'cool' and acceptable, increase aggressive behaviour and/or make children wary or frightened of the outside world in unhelpful ways.

In the nursery, if a child wants another toy, then the most efficient way of getting it is to take it by force. Parents and teachers know how long it takes to demonstrate and convince about other ways of acting. The key question in relation to media is how they position themselves in this constant process of the production, negotiation, and transfer of social values.

Greg Philo, Glasgow Media Group[8]

In all this, three key messages emerge. TV, videos and computers are great tools and great fun if handled with care. Parents can encourage this by:

1   Limiting the time children spend before TV and computer screens. We now have enough electronic gadgetry to keep children quiet for hours, but a virtual childhood is a waste.

2   Monitoring the content of what children are watching and playing. The advent of videos, the Internet and other technological advances mean parents can no longer rely on the law and film classifications to restrict children's access.

3   Watching with children – and talking to them about what they see and do. This may increase the value of what they see and help them separate fiction from fact. It also helps parents judge what effects programmes or games may be having on how their children feel and think.

It is clear that the context in which a child views violent images, and the presence or absence of a critical commentary not approving of violence, is likely to influence whether or how the child is affected.

The Commission on Children and Violence[9]

LEARNING

Parents have a crucial role to play in inspiring their children to learn and in supporting them when they find it a struggle. All evidence points to the fact that encouragement, not force, is the most effective way to unlock children's potential in their early years.

Encouraging enjoyment

Children learn better if they are enjoying themselves. Right back in ancient history children were taught to read with enjoyment – for example Jewish children were allowed to lick the honey off the letters they were learning. If you are not enjoying yourself you are usually obsessed with failing. With enjoyment you want to go on because you are having a good time.

Nicholas Tucker, educational psychologist now lecturing in Cultural and Community Studies, University of Sussex

This most obvious point is often the first to be forgotten. Parents can make learning enjoyable. The pleasure principle can begin from your child's earliest encounters with play materials and books – if he associates books with cuddles and fun, you are off to a great start.

Play games where you can and when you are both in the mood – nursery rhymes in the car, I Spy in the doctor's waiting room. Try reading silly poems and books you know will whet his imagination and interest (see Between the lines, opposite). Encourage confidence and pleasure in numbers by letting him dial a grandparent, count the cars on the way to the shops together or the stairs on the way to bed. Allow him the freedom to find pleasure in the means as well as the ends – weighing and measuring, playing shops with real money, making rockets out of rubbish, drawing, painting, exploring, imagining. Most children can enjoy the process when they couldn't give a hoot about the educational goal.

Between the lines

Adrienne Katz, author of *You Can Teach Your Child to Read*

'Parents need to spend time on anything that sparks their child's interest. Children have to be interested in the story to enjoy reading it. Some are forced through boring reading schemes then expected to make a huge effort to learn. It does not make sense. If you take time to find out what books they really like and why they don't like others, it will help enormously. One little girl hated reading books about animals because they so often got lost. She was associating the pain she felt on reading the story with reading and it was putting her off. We all need to be more sensitive to these things.'

Doing it for themselves

My five-year-old got a real buzz out of doing his own shoelaces, being allowed to be more responsible for himself and knowing he'd get a lot of praise, too. There are parents who throw themselves like saints into looking after their children in every way. It comes as a great surprise to them to see how children thrive when given the chance to do it themselves, what a boost it is to their self-esteem.

Kate K

Allowing children to decision-make and do whatever they can safely do for themselves is an important first step towards enquiry and discovery (see Encouraging enquiry, p.298). A child who is allowed to problem-solve and tackle situations in life is going to be better equipped to do the same in the classroom.

You can begin this process from babyhood on by letting your baby reach for things on occasions instead of handing things to him, by letting him attempt to feed himself, even though much of it ends up in his ear. As your toddler begins to insist 'Me do it, me do it', let him try whenever possible. As he grows, aim to involve him in early decision-making – 'If we stay in the park now we won't have time for a play at home before bathtime. Which do you want to do?' As a rule of thumb, try not to do the things for your child that your child can do without you.

Next time your child wants to go one rung higher on the climbing frame, ask yourself whether you want to hold on to him because it is best for him or best for you. If he can hold on well and you are there to catch him if he slips, letting him explore and test his own limits will increase his understanding of potential dangers and of his own capabilities.

When you teach him a new skill, try to ensure you follow this up by letting him do it for himself so he fully understands and is confident in his new ability. This way you can begin to equip him with the confidence he will need to tackle new challenges, test his capabilities and 'think on his feet' even when you are not there to guide and support.

One of the most effective ways in which children learn is when a more able person helps them to see what they can achieve with a little help. Psychologists call this 'scaffolding', suggesting that a structure is put up to help build new skills, and then the scaffolding is gradually removed, allowing the child to consolidate their new-found skills for themselves.
John Oates, developmental psychologist

Building confidence

Your child's view of himself is based almost entirely on what you tell him. So try to praise him, not just for achieving things but for trying too.
Eileen Hayes, Parenting Advisor to the NSPCC

Parents have natural fears about how children are going to cope in the world but they need to keep some limits on their anxiety. The moment you get anxious, children will pick that up and this will just lead them to make more mistakes.
Angela Gruber, psychotherapist

If your child is confident about learning – rather than simply confident in what he has learnt – if he is happy to face challenges and to try even when he's not assured of success, he has a skill that could benefit him for life.

Letting your child shine The pleasures of success and doing something well are crucial to a child's sense of self-worth and perhaps the greatest motivator in all areas of learning.

It is really important to keep looking for things your child can excel in and enjoy, whatever that may be, and to focus on that. It may be that he loves to laugh, or that he loves to tell stories, or that he's great at drawing, whatever. Competition is in the air at school and I don't think one has to foster it at home. This is the place to focus on the strengths of the child. Not to can often make them feel worse.
Vivienne Gross, Clinical Director, The Institute of Family Therapy

Switching focus We are so concerned that our children 'get it right' that we may spend too much time showing them what they've done wrong. The huge danger of allowing any child to feel a failure so young is that it becomes part of their self-image and is hard to reverse (see Correct without crushing, p.292 and Descriptive praise, p.154).

I was shocked by my response. I really wasn't the patient parent I thought I was. I got so wound up, it was like I couldn't believe she couldn't do it. I went over it and over it and she still made the same mistake.
Helen P

Making it manageable Throughout children's education, but particularly in the early years, it helps to match tasks to their capabilities and to keep them stimulated enough to want to take the next step forward. This involves being aware of a child's emotional as well as educational needs. He may be developing quickly in one area and taking longer in another, he may be having a good day or bad.

Bite-sized tasks are generally much easier for a young child to face than an apparently insurmountable mountain of learning. They also provide more opportunities to succeed. Writing four words three times each rather than one word 12 times, for example, can add a much-needed sense of variety and progress.

Children develop different skills at different rates and do not achieve like rungs on a ladder. Look at your child and respect those skills he is developing. He may be desperately interested in nature or science and you are ramming reading down his throat. He may choose to do things in a different order.
Adrienne Katz, author of *You Can Teach Your Child to Read*

Correct without crushing

We can crush children's wonder and curiosity if we are not careful.
The other day I heard a little boy say to his Dad, 'WOW! That is the biggest
car in the whole world!' and he said 'Don't be so stupid, of course it isn't.'
There is often no need to correct, just agree with the sentiment. The father could
have said, 'Gosh, that is a big car.' There is no need to be over-conscientious
about every word when your child is learning to read, for example. If you
feel relaxed and want to enjoy the story I think children pick this up and
can take risks in what is for most children a bit of a risky business.

Angela Gruber, psychotherapist

Children may need to have their mistakes pointed out to them so they know where they are going wrong. But not always.

If a child is corrected for every misread word or badly formed number or letter, he will quite understandably stop wanting to show you what he can do. Focus on what is most important at that time.

If it is his first attempt at writing words with finger spaces in between, praise him when he gets that right. If he is working on capital letters and full stops at school, concentrate on those rather than every spelling.

When he is reading, quietly and simply say a word he is struggling with but try not to interrupt his 'flow'. If he is attempting to write a sentence or work out a sum, make a mental note of any numbers or words he needs to practise later but try not to interrupt the task in hand.

Also beware overuse of 'But', as in 'That's lovely, but next time see if you could do it more neatly', or 'Those are very good, but those ones are wrong'. Praise doesn't count if it is only used to sugar-coat criticism.

It is very easy to always end on a high note, with praise for something your
child can do. So if he fails on one word, make sure you end on a word they
do know and say 'Oh, good'. You can always end positively.

Nicholas Tucker, lecturer in cultural and community studies

I watched my child's teacher go through a spelling test with her and it
was fascinating. She pointed out every word my daughter had got right or
very nearly right and said 'Well done'. She didn't have to point out the mistakes,
because they were obvious – they were the ones that didn't get praised.
It was the same information, just delivered in a positive way.

Jane P

Teaching children about learning Explaining how people learn – and need to make mistakes to learn – can boost a child's confidence to try. Reminding them of something they can now do – perhaps reciting the alphabet or drawing a shape – will help them see that they have already achieved what they once found difficult.

It may also help to state the obvious – how different people learn different things at different speeds, that everybody is good at something and no one is good at everything. To a child, this can be revelatory.

It is our responsibility to make clear to the child that getting something wrong is part of learning and you cannot learn unless you make mistakes. Parents and teachers should also be big enough to say, 'Oh, you didn't understand that. I didn't explain it well enough, let me try and explain it again' – ie. it is my duty as a teacher to try and explain it better rather than 'You've got it wrong'. We have to take responsibility rather than blaming the child.
Corinne Abisgold, educational psychologist

Being honest Slightly older children, especially those who know from experience that school isn't always a fun factory, may appreciate a parent's acknowledgement that it can sometimes be a slog. Let them know that hard work and application do make a difference – that sometimes you do have to work at something that seems boring just to be able to move on to the next, more interesting stage. Praise them when they stick with a problem and explain that there would be no need for teachers and schools if learning was always easy.

It is often helpful for parents to explain the process of learning and how the mind works. Explaining how memory works, for example, that sometimes it is easy, sometimes we forget, that we have short- and long-term memory and how normal it is to find some things harder than others can be very reassuring.
Camila Batmanghelidjha, psychotherapist, Director of Kid's Company

Learning to concentrate Sitting still does not come naturally to all children. When children are having difficulty, these skills can be best learned doing something they enjoy (painting, cooking, construction kits, etc) perhaps with a parent sitting alongside until they are happy being left to their own devices.

Board games may help older children concentrate for increasingly longer stretches. If your child can't cope with a full-length game, do it in stages, keeping a note of where you left off the previous day.

Changing tack

All of us learn in very different kinds of ways. People have not thought about this enough in schools or in homes: some children like to learn alone, others learn better through interaction with others, some learn through words, others through visual or musical cues, some learn by doing. I think many parents are very aware of how their child learns just by trying different ways.

Professor Katherine Riley, Director of the Centre of Educational Management, Roehampton Institute, London

If your child doesn't understand an explanation, repeating it may mean he gets bored and you become frustrated. Simply shifting from abstract to concrete examples can work wonders. A child who shows no interest in adding six plus five may be more enthusiastic working out the footballers needed to make an 11-man squad.

If you are still getting nowhere, and you feel yourself getting impatient, it may be best to let the matter drop. A few days without reading or whatever task you have in hand will do much less damage than you getting cross or exasperated.

If the child can't do something, never get cross. Parents are not always very good actors, and if you are going to show disappointment you are doing more harm than good. Children hate disappointing their parents and easily lose confidence.

Nicholas Tucker, lecturer in cultural and community studies

Avoid comparisons Telling children they are performing better or worse than their peers may fuel anxiety and a counterproductive fear of failure, as there will always be others more able in certain areas. Your child will be bombarded with comparisons with other children once he starts school, from teachers and from other pupils, and there seems little to be gained by you joining in.

You will, however, need to know how your child is progressing and whether he is attaining the levels expected for his age so you can pinpoint any areas where he needs extra support.

Yesterday I was talking to children who had been taken out of mainstream school for a few weeks to learn some of the basic skills they were struggling with. It saddened me how they all talked of being bullied. Children who are struggling may also have to cope with what goes wrong around that, feeling left out, being called names and so on. It is very important for parents to know how their child is doing.

Professor Katherine Riley, Director of the Centre of Educational Management, Roehampton Institute

Ease test pressures Almost every child will now sit tests at a very young age. How well such tests are handled will vary hugely from school to school, but your child's ability to cope will also be influenced by your attitude.

I have seen seven-year-olds having anxiety attacks before their SATS – actually shaking and hyperventilating – and this is at a school where we try to be so low key about tests at this young age they'd hardly know they are happening. In each case, they had picked up their parents' anxieties. Parental aspiration is understandable, and children do need parental support. But all parents, especially those of children who require extra help, need to be skilled in not transferring their anxieties on to their children.

Carol Munro, primary headteacher

Hothousing

Some people who work in selective schools talk about a syndrome that occurs around the age of 13 – the children peak. They have had their finest hour because they have had tutoring and parental squeezing for years and have been working flat out at their limit for so long they simply cannot keep it up. Their performance has had to be impressive to get into certain schools, but it is not a true reflection of their learning – more of the incredible input they have had. They come out of the hothouse and are expected to grow at the same rate and they simply cannot do it.

Robin Freeland, educational psychologist

Encouraging your child to learn happily, presenting him with opportunities and helping him think for himself does not mean hothousing.

Homework

How much homework your child does in his early school years will depend on many factors – school policy, government recommendation, your attitude, your child's mood. You can help by ensuring the following:

— He has the space, the equipment (pencil, rubber, etc) and the time to do what he needs. If he has regular homework, try to build it into the afternoon/evening routine.

— You are available to help – sit with him if he likes – but do not hang over your child's shoulder or interfere unless requested. If you help, tell his teacher, who needs to know his true ability levels.

— He is physically tired enough to want to sit down but not too tired to work. Some exercise after school often helps.

— Explain how he could best organise and present his work if he seems unsure. Uncertainty of what is expected creates unnecessary pressures, and children have enough of those already.

— Many parents report success playing schools when children become resistant, giving the child an opportunity to be 'teacher' with the parent as 'pupil'. This eases the tension, enables the parent to discover what the child knows, and allows the child to learn while having fun.

Hothousing, where a child is bombarded with task after task in an attempt to push him to some adult-ordained peak of performance is one of the most unlikely ways to get your child to learn willingly and effectively in the long-term. It can backfire seriously and is actively discouraged by leading educationalists and child professionals.

Recent history is peppered with tragic examples of parents who have pushed their children too far, too soon, sometimes out of fear for their future, sometimes out of a need to compensate for their own unfulfilled ambitions, sometimes out of raw competitiveness. This is nothing new: in the 1890s, a father kept his talented children off school to hothouse them at home. After two of his sons committed suicide he sent his youngest and most unpromising son to the local technical school. That son was Ludwig Wittgenstein, considered by many to be the greatest philosopher of the 20th century. Yet our society seems increasingly obsessed with speeding development and achievement – we have French for tots, baby gymnastics, 'pre-reading' toddler tapes to play while they sleep and a raft of national assessments and tests to feed parents' neuroses. It may help to consider that:

Pushing children too fast denies children the experience of success It allows them no time to feel great about what they have achieved – the greatest motivator of all. Every time they reach the top of one mountain they are faced with another to climb rather than being allowed to draw breath and admire the view.

Pushing too hard makes failure inevitable There is no surer way to undermine a child's confidence than to push him beyond his natural capabilities.

It does not equip a child to continue learning without parental pressure Exceptional performance at an early age does not mean exceptional performance later in life. A child's own motivation is the key to his future success, not his parents' demands.

A child may reject later what you force now Encourage when you can and coax when you need to, but try to avoid forcing any 'educational' issue. Resentment only fuels resistance and the likelihood of rejection.

I knew a boy who was an exceptionally gifted pianist at a very young age. He was forced to practice long and hard by his parents. Then, when he was 18, he announced he was leaving home and leaving the piano behind, too. I don't think he's touched one since. What is the point of destroying a child's pleasure? Surely it would have been better for him to have not been so pushed, perhaps not achieved such excellence so young, and still be playing music today?
Jane Cutler, Head of Music, Da Capo School of Music

Stress is bad for your health The effects of stress on health are well documented. A child's anxieties may find expression in very real physical symptoms, from stomach cramps to headaches, skin disorders to other chronic and debilitating conditions.

I see so many stressed children. London is full of them. Often their natural ability to learn is blocked because there is a difference between hammering information in and allowing the child to acquire learning skills. Good education is not really the information they have but rather the encouragement of their desire to learn, and that has to be emotionally genuine.

Camila Batmanghelidjha, psychotherapist, Director of Kid's Company

Hothousing takes time This time could be spent doing things that are much more important to a child's healthy development.

Hothoused children rarely have sufficient free time to just potter around, follow their own leads and learn that it is OK to be still, relaxed and quiet. Children I see are so often zoomed around from school to class. Taking this quiet time away at an early age will have important consequences for them as adults because they will have difficulty relaxing and being on their own.

Corinne Abisgold, educational psychologist

Encouraging enquiry

The advantage of being more democratic and admitting you don't know, and that you are wrong sometimes, is that the child is respected more for himself and has to make some of his own decisions.

Elizabeth Newson, Emeritus Professor of Developmental Psychology, University of Nottingham

I've been thinking. I think Father Christmas is God's cousin.

Joshua, six

I'm glad I'm not a porcupine.

Holly, four

Learning, for children of the information age, will be less a matter of memorising facts which can be found elsewhere and more a matter of knowing what to do with them. This ability to think, rather than simply being a receptacle for received information, can be aided even at pre-school and primary level, by encouraging your child to ask questions, to enquire and to explore, to think creatively and courageously.

The importance of children learning to think for themselves is

Questions, questions

Children's natural desire to enquire is blossoming at around the age of five and you are simply tapping a natural resource at this age. The questions a child formulates for himself will be incredibly motivating and often remarkable – 'Does the wind have a mind?' We can close this question down because it is difficult to answer, or close down further enquiry by answering it, but our role as a parent is to facilitate the enquiry. This is not about giving a quick answer but about the trying to understand and keeping the enquiry open. The ability to ask original questions, enquire and be adaptable becomes even more essential now with the speed of technological change.

Robin Freeland, educational psychologist

Help your child also by keeping a sense of perspective and humour. Get too intense and your child's eyes may glaze over. 'The worst thing to do is make something the child has expressed interest in into a really big deal,' explains Nicholas Tucker, an educational psychologist now lecturing in Cultural and Community Studies at the University of Sussex.

'Try not to be too heavy, and take the lead from the child. There is this old story where a little boy says to his mother "What is lightning" and she says, "I'm not sure go and ask your father," and the little boy says "I don't want to know that much!" Children do not want lectures. Unfortunately, parents often see an opportunity and then squeeze it to death.'

increasingly recognised by parents and professionals. Whether it is new initiatives to encourage mental calculation in maths classes[10] or new research into 'cognitive acceleration', the message is clear – adults can encourage children to think and this can have remarkable benefits for their education as a whole.

At its simplest level, this requires parents to focus on active enquiry rather than passive learning – to welcome questions, to admit when they don't know the answers and to fuel their child's interest in wanting to know more. Recognising a few common parental bad habits may help:

Child: How does the jam get in a doughnut?
Parent: Pass me that cup would you? Thanks. (Child ignored)

Child: How does the jam get in a doughnut?
Parent: What are you on about now? (Child treated as an irritant)

Child: How does the jam get in a doughnut?
Parent: Ask your mother. (Child fobbed off)

Child: How does the jam get in a doughnut?
Parent: Well, I'm pleased you asked me that. After first being deep
    fried in extremely hot oil the soft dough rises until it is the
    familiar doughnut shape. Then, once cool and firm, it is pierced
    by a long needle and . . . (Child asleep)

The remedy is relatively simple.

Child: How does the jam get in a doughnut?
Parent: That's a good question. How do you think it might? (Child
    encouraged to think for themselves)

If the response is, 'I don't know', you can still encourage him to
think it through by giving him a series of possible answers to choose
from. Throw in a few funny ones for good measure.

On a deeper level, we have to recognise the importance of the
process of enquiry, the doing and the discovery rather than simply the
end result or final mark – and to explain that to our children. We can
encourage the enjoyment of enquiry through games and stories (see
Stories and games for thinking, opposite) and also by showing the significance of things they learn by explaining how they link to the world
around them.

We also have to recognise that what we do has a far greater impact
on our children's attitude to learning than anything we say. If we are
open, enthusiastic and constructive about our own opportunities to
learn and problem-solve, the chances are our children will be, too.

*Many psychologists believe, and I agree, that what happens on the mental plane is
first experienced on the social plane. Thus, for example, if a family solves problems
with democracy their children will show good problem-solving abilities whereas if
they see us shouting or becoming depressed if there's a problem, these children become
very poor problem-solvers. The kind of things we model in the everyday are
absolutely crucial to what our children learn and how they learn it. People do not
seem to be aware how critical these things are in the forming of children's thinking.*

Robin Freeland, educational psychologist

Stories and games for thinking

Adapted, with kind permission, from *Stories for Thinking* by Dr Robert Fisher
(see Contributors, p. 350).

*The world is an unpredictable place and the job / career for life increasingly
unlikely, so children need to learn flexible thinking and problem-solving
skills to enable them to be life-long learners.*

*Parents can broaden and focus on their children's interests and equip them
with the flexible thinking they need in a way that teachers cannot because of
the number of children they teach. It is important for parents to give children
as wide an experience of life as is possible, including music, art, 'finding out',
sports and so on. There is also such a focus in schools on reading, writing
and arithmetic that the fourth 'R', 'reason' is neglected. Parents are in a very
good position to talk through things that are of interest to their children, reflect
with them on what learning means and to build on their talents.*

*This can be done through stories (see below), discussing their meaning in terms of
a child's own experience of life. Games (see p.303), on occasions, can also be
turned into thinking games. For example, parents can discuss with a child a
plan of playing the game before it begins, then review why they were
successful or not. In this way the child can see what the game is about,
see how to play it better, and to enjoy it more by discussing it with
those they love. This ought to be fun, not work. Part of the fun for
both of you is finding out what and how your child really thinks.*

Dr Robert Fisher, Head of the Centre for Research in Teaching Thinking,
Brunel University

A story for thinking: The Timid Hares

(Folktale from India, which also appears in similar versions in Europe and Africa)

There was once a timid hare who was always afraid that something terrible was going to happen. He was always saying: 'What if the sky were to fall down on us? What if the earth were suddenly to fall in? What would happen to me then?'

One day after he had been saying this to himself many times, he heard a loud noise.

Bang! The ground seemed to tremble. The hare almost jumped out of his skin. 'What was that!' he cried. 'The earth must be falling in!' So he ran off as fast as he could go. After he had gone some way he met another hare. 'Brother hare,' he said, 'run for your life! The earth is falling in!'

'What's that?' cried the other hare. 'Hey,

continued overleaf

wait for me!' So he ran after the first hare, who told another hare, and soon all the hares were running as fast as they could. And each one cried. 'Run, run, the earth is falling in, the earth is falling in!' Soon the larger animals heard and they began to run, crying: 'The earth is falling in! Run for your lives!'

A wise old lion saw them running, and heard their cries. He looked around. 'I cannot see the earth is falling in,' he said. So in his loudest voice he roared, 'STOP!' At this all the frightened animals skidded to a halt.

'What are you saying?' asked the lion. 'Haven't you heard?' trumpeted the elephant. 'The earth is falling in!'

'What makes you think so?' enquired the lion. 'The tigers told us,' said the elephants. 'What makes the tigers think so?' 'The bears told us,' growled the tigers. 'What makes the bears think so?' 'Why, the deer told us,' said the buffaloes. 'Why do the deer think so?' 'The monkeys told us,' murmured the deer. 'And how do the monkeys know?' 'The jack-als said so,' chattered the monkeys. 'And how did the jackals find this out?' 'The hares told us,' yelped the jackals. 'And how do the hares know?' One hare said that the other hare told him, and so on, until finally they came to the first hare. 'I know,' he said, 'because I saw it happen.' 'Where?' 'Under the big coconut tree.'

'Well, come and show me,' said the lion. 'Oh no, I'm too scared! It might happen again!' squeaked the hare. 'Well, climb on my back and I'll take you,' said the lion. So, still trembling, the hare jumped on the lion's back, and slowly they plodded to the big tree. Just then . . . BANG! A coconut came crashing to the ground. 'Run, run,' cried the hare, 'we're all going to be killed!'

'Stop and look!' said the lion. 'Well, what is it?' 'I . . . I think its a coconut,' said the hare. 'Then you'd better tell the other animals that the earth falling in is only a coconut falling from a palm tree.'

One should not always believe what one hears.

Thinking about the story

Key question: What does the story mean?

1 What made the hare almost jump out of his skin?
2 What did he think the noise was?
3 Which animals joined the hare in running away?
4 Which animal did not run, and stopped the other animals?
5 Why did the animals think the earth was falling in?
6 What did make the noise? How did the animals know?
7 What advice would you give the hare?
8 Can you think of a time when you believed something that turned out to be wrong?

Thinking about knowledge

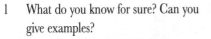

Key question: What do knowing and believing mean?

1 What do you know for sure? Can you give examples?
2 What does 'knowledge' mean?
3 If you know something does it mean it must be true?
4 If other people say they know something, does it mean it must be true?
5 If you read about something in books, does it mean it is true?
6 Are there some things you believe in but are not sure you know about? Give an example.
7 Do you believe everything you see? Why?
8 Do you believe everything you are told? Why?
9 What do you know that nobody else knows? Can you give an example?

Further Activities

Make up a play about someone who was very scared of something that was not true.
Make a list of things you know and things you believe but are not sure of.

A game for thinking: Improve the human body

How to play

Players are given paper and pencil and told to design and draw some improvement or improvements to the human body. At the end of a given time, say 15 minutes, each player shows their drawing and explains what improvements they have designed. Players may then vote to find out whose design was thought to be the most creative and original.

CHAPTER FOURTEEN

GROWING INDEPENDENCE

I look at him and I can't believe how much he's changed.
He seems so grown up, it can take me by surprise how much he needs me.
Jenny T

I never know who I'm going to meet – the six-year-old going on 16,
or the six-year-old going on three.
John S

Your child's increasing independence brings huge changes and opportunities to both your lives. She will be venturing out into the world, often into unfamiliar territory without you to lead the way – yet you are still the central figure in her life and what you do will profoundly influence her ability to cope and enjoy her new experiences to the full.

Preparing for school

Imagine. You are starting a new job tomorrow. You can't remember where it is or what the office building looks like and how or even whether you'll get back home again. You don't know where you'll sit. You don't know who you'll be working with, who your boss is or what you're expected to do. You have no idea when or whether you'll be able to eat or even go to the loo. Everything you know well and love deeply will be somewhere else – and everyone's telling you you'll have such a wonderful time. No wonder many children find starting school so hard.

Acknowledging those fears and anxieties is the most effective means of dealing with them (see Dealing with feelings, p.94). You can also help by gently and calmly giving your child as much preparation and information as she needs. Make sure she knows the sorts of things she may be doing and the rough structure of her day.

If you have a chance to chat to the teacher before her first day, try to find out what will be expected of her. Don't just think of schoolwork – how do they like children to ask to go to the loo? Will she be expected to shut the loo door? Will she be expected to sit at a desk? Simple things like this can throw a child, especially if she risks being chastised for something she is allowed to do at home. Reading books together about going to school, even playing school with her toys, can help familiarise your child with new routines such as assembly or going to the school canteen for lunch.

Letting her play with crayons, paper, scissors and books and, crucially, letting her mix with other children before she starts school will all help her feel less fearful. Meeting up with children who may be in your child's class before school begins can also ease the transition. The school or local playgroups and nurseries may be able to put you in touch with other parents in your area.

Smoothing the way

Adrienne Katz, author of *You Can Teach Your Child to Read*

'This is one of the most important boosts you can give a child. Their first impression of school and their feeling of coping with it colours their view of school for a very long time. The happier you can make this transition the more positive the child feels about it.

'It is the little things that matter, the sort of shoes you choose – laces or Velcro for ease, trousers that are easy to take down in the toilet, etc. Another important preparation is helping your child understand and follow instructions. Teach them prepositions – underneath, on top of, behind – because teachers are forever giving instructions such as 'Stand behind Jonathan', 'Put your books next to my table, please'. If young children do not understand these, and not all do, they may appear unco-operative or hesitant and the child feels nervous and unsure.

'Using these words in a fun way yourself will help – "Put teddy on the table. Where has he gone? On the table." It only takes a few minutes here and there and is, I believe, even more valuable than teaching children the alphabet.'

If possible, discuss in advance the school's attitude to you staying for a while in the mornings until your child is happy without you (see Separation anxiety, p.116). Many children respond best to a gradual introduction, others may be happy with a clean break. Some schools welcome parents' support in the early days, others see it as unnecessary interference. There is little way of knowing how your child will respond until you get there, but thinking through the school's preferred approach and your possible responses will help.

Also think about your own attitudes to your child starting school. If you are very anxious or simply not ready to let her go, she will pick this up. Try to communicate positive messages about school, and your faith in the fact that she will be OK. If she knows you feel relaxed about it and sees you relaxed in the presence of her teacher, she will expect to feel the same. It is a big step and most children stumble a little when they begin. But they get there in the end.

I have seen children going from almost solitary reclusiveness at age five going into primary school. They have never experienced playgroup, they have never experienced nursery, they have never had brothers and sisters or anyone else to play with and the first few months of integration into the school is traumatic. Parents should never allow children to be divorced from others of the same age. But even children as deprived as one or two I've seen coming in to primary school, within a few months will settle down and will be OK. It can be achieved, so never despair.
Professor Hugh Foot, specialist in child psychology and social development

The parent-school relationship

A good relationship between a child's teacher and parent(s) benefits children at a number of levels. For younger children, there is a connection between different parts of their lives, so what happens to them at school is not a completely different world but very much linked to their home life. This is enormously important to a young child. What parents know about how their child learns best is also very useful when fed back into schools, but this will only happen when the relationships are good.
Professor Katherine Riley, Director of the Centre of Educational Management, Roehampton Institute

Hone your diplomatic skills. If you are able to build some rapport with your child's school and teachers, you should get more information on her progress and needs and your own input and opinion may get a better hearing. This may be crucial if your child encounters difficulties with her work or with other children (see Bullying, p.318). Parent-teacher meetings tend to focus on school work rather than how your child mixes and communicates with others, but ask for this information, too, as it will help you gauge how she is developing and coping.

The aim should be an open rather than defensive dialogue. Presuming your child is always in the right may limit your chances of productive discussion and blind you to possible problems and solutions. On the other hand, always defending teachers' actions in the hope of presenting a 'united front' may force your child to question her own feelings and experiences and make her reluctant to tell you when she encounters difficulties (see Dealing with feelings, p.94 and Communication, p.70). School life isn't always straightforward or fair, and it helps parent and child to be aware of that.

If your child gets told off for something somebody else did at school and they feel an injustice has been done, I would advocate talking with the child about unfairness, acknowledging that it is unfair and upsetting, and thinking together about what you want to do. I wouldn't advocate taking every single case to the headteacher. Some children who feel their parents are going to write a letter or go marching up to the school about every single thing will then hide things because they fear their parents are a loose cannon. You want to keep your child telling you about what's happening to them so you can help them manage it. There may be issues that you do want to make a point about but at other times you may agree with your child that an incident was unfair but minor, that the teacher was mistaken and it is best to let it go. If you protect your child from every possible disappointment, these are the children who end up seriously ill-equipped to deal with the real world.

Vivienne Gross, Clinical Director, The Institute of Family Therapy

Friends

Having a good friend will lessen the harmful effects of bullying. If you are excluded by the general peer group but you have a friend who is saying 'You are not so bad as they say you are', this can be enough to satisfy your need to belong. You will not be damaged if somebody special is valuing you, even if you are not valued by everyone.[1]

Dr Michael Boulton, child psychologist, Keele University, specialising
in research into aggression, bullying and victimisation

*I wince when I hear my daughter and friends' conversations
about who's bestest friends with whom.*

Carolyn P

*After I lost my baby I heard my daughter talking to her friend about
it with such brutal honesty. It was so matter-of-fact and what she obviously
needed to say but in a way she would never have said to me. In that way
kids do support each other, even when they're quite little.*

Helen O

Friends matter. Your child's general happiness, behaviour, language, sense of worth, physical and emotional safety and educational aspirations and achievements are likely to be greatly influenced by her peers in general and her friends in particular.

As any adult knows, friends can help you through the toughest of times and falling out with friends can make even good times hard to bear, yet the intensity and importance of childhood friendships is often overlooked. Strong friendship bonds can develop from nursery and reception age on. It doesn't matter much whether your child has one special friend or many, whether she has close friendships or seems generally liked and accepted. What matters is that she has at least one other child at school she considers a friend (see Bullying, p.318).

Your role is to help your child develop the skills she needs to make friends while also boosting her confidence, resilience and understanding of values, so she knows when not to run with the pack. You can do this by:

Providing opportunities for your child to play with others
Asking your child who she would like to get to know better and inviting them on a trip to the playground or home to play may help budding

friendships. Try also to show her the benefits of friendship and socialisation in your own life. Out-of-school activities may help her widen her circle of possible friends and boost her social confidence.

Boosting your child's self-esteem (see Dealing with feelings, p.94). This will increase her confidence in forming friendships and

Peer influence

Parents of school-age children will be well aware of peer influence. A craze can sweep through schools in a matter of weeks (remember yo-yos!) and your six-year-old may start talking playground-speak or develop a deep hatred of carrots for no other reason than that her best friend doesn't like them. Such manifestations of peer pressure are relatively insignificant and often funny, yet others are extremely important to your child's future.

There is increasing evidence on the potency of peer pressure, much of it US research into drug use among children (see Boosting your child's resistance to drugs, p.332). While arguments rage about the extent of peer influence, it is also clear that parents have a role to play in this – in influencing children's attitudes and behaviour, and thus their choice of friends, and in checking out who their children mix with.

'Peers are very important. They are likely to be every bit as important as parents in, for example, the development of delinquency,' explains Gavin Nobes, lecturer in psychology at the University of East London. 'It is likely that these sorts of influences begin very young, possibly pre-school. Importantly, parents should avoid being authoritarian, harshly punitive or aggressive. These parental styles lead children to develop anti-social behaviour and to them becoming attracted and attractive to other aggressive, deviant peers who, in turn, encourage and reinforce that anti-social behaviour.'

Peers are nevertheless very important to a child's healthy development. 'Peers have something unique and significant to contribute to development because they are equals: they tend to be equally knowledgeable, skilful and strong, and have similar interests,' Gavin Nobes explains.

'Negotiating rules with peers might well be an important first step in the process of learning about the rules that regulate social behaviour. With peers, children have almost unique opportunities to develop social skills, such as those of negotiation, co-operation, competition and conflict, in ways in which they usually cannot when with parents or teachers because adults are too big and too powerful.'

prevent her becoming over-dependent on them. Talking together about how friendships come and go, that some last a lifetime and others a day, may also be useful.

Friendships can become crucial out of desperation that at least somewhere a child has an affirming relationship. This creates a fragile situation because when peers don't respond the child can feel desperate. They then try too hard, which backfires, and they are then vulnerable to behaving in any way to be acceptable to their peers.

Camila Batmanghelidjha, psychotherapist, Director of Kid's Company

Equipping your child with basic social skills

It is not the kind of world where shy people get noticed. So all children but especially shy children need to be taught the basic skills of communication and being sociable to get them started. You start the rollercoaster by practising with your children at home: 'Hi my name is. . . what's yours?' Tell them about eye contact if someone talks to them and about asking how someone is, and practise these until they don't find them a problem any more. From this, they will find people are nicer to them and they can learn the next response until it becomes more natural.

Steve Biddulph, psychologist and author

You can help your child negotiate her social life and playground politics by encouraging and praising those social skills she already displays and working on those she does not (see Social skills, opposite). Think together of different ways to start a conversation – 'I liked your drawing. What do you like drawing most?', 'Have you got any brothers or sisters?' 'I can touch my nose with my tongue. Can you?' Talk about different ways to join in or start up a game.

We are teaching and equipping our children for life so it is essential to teach them how to communicate and interact with people. A friend of mine's child went through a stage of never smiling at anyone and looking very sulky, so she actually told him to smile. She explained it was a signal to other people. It may not mean you want to be their friend but it is saying 'I'm friendly', so you then have the opportunity to find that out. It is about socialisation and survival in the real world.

Pat Elliot, psychotherapist

Social skills

Dr Michael Boulton, child psychologist

'People are waking up to the fact that children's social relations are just as important as their cognitive development. Many children are adept at socialising from an early age with very little coaching, perhaps because parents are providing these learning opportunities in the home. A small proportion of children lack these social skills.

'Some kids are happy being on their own. Others, however, may be on their own against their wishes, which may make them vulnerable to bullying. They just simply don't know how to join in, hover on the periphery of a game and are ignored.

'Some are outgoing but tend to make statements that put the peer group off – "I can do that better than you", "Don't do it that way, do it this", "Don't play that play this". They are then rebuffed. It is far better for a child to actively fit in with what's going on – "That's a good game, whose side shall I be on?" They assume they are welcome and accept the rules of the game. A parent can help a child develop these skills.'

Encouraging your child to think for herself Show your child that her opinions matter, both in her learning (see Encouraging enquiry, p.298) and her home life (see Encouraging positive behaviour, p.143 and The value of values, p.333).

In America where the problem of drugs is much more prevalent, schools do projects with younger children to show them the value of their own thoughts and decisions. One example was a group of children who had to choose between two boxes, one of which contained something the children really wanted and they had to guess which one by placing a counter on it. After a while the children just placed their counter on the box that had most on. This was used to demonstrate to the children that it wasn't always the best option to go with your peers, ie. you have to think for yourself.
Corinne Abisgold, educational psychologist

Admitting that appearances matter Sad but true. In playground culture, outlandish or very unusual clothes or haircuts will not help your child feel she belongs. You can help her conform enough to be accepted without making her a class clone.

Parents' eyes can be so closed to this. I am not recommending parents having to buy the best trainers etc but being aware of the impact that fitting in has on a child. You have to be alive to what it is like to be your child in that environment.

Mary MacLeod, Director of Policy and Research, ChildLine

Knowing what's happening in your child's life It is much easier to know when she needs your extra support or intervention if communication between you is good and she feels confident enough to admit to problems or mistakes (see Communication, p.70 and Dealing with feelings, p.94). Try to have a general idea of the work she is doing, the friends she is playing with, what happened at breaktime, what she had for lunch. Ask to see her timetable so you can talk about the specifics of her day rather than generalities. 'How was today?' may be shrugged off much more easily than 'What songs did you do this morning?'

Also beware after-school activity frenzy. One recent survey[2] identified a 'critical time' after school when children want to talk through their day. The person they talk to need not be you, but children should be able to speak to someone they know and trust about how they feel. Some organised activities are fine and fun; too many may exhaust you both and limit opportunities for relaxed conversation.

Being aware of your child's vulnerabilities If she seems to be finding it difficult to make or keep friends, try to spot any aspects of her behaviour that may be making her vulnerable to being picked on, excluded or ignored by others. Try not to 'fix it' but rather allow her to come up with suggestions (see Communication, p.70). Talking together about what makes a good friend may encourage her to think about what she could do differently. You could also draw a picture or make a list together of what she may like in a friend and friends may like in her.

It is key to listen to your children's feelings without dismissing them, or giving solutions. It is helpful to let them tell you what is going on. Even young children are amazingly resourceful at finding their own solutions given the opportunity – 'I understand this is difficult (eg. best friend won't play with them) and what do you think would help?'

Kitty Hagenbach, psychotherapist

Modern manners

There is this view that with strangers we should be on our best behaviour but at home you can do whatever you like, which is wrong. Those closest to us deserve to be treated with respect and dignity and common politeness.

Dr Dorothy Rowe, psychologist and writer

Social conventions are often arbitrary and often broken, so it is hardly surprising that most children sometimes forget what they are supposed to do when. Yet how your child behaves will influence and be influenced by how she is viewed and treated, both inside and outside the family, so it is only fair to equip her with the basic skills of courtesy and consideration.

Children pick up most of these through observation, but almost all will need some guidance along the way if they are to survive and thrive in school and other social situations. You can help by explaining very clearly what behaviour is expected and effective in particular circumstances, and by allowing her to practise with you until she gets it right and seems comfortable.

By about six years old your child will be old enough to understand that social codes and conventions vary between families and groups (see Swearing, p.314). Explaining this clearly will help her when she comes across other children and other families doing things differently – which she almost inevitably will.

My partner, Shaaron, noticed that at about the age of four our little girl needed help to know how to wait. She was so concerned she would forget what she was going to say, she would get more and more frantic to be heard, especially if Shaaron was on the phone. She needed a task to begin to learn a new skill of waiting for the right time to speak, so we asked her to repeat silently in her head what it was she needed to say, until the right moment to tell us. This is more helpful to the child than saying 'Be patient' or 'Wait there'. Other skills to build on from waiting are listening, joining in on conversations on the right subject, noticing pauses in the conversation and asking permission to change the subject.

Steve Biddulph, psychologist and author

Assertion v. aggression

You are aiming to educate to find solutions, ways to do things that suit everyone. We are not aiming for frozen, compliant children but children who can decide for themselves, learn from life and interact. The aim here is to

---

Swearing

We used to make our own swear words up. We had one – horhors – which meant poo and we thought it was so rude and so hysterically funny. We'd say it endlessly and fall about laughing.

Angela S

I remember getting into such trouble for saying something when I had no idea what it meant. That really sticks in my mind as one of my childhood's great injustices.

John B

Most children occasionally bring home the playground's choicest grimaces, gestures and expletives. How their parents react will depend on what is done, how and when. It is part of a parent's role to equip a child with the knowledge that many people find certain words and gestures offensive, but also to keep minor misdemeanours in perspective.

Sniggering with friends about 'rude' words and body parts is a perfectly healthy part of growing up, and most adults can remember the childhood glee of sharing 'swear words' with their friends.

But the likelihood is that your child, at some stage, will utter something either that you find offensive or which you know will offend others. What this is will vary between families and cultures, but it helps to think through your possible responses in advance.

First check whether your child knows that what she has said or done is not OK (which is not the same as explaining the word or gesture's meaning. For a young child, this may be bewildering and counter-productive). It may also help to explain that words are strange things and that it is very

There was a tree in our playground and we used to dare each other to climb up to the top, shout 'bum', then all run away.

Christina C

have a child with heart and backbone. You do want a child to be kind to other children and they will do this if they have been shown enough kindness, but you also want a child who can be themselves and not just give in to others, who has the discipline to move through life, make decisions, get things done and make the best of their abilities.

Steve Biddulph, psychologist and author

---

difficult to know why some people are offended by some words and not others, so to make it easier to remember, you have a house rule that xxx isn't said.

No child is going to take much notice if you don't follow the house rule yourself. You need to be able to say 'I don't speak to you like that and you don't speak to me like that. OK?'

If your child is knowingly and repeatedly rude in ways that worry or offend you, it is time to think of methods to turn around her behaviour (see Encouraging positive behaviour, p.143 and Effective discipline, p.170). One way may be to change your own responses.

'I recommend the parents sit down with the child on a day where things are quite calm and say, "From now on I'll answer you whenever you speak to me in a friendly tone of voice." Then pause,' says Noel Janis-Norton, director of the New Learning Centre. 'Some discussion will probably take place about what happens when this is not the case. The parent can even say "When you speak to me in a way I don't like I will look at you and smile so you know I have heard and that I am not being rude but I will not answer."

'You can cover yourself by saying, "This is a new rule I'm making for myself here and I might get it wrong sometimes but I am practising and I will get better and better over time." This is a rule for the parent. The child will of course adjust to the new situation over time, but you are not making the rule for the child. You are not saying the child should always be polite. The child will become much more respectful if the parents do not react to the disrespectful comments.'

I'd always been told never to make a fuss when a child swears because to react draws attention to it. That worked until he was about six when he came out with a phrase that I find really offensive. When I said I didn't like it his friend said, 'My dad says it all the time.' I said something like, 'Well, every house has its own rules and that's one of ours.' I know they'll probably use it to each other but they haven't used it in front of me since, so they can control it and I guess that's what matters.

Laura F

To mix happily with other children your child will have to learn how to give and take, to not only understand and consider others' feelings but also how to express her own needs and wants clearly, appropriately and effectively.

It may help to explain, in words your child understands, that there are three ways of responding to situations:

Aggressive Aggressive people think their needs matter more than anybody else's. They will do whatever it takes to get what they want. Push. Grab. Say horrible things. They will get some of the things they want this way, but lots of people won't like how they behave. Their behaviour is likely to get them into trouble.

Passive Passive people think other people's needs matter more than their own. They have trouble getting what they want or standing up for what they believe is right.

Assertive Assertive people think their needs matter and that other people's needs matter, too. They try to get what they need or want by being clear and firm when they need to be, in ways that don't hurt other people's bodies or feelings. This is usually extremely effective. Other people understand and respect their behaviour.

This is sophisticated territory, but young children can begin to grasp the difference. When they do, they have a skill for life which many adults have yet to master. Thinking through different situations together may help clarify the issues.

You want to use your friend's pen. What's the best way to get it?
1   Grab it or shout 'Give me your pen'? (Aggressive)
2   Decide to use a pencil instead? (Passive)
3   Ask calmly and clearly, 'May I use your pen, please?' (Assertive)

Someone in your class has taken two books and there isn't one left for you. You've asked him to give it back and he won't. What would be the best thing to do next?
1   Hit him? (Aggressive)
2   Keep quiet and let him keep the book? (Passive)
3   Calmly explain to the teacher that you have a problem and ask for her help in sorting it out? (Assertive)

Talk together about different ways of being assertive (see Self-assertiveness skills, opposite) and try to illustrate its effectiveness in your own responses – by not caving in to aggressive behaviour, being firm but not threatening etc (see Effective discipline, p.170).

When two children cannot agree it may be time to negotiate. Even young school-age children can often grasp the importance and finer points of negotiation and resolving disputes fairly and peacefully. The following conflict resolution technique is especially good for serious disputes between siblings (also see Standing back, p.184). It looks as though it involves a lot of effort, but becomes second nature with practise. It is straightforward, fair and constructive, lets every child have

---

Self-assertiveness skills

Adapted, with kind permission, from *Preventing Bullying! A Parent's Guide* by Kidscape (see Contacts, p.355)

The children's charity Kidscape (see Contacts, p.355) has compiled a list of skills to help children who are bullied or bullying to become more assertive. The following points will help children in any situation.

Making requests

— Be clear about what you want.
— Plan ahead and practise.
— Make your request short and precise ('That is my pencil and I want it back').
— Decide what you want to say and stick to it ('I would like my pencil back'). You don't have to be rude but don't get side-tracked.

Saying No

— When you say NO, say it firmly.
— If you don't want to do something, don't give in to pressure. Be firm. Remember we have the right to say NO.
— If you are not sure and somebody is bugging you for an answer, say 'I need more time to decide' or 'I need more information'.
— Don't make excuses: keep your body posture assertive (don't stand all hunched up in victim-mode) and look the person in the eye. The other person will know from the decisive way you are speaking and standing that you mean business (If you find looking people in the eye hard, practise keeping eye contact within your family).
— Offer an alternative: 'No I don't want to play football. Let's go for a walk instead.'
— When we say No to someone, we are only refusing the request. We are not rejecting the person.

their say, teaches the importance of assertion and compromise – and saves more parental time and effort in the long-run than letting bitter disputes simmer and boil.

Your role is to guide rather than impose solutions and to let the children themselves decide how to change their behaviour or make better choices in future.

1 **Explain** Tell the children that for disagreements to be sorted out in ways everyone agrees with, everyone needs a chance to speak. Express confidence in the children's ability to help sort the matter out.
2 **Take turns to identify the problem** Each person has a chance to say what they think is the problem. No one may interrupt the person speaking. (Giving the speaker an object to hold, such as a spoon, can encourage turn-taking and discourage interruption.)
3 **Agree the problem** Once each child has spoken, can they agree what the problem is?
4 **Suggest a solution** Once that is agreed, let everyone have a turn to suggest solutions. If they are struggling, you could suggest some.
5 **Agree a solution** Ask the children to agree a solution between them.
6 **Review** Once agreed, express your confidence that they will follow it through and ask everyone to get together again to discuss how it has worked (in an hour, a day, two days depending on the dispute).

Bullying

In my experience most victims are sensitive, intelligent, gentle children. They don't come from homes full of conflict and shouting so when a bully comes at them they don't know quite what to do.

Michele Elliott, Director of Kidscape, the charity for bullied children and their families

Bullying will never be eradicated but there is much parents can do to help children become bully-aware and bully-resistant. The first is to know the facts.

Bullying – the hard facts

— In a ChildLine study into bullying in schools 64% of primary school children said they had been bullied at some point at school, 50% in the last year.

— In one recent survey [3] of 1,000 children and parents, a quarter of parents surveyed said their child first encountered bullying at five or younger.

— 94% of children said they had experienced verbal abuse, 56% physical abuse and 51% both.

— Half of those children who said they were bullied said their school had been unhelpful.

Bullying can be physical or psychological Professional definitions vary but children themselves consider bullying to incorporate everything from serious physical harm to teasing, including acts such as name-calling, spreading malicious gossip, destroying property, humiliation, rejection and exclusion. They also include one-off incidents, as well as long-term campaigns of harassment.[4]

Evidence is growing that psychological bullying can cause the greatest long-term damage to children's view of themselves and their world. It can also be the first step on a downward spiral of intimidation that ends in physical attack.

Children are not always playing when they tease or name-call.
The typical excuse is 'I was only playing' but we now know children use
this as a smoke screen, and they are motivated by the desire to cause distress
to their victims. In our research, psychological bullying was found to be
more damaging than physical bullying and there is no greater example of
psychological bullying than being left out by one's peers.
Dr Michael Boulton, child psychologist

Any form of bullying, however 'mild', should not be ignored
If left unchecked, bullying can result in depression and other mental health problems, low self-esteem, shyness, poor academic achievement, truancy, self-injury and, very rarely, suicide. It can also seriously damage those doing the bullying, who learn that aggressive, threatening behaviour gets them what they want, which in turn

increases their chance of violent behaviour and relationship problems in adulthood.[5]

Help your child avoid bullies

Prevention

Invest in your child's resilience Much research has shown that being unaggressive and having good social and communication skills and self-esteem diminishes the likelihood of being bullied[6] (see Communication, p.70). Assertion skills help (see Assertion v. aggression, p.314) and at least one friendship seems crucial (see Friends, p.308).

It seems children try out subtle forms of victimisation initially. They try out the chinks in the peer's armour, maybe call them a little name to begin with and watch the reaction they get. If you are a child who has been brought up in a family that has led you to believe you are important, worthy and undeserving of these sorts of behaviours you are more likely to stand up to another child. If you are doing well in other areas of your life it may be easier to shrug off the effects of victimisation.
Dr Michael Boulton, child psychologist

Talk about bullying Discuss the issues with your child – what bullying is (ie not only physical threat or attack); where it might happen (are there any 'hot' spots – school cloakrooms, etc); how to minimise opportunities for bullying (not carrying valuables, staying in groups, walking on if confronted, etc).

Include the vital message that being bullied is not a child's fault. Sometimes a child is picked on because of differences of race, gender, class, accent, appearance, disability, hair colour, academic ability, height. Sometimes there seems no discernible reason at all.

Let your child know that showing bullies you are upset can encourage them to carry on. Also that ignoring a bully (see Dealing with taunts and insults, opposite) is not the same as ignoring bullying or hiding feelings.

It is important to remember that children assume everyone will treat
them as their parents do. It is very important to tell them that this is not the
case both with teachers, peers and strangers. It does not need to be terrifying and
it helps with young children to give examples from the animal kingdom.
At different times in different situations some animals protect, some attack,
some do both, some are gentle and some are to be avoided.

Camila Batmanghelidjha, psychotherapist and Director of Kid's Company

---

Dealing with taunts and insults

Adapted, with kind permission, from *Preventing Bullying!*
A Parent's Guide by Kidscape (see Contacts, p.355)

If children respond to insults with more insults, they can build up until they become unbearable. Tell them about 'fogging':

How 'fogging' works

When other people make hurtful remarks, don't argue and try not to become upset. Imagine that you are within a huge, white fog-bank: the insults are swallowed up by the fog long before they reach you. Nothing touches you.

Reply to taunts with something short and bland: 'That's what you think.' 'Maybe.' Then walk away. This might seem very strange at first and very hard to do but it does work and it can help you blot out insults.

Speak up Let children know they *must tell* as soon as a situation feels difficult. Be explicit about this – children are bombarded with images and stories that say it is wrong to 'tell tales'. Around 50% of children who are bullied at school do not report their experiences, often because they are afraid of further intimidation from their tormentors.[7] So reassure your child that telling makes matters better, not worse, and do all within your power to ensure this is the case.

Let your child know who she needs to tell and how she can do this (see How the school can help, p.323). Also tell her of at least one other trusted adult she can turn to.

Action

Be direct. Say something like 'I think you are being bullied or threatened and I'm worried about you. Let's talk.' If your child doesn't tell immediately, say you are there night and day, whenever she is ready to talk. Then keep a watchful eye.
Michele Elliott, Director of Kidscape

Gently encourage your child to talk (see Communication, p.70). If your child does tell you about bullying:

— Offer praise ('It is very brave to tell'), support ('I will help in any way I can. There is much we can do together') and reassurance ('I love you very much. Always have, always will').
— Check back that your understanding of the situation is the same as your child's. This will help clarify the situation and prove to the child that the message has been received and understood.
— Act.

Bullying is complex and you will need to consider a range of options. Ask for your child's suggestions, let her describe her worries about any of them and agree a joint plan of action. Avoid imposing 'solutions' without consulting her or she may feel even more powerless and vulnerable. If the bullying is school-based, it is important the school is informed.

Advising your child to get her own back or to hit back harder if physically threatened could make matters much worse.

— It may not work and your child could get seriously hurt.
— It reinforces the idea that might is right (when your child has been the victim of it).
— It can make children feel abandoned to fight their own battles.
— It can turn the bullied into a bully.

Yet also be aware that children do need to keep themselves safe. This may mean them running away, using verbal assertion, seeking adult help immediately or sometimes – when all others have been tried or circumstances are extreme – defending themselves physically. Not all children can do this or want to, and parents should be aware of the dangers of telling children they should. Yet children who are expressly forbidden to use force in any circumstances may feel exposed. Talking to children about self-defence in the context of safety rather than

How the school can help

For most of the children we talked to, the problem was not a reluctance to tell but the reluctance of adults to act or act effectively. They bitterly complained about adults who advised them to ignore it and it would stop. They cannot ignore it and adults should stop telling them to do so.

from *Why Me?* A ChildLine Study[8]

No school is bully-free and all should be doing their best to tackle the problem. Ask if your child's school:

Adopts a whole-school approach
This involves the school developing a 'culture of decency', in which positive behaviour is promoted generally as part of the anti-bullying strategy. Many recent studies show such approaches to be more successful in tackling bullying than those relying solely on the punishment of wrongdoers.[9]

Encourages children to tell Are children told who they can turn to? How can they register their fears or report incidents confidentially? What happens after children have told? Are procedures in place to take reports seriously, investigate thoroughly and act effectively?

Minimises opportunities for bullying
Is there adequate supervision at lunchtime? Is there a 'quiet area' where children can escape rougher play? Are all teachers and supervisors trained to spot psychological as well as physical intimidation?

Provides opportunities for children to explore the issues How are discussion and thought encouraged?

Allows children to be part of the solution Teaching children how to resolve disagreements peacefully has proved extremely effective in many schools, even at primary level (see Assertiveness v. aggression, p.314). Some have successfully introduced peer counselling, mentoring and mediation.[10]

If bullies can be made to feel their behaviour is unacceptable to other children they are much more likely to change than if they are simply told by adults to mend their ways. Involving other children ensures bullying is stripped of glamour and condemned as wrong.

Michele Elliott, Director of Kidscape

revenge or tit-for-tat exchanges, making the distinctions clear and emphasising that it is something they may feel they need to do in emergencies as a last resort, may help them feel less vulnerable (see Skills for safety, p.330).

It is hard to know the balance. Quite often parents advise children very strongly 'You mustn't hit' and I am not advocating that we urge frightened children to take a stand against bigger, more threatening ones. However, occasionally, if a child is capable of being physically assertive it can stop matters escalating. So, yes, I have talked to my own children about self-defence. One feature of bullying is that if the person finds out they can get away with it, they will repeat it and it can spiral out of control. Tackling bullying is about trying to get in there very early on, if possible, to stop it escalating. Either by the child himself saying I am not going to put up with this – 'You are not to hit me again' – or calling for help there and then and adults responding. Sometimes if the child is able, self-defence can put an end to it, too.

Mary MacLeod, Director of Policy and Research, ChildLine

Bullying can take a long time to resolve and the damage done to a child's confidence and self-esteem lasts much longer, so be prepared to provide your child with considerable emotional support. Anti-bullying support groups and charities such as Kidscape, the NSPCC or ChildLine (see Contacts, p.355) can offer expert support and advice.

Help your child avoid becoming a bully

Prevention

If 'taking it out on others' is a major cause of bullying behaviour (as children tell us), then younger children with less developed social skills and means of communicating and managing feelings are bound to be involved in nasty and mean behaviour towards each other. Prevention of bullying has to start here.

from *Why Me?* A ChildLine Study[11]

Bullies come in many guises, can be of either gender and their reasons for bullying are as diverse as they are. Some feel inadequate or unloved and bully to feel dominant and significant, others bully because they follow the crowd; some are unpopular among their peers, others are popular and misuse the power vested in them by other children; some are bullied or treated harshly at home, others have always had their own way and so have never learned to negotiate or compromise; some do it very infrequently, perhaps in response to a difficult or sad experience, others habitually.

You minimise the risk of your child bullying by:

Being constructive Does your child need to develop skills to negotiate conflict and to communicate and manage their emotions?

Being alert Name-calling, taunts, exclusion and other forms of 'mild' bullying should be nipped in the bud.

Being honest Bullying behaviour can be reinforced by parents' behaviour. If you intimidate, humiliate or threaten your child, you dramatically increase the chances of your child using similar techniques.

> *Parents are such strong role models. Children may think this is the way we should be in our dealings with other people. So if I am more powerful than you, I am justified in making you feel lousy, and making you do what I want you to do.*
> Dr Michael Boulton, child psychologist

Discussing the role of the bystander An estimated 70% of bullying is done in groups rather than by individuals acting alone.[12] Discuss with your child what they should do if they are part of a crowd in which bullying takes place. How could they avoid being pulled along by the crowd? What if a friend bullies another child ('I like you but I don't like what you are doing' may be a useful line to know)? How could they help the person being bullied?

Explain that bullying does not pay This can be the hardest point to put across to children, especially if they have seen bullies succeed where non-bullies don't. It may help to explain that boy or girl X may have got the toy, the turn, the position that time but they didn't behave well. They will know they should not have done that and so will everyone else.

Channel aggression Sports and rough-and-tumble play can act as a release and also teach children self-control. It should be monitored closely so it does not become a vehicle for bullying behaviour.

Review recreational and academic stimulation Children who bully sometimes need something better to do. Is it possible that your child is bored or insufficiently challenged?

> *In our research we asked children why they bullied. They cited three major reasons: 1. They did not like the person. 2. They were bored. 3. They were taking their feelings out on someone else.*
> Mary MacLeod, Director of Policy and Research, ChildLine

Action

If your child has done wrong she needs to be told, but she also needs help to do something about it:

— Keep calm. Becoming angry or defensive if your child is criticised won't help.
— Tell your child you love her but you don't like her behaviour. Try to talk about the behaviour as bullying rather than the child as the bully (see Ripping up labels, p.108).
— Explain the basics. Some young children need reminding of exactly what bullying behaviour is and why it can hurt and frighten others.
— Role play. Practise different ways of handling difficult or volatile situations.
— Has your child any ideas on how she could stop bullying? If not, suggest some. Aim for your child to agree to an approach rather than have one imposed. This makes them feel a part of the solution rather than simply 'a problem'.
— Saying sorry, or writing a note to the victim, may help but wait until apologies are sincere.
— Be patient. Breaking any habit takes time and often has to be done in stages. Monitor progress (keep in touch with the school if bullying is school-based). Praise your child for reducing bullying behaviour.
— Don't struggle alone. A parent's role in this situation is difficult and draining. Seek professional help, support and advice from anti-bullying charities when you need it (see Contacts, p.355).

Protection v. exposure

*I found a needle and syringe in my garden, right near where the children play.
It must have been thrown from a window from the flats behind.
My eldest is six.*

Carolyn V

*My kids got stuck in the lift in BHS and shouted for ages before anyone
realised they were stuck. When I asked why they hadn't pressed the alarm
button they both said 'You always told us not to touch it'.*

Richard P

*So many parents are in this terrible state of siege where they believe
monsters and paedophiles are behind every lamp-post so we mustn't let the
children out of our sight. That creates such a stifling, constraining atmosphere.
The child feels loaded with the parents' anxieties and almost feels as if
he or she is doing something wrong.*

Peter Wilson, child psychotherapist and Director of Young Minds

We are losing our sense of perspective. As a society we tend to warn our
children most about dangers which threaten them least and gloss over
or ignore those which are much more likely to do them harm (see Fears
and facts, p.328). Parental neurosis is good for media ratings but we
must also be aware that children are extremely sensitive to their parents' panic and fear. We owe it to ourselves and to them to look at the
issues calmly.

Our fear of the outside world is pushing children indoors where,
ironically, many risks are higher. Most abuse takes place inside the
home by people children know. The full extent of problems caused by
'home-locked' childhoods is only beginning to be recognised but can
include:

— almost constant adult supervision (which can delay development of
  independence)
— long periods spent in front of a TV or computer screen (which can
  delay speech and social skills)
— insufficient physical exercise (which increases the risk of becoming a
  couch potato)

Fears and facts

We and our children are much more aware of the dangers of paedophiles, abductors and abusers than previous generations and we cannot pretend otherwise. It is our duty to make children be safe and feel safe, so such issues must be addressed. But we must be equally alert to the dangers of over reaction and of focusing on these matters to the exclusion of others.

— Twice as many children fear an attack from a stranger as are worried about being hit by a car while crossing the road. Yet in 1996, ten children were murdered by a stranger in England and Wales, while 270 were killed and 45,000 injured crossing roads. Road accidents are the biggest cause of accidental death in children under 15.[13]

— Parents feel their children are more at risk from abduction than from drugs, alcohol, horror videos or violence on TV. In London 98% of parents put abduction above any other fear. In country areas the figure was 96%.[14]

— In 1971, 80% of seven- and eight-year-olds were allowed to go to school on their own. By 1990 this had dropped to 9%. Nearly a third of parents now take their children to school by car.[15]

This is not a good preparation for a full and happy life.

Parents must wise up about the dangers in the home. Let's be sensible about it — you are not doing kids any favours if they are always in the car and they do not learn to cross the road. The real risk to their children lies at home and not in the street but it is far harder to think that the man you are just starting to go out with may be more of a threat to your three-year-old than a stranger.
Caroline Abrahams, Head of Public Policy, NCH Action For Children

Every parent has to negotiate their own route between equipping children with the skills they need to stay safe and not restricting or terrifying them unnecessarily in the process (see Skills for safety, p.330). It helps to give your child only the information she needs, as simply and clearly stated as possible.

If you are calm and matter-of-fact your children are more likely to listen and remain calm and matter-of-fact themselves. Also try to check that your child has understood an issue fully by posing occasional questions or acting out situations. Just as you wouldn't simply tell a child once how to cross a road or cut with scissors on her own, don't presume she will know how to put your words into action in an emergency without a little practice.

I remember my dad pressing a coin into my hand as I left for my first scout camp, saying something like 'Ring me if anyone dares to touch a hair on your head'. I spent the next week wondering why anyone would want my hair and why he was so concerned about it all of a sudden.

Rob C

Even when children are too young to comprehend or cope with the full facts surrounding a safety issue, there may still be much that parents can do to help equip and protect them. Drugs education for young children, for example, worries many parents who fear a premature loss of children's innocence and that increased awareness may fuel curiosity. What young children need to know will vary according to their particular circumstances and experience, and knowing what information to impart and what to withhold is a hard call for any parent. Yet the vast majority of under-sevens need only basic and simple information to keep them safe, such as safety around medicines, not to touch needles, etc. Importantly, effective education at this age includes encouragement of skills such as decision-making and problem-solving, dealing with disagreements and resisting peer pressure (see Boosting your child's resistance to drugs, p.332). These may prove crucial if they encounter drugs as they grow up and will also benefit them in other areas of their life.

What you tell your children about the news and news-related issues has to be a matter for you and your family. Some psychologists believe no young children should watch or hear the news because it focuses on horrors they are not equipped to deal with. Others believe such censorship does not equip them with a balanced view of life and is unnecessary if they are growing up in a loving home that shows them a very different view of the world. Where you decide to draw your line will depend on many factors, including your child's age and temperament. You may also want to consider that:

— Total censorship is virtually impossible even if you wanted it. A newspaper may land on your doormat in the morning, shops play radio news, children talk to each other in the playground. It is inevitable that your children will get to hear of some events and issues you would prefer them not to know.

— Total exposure without any parental censorship could give a child a

Skills for safety

The Kidscape charity suggests all parents should teach their children:

1 **To be safe.** Tell your children they have a right to be safe. No one can take that away.

2 **To protect their own bodies.** Children need to know their body belongs to them.

3 **To say no.** Tell your children it is all right to say no to anyone if that person tries to harm them. Many children are told to always do what grown-ups say.

4 **To get help against bullies.** Tell children to get friends to help them, to say no without fighting and to make sure they tell a grown-up. Tell them to give up something a bully wants (eg money, a bike etc) if they are going to get hurt – you will not be angry with them and keeping themselves safe is the most important consideration.

5 **To tell.** Assure your children that you want them to tell you of any incident and that you will not be angry. Children can also be very protective of parents and might not tell about a frightening occurrence because they are worried about your feelings.

6 **To be believed.** If your children want your help, they need to know they will be believed and supported. This is especially true in the case of sexual assault as children rarely lie about it.

7 **To not keep secrets.** Teach children that some secrets should *never* be kept, no matter if they promised not to tell. Child molesters known to the child often say that a kiss or touch is 'our secret'. This confuses the child who has been taught always to keep secrets.

8 **To refuse touches.** Tell children they can say no to touching or kissing if they don't like it. If someone touches them and tells them to keep it a secret, they *must* tell you. Never force children to hug or kiss anyone.

9 **To not talk to strangers.** Tell your children not to talk to strangers when they are by themselves and to ignore any such approach. Explain that they can pretend not to hear and quickly walk or run away. Tell them you want to know if a stranger tries to talk to them.

very distorted view of the world for the simple reason that good news rarely makes the front page.

— Feeding children information about the cares of the world may give them a sense of fear and powerlessness unless it is also balanced with information about what they can do and how they could respond.

---

10 To break rules. Tell children they can break rules to stay safe. They can run away, scream, lie or kick to get away from danger.

In addition to these key safety messages, parents have also suggested:

— Teaching children their full name, address and telephone number as early as possible. Explain how to dial 999 in emergencies and check they know how to use the telephone.

— Discussing what an emergency is. Children sometimes imagine it means great calamity or threat of death rather than danger.

— Explaining the difference between surprises and secrets. Tell your child that adults can ask a child to keep a surprise (birthday gifts, etc) but never a secret.

— Letting children know the difference between a stranger approaching them (strange behaviour, to be avoided) and them asking a stranger for help in emergencies (sometimes necessary).

— Talking about drugs. Give age-appropriate information and education, such as never touching and always reporting any needles they may find (see Boosting your child's resistance to drugs, p. 332).

— Only let your children stay the night at friends whose families you know and trust. Gently tell them they can phone you day or night, at any time, if they need you.

— Talk about what to do if separated in crowds. Advise children not to wander off in search of you because you won't know where to look. Ask them to stay where they are, shout for you and wait. If you don't come or respond after they have shouted and waited an agreed number of times, tell them to ask for help from a female shop assistant or an adult with children.

— Practise road safety. Once children are confident about the basics, get them to tell you when it is safe to cross the road together.

— Never let young children go into public toilets or changing rooms on their own.

— Talk about telling. Let children know that part of a parent's job is to protect them. You are there to listen and help and they can tell you anything, any time.

Boosting your child's resistance to drugs

Teaching life-skills to primary school children may reduce the risks of drug misuse in their teenage years. Home Office research[16] into one such drugs prevention programme – Project Charlie – shows that children taught how to resist peer pressure and encouraged to value themselves, make decisions and solve problems were less likely to have smoked cigarettes or tried drugs by the time they were 14 than those who had not taken part.

Nancy Hobbs, a drugs education consultant with the project, explains: 'Children need information but they also need the confidence to think matters through, to make decisions for themselves and to feel good about themselves. They need skills to reach out to other people and to cope with peer pressure.

'No teacher or parent can guarantee that a child will not experiment with drugs, but we can give them the skills that will help them as they grow. Feelings are what connect us with other people. If children can't understand and deal with their feelings – embarrassment, fear, anger, etc – they are not in a strong position to cope with the pressures to take drugs.'

The project uses games to help children address the issues and express and explore how they feel (also see Dealing with feelings, p.94 and Friends, p.308). One game has a different emotion written on each side of a die. Children are encouraged to discuss whichever emotion the die lands on and to say when they last experienced it themselves. Other discussions are tailored to the children's age, knowledge and experiences.

'You can't talk usefully to five-year-olds about heroin, but you can talk to them about medicines. About the difference between their medicines and someone else's, about who they would take medicine from – their mother? their teacher? their brother? What if their friend offers them some? By six and seven, you can begin to talk about legal drugs such as alcohol and cigarettes. It's a question of gauging where the children are and working at their level.'

The project, operating in schools in Leeds, Newcastle and London at the time of the Home Office study, faces up to the fact that children are likely to come into contact with drugs, especially as teenagers. Nancy Hobbs suggests parents also wake up to reality.

'It is so important for parents to talk about these issues in an age-appropriate way, so it doesn't become a taboo subject. As children grow older they need to know they can talk to their parents about such matters, but the roots of openness and understanding can begin to be encouraged at a much, much younger age.'

As the Home Office evaluation report states: 'For a growing number of young people, it is too late to attempt early prevention at secondary school. If programmes aim to give pupils resistance and other life skills, they need to give young people these skills before they encounter situations [where they are offered drugs] and at an age when they are prepared to accept advice.'

My son came home from school like Chicken Licken because he'd been told the hole in the ozone layer was letting in all these rays that were zapping us. I told him there was a hole, but people now knew what we needed to do to keep it under control and that you can protect yourself from the rays by using sun cream. He was still concerned, but at least he wasn't terrified.

Anne I

— When and if children hear of an horrific event, it may help to stress that these are rare incidents and to say what grown-ups are doing to find the person(s) responsible and to ensure it doesn't happen again.
— Talking through issues to which your children are exposed can help you allay their fears. Ignoring issues provides no such opportunity.
— Lying can seriously backfire. It is usually possible to answer even tricky questions in a way that gives children the information required but which doesn't overload them with unrequested and unnecessary details. If in doubt, err on the side of caution. If children want to know more, they generally ask.

The value of values

It is accepted that children get their ideas of right and wrong, including their attitudes to violence, from important, caring adults, but they get them first and foremost from adult behaviour that they can see; only secondarily from adult words that they may not understand.[17]

The Commission on Children and Violence

To an extent, children can be trained like rats or dogs by punishing and rewarding their behaviour. But much more importantly, children can also internalise rules, adopt them as their own and understand them. When this happens, children behave for the right reasons, not because they are scared of punishment or withdrawal of love but because the reasons for behaving in certain ways make sense to them and they want to co-operate

Gavin Nobes, lecturer in psychology

Your child's moral sense

Gavin Nobes, lecturer in psychology

'We know that even young children are much more morally sophisticated than we used to believe. Even 20 years ago it was thought that children under the age of 12 had no real understanding of why things are right and wrong and that they obeyed rules simply to avoid punishment and gain rewards.

'We now know that children as young as three show surprising understanding. Many will say that not hitting someone is a more important rule than, for example, not eating with your fingers. Many five-year-olds can tell you that social conventions – rules about eating, dressing and being polite, for example – can be changed and that moral rules – rules about not hitting, stealing, lying and so on – cannot.

'We used to believe that children could not make these distinctions and that they thought all rules were equal in importance. Now we know they are aware that hitting is wrong not just because there is a social command to not do so, but also because it causes distress.

'Parents can help children understand what is right and wrong by explaining clearly and being consistent. It is also important to use simple language and ideas. We should expect children to sometimes forget rules, especially ones that are hard to understand, and try to explain rules rather than punish children for making mistakes.'

By their early school years most children have a sophisticated understanding of right and wrong and an awareness of other people's feelings (see Your child's moral sense, above).

The challenge for us as parents is to recognise and develop this understanding and so equip our children for a life of increasing experience, independence and choices. This gives them the capability to make the right choices even when we are not there to guide them. Equipping them includes:

Developing your child's self-esteem and self-awareness She is more likely to understand and value others if she values and understands herself.

Encouraging respect of other people's feelings Only then can she fully understand the consequences of her actions.

Establishing consistent, firm and fair ground rules for behaviour, encouraged through praise and the controlled use of sanctions.

Helping your child build and enjoy relationships with others

Encouraging your child to articulate emotions and opinions, helping her better understand her decisions and take responsibility for her actions.

Developing your child's ability to handle frustrations and tackle mistakes Help her view them as temporary situations to be dealt with rather than matters to overwhelm or devastate.

Encouraging your child to question, reason, consider and think for herself, so she not only knows how but why she should behave in certain ways.

Showing her the power she has to make choices and change outcomes, to break habits and create her own path in accordance with her own principles.

Which may all sound absurdly optimistic if your sophisticated six- or seven-year-old sometimes sighs in exasperation at the mere sound of your voice. But it can be done.

Reflect on your own behaviour If you have managed to create a family in which self-esteem is generally high and human fallibility understood, in which your unconditional love is a given, children are respected and communication is open and honest most of the time, your child will have already learned a huge amount about tolerance, compassion, co-operation, respect, responsibility and consideration.

Be clear Letting your child know not only your expectations of her behaviour but also the reasons why will help to reaffirm your principles and priorities.

Avoid parent traps The two most common ones almost every parent walks into occasionally are:

— *Absolutes.* As in 'never', 'always', 'worst', 'best'. Only use these if you know you can stick to them yourself and expect your children to do the same. 'Never lie' may rebound in a way that 'it is wrong to lie' or 'it is important to tell the truth' may not. 'We don't hit in this house' holds no water if you sometimes do. Simple statements like 'Sorry is the hardest word' may trip you up if your child finds a harder one. 'Sorry is very hard to say' leaves you less vulnerable to contradiction.

If you say 'always tell the truth', the moment they see you break from the 'always', the whole scheme is broken, and life isn't like that, it is much more graduated. Most days we fall from our own standards by some percent. Parents should try to help children see there is something to aspire to rather than to see life in terms of either all good or all bad, or associating doing something your family prefers you not to do with being a bad person.

Vivienne Gross, Clinical Director, The Institute of Family Therapy

— *Talking above children's heads.* Children's moral sense may be more sophisticated than we generally give them credit for, but it is also easy to overburden them with complexities when they are still getting to grips with the basics. Life throws up imperfections and dilemmas, and these can be discussed as they arise if your child seems ready or interested, but it is probably best not to overwhelm them with real-life exceptions to rules until the rules are set in place.

With young children, where you have a clash of moral issues things become more difficult. For example, to say you love the jumper your grandmother has knitted when you clearly don't, throws up the moral dilemma of deciding between lying and not hurting somebody. This is quite complicated and it is not really fair to expect children to understand.

Gavin Nobes, lecturer in psychology

Such morally ambivalent and adult concepts as 'white lies' are likely to confuse young children and are probably best avoided. Keep things as clear, simple and positive as you can, explaining, say, that you know it is good to tell the truth and you also know it is good not to hurt people's feelings unnecessarily but you had to decide what to do for the best in that situation.

Check, too, that children understand the words you use. 'Respect other people' isn't going to cut much ice if they don't know what

THE VALUE OF VALUES

Exploring tales together

Carol Munro, primary headteacher

'Our school is tremendously diverse. We don't have a dominant culture and there are 42 languages spoken by pupils. In such an environment we have to develop understanding among us, we have to get along and all be aware of what behaviour is expected and why. All our children have to feel comfortable and accepted. We have to build their self-esteem and self awareness, and their respect for themselves and each other. All these spring from a growing understanding of themselves, other people and the world around them.

'How to encourage that understanding? Stories make the issues come alive for children. You can draw them in through their imagination and their own experiences and encourage them to explore new situations and considerations – How would you feel if . . ? How did they feel when . . ? What could she have done . . ? What will happen now . . ?

'In this way, stories can be used to develop children's moral sense. Through them they can reflect on what they know or feel; put themselves in somebody else's shoes and broaden their understanding of other's experiences and emotions; examine actions and consequences; explore moral dilemmas; challenge their own experiences and view issues from a distance when sometimes personal experience is too close to unravel.

'Most reception-age children will take stories at face-value, but that's OK. Important messages are still going in. By year one (age 5/6) children are able to analyse and consider, understand and feel. The more sensitive and brighter ones in particular really benefit from this kind of interaction.' (See Stories to explore with your children, p.348 for details of books dealing with issues of relevance and interest to young children).

'respect' means. Simple language and examples of how respect can be shown to others may be much more useful.

Children are very concrete. You will probably have to say to a child of five, 'Tell me what you saw happen'. If you say 'Tell the truth', it is loaded with values and moral imperatives they may not understand.
Vivienne Gross, Clinical Director, The Institute of Family Therapy

Explore issues together It helps to explore the relevance, application and complexity of moral issues in ways children enjoy and understand (see Exploring tales together, above). Try to avoid anything that smacks of knitted brows or ponderous instruction – stories can be told in books, films, videos, songs, television programmes. Excite and entice your child's curiosity and invite her to think through situations for herself – 'How does that character feel?', 'What would you do in that situation?' 'Why?' (see Encouraging enquiry, p.298).

Once children understand why morals matter, they can claim them as their own rather than have them imposed upon them by their parents. This lies at the root of self-regulation, of children managing their own behaviour and making moral decisions even in their parents' absence, of choosing for themselves the best way to behave even in difficult or challenging situations. It is fundamental to their ability to respect others and to respect themselves, of their consideration, resilience and confidence from now to adulthood.

As ever, focus first on those approaches you feel would benefit your child most. Remember, too, that every small, positive step you take as a parent will have an impact on your child's life. Do what you can, when you can and you will make a difference.

No parent can know what the future holds, but supporting and encouraging our children now will help them develop the courage, confidence and understanding they need to be themselves, to face the future and take their place in it.

APPENDIX 1

References

CHAPTER TWO

Baby's needs, your needs

1   Film on premature infants, Van Rees, S and de Leeuw, R (1987) *Born Too Early: The Kangaroo Method With Premature Babies*. Video by Strichting Lichaamstaal, Body Language Media Centre, The Netherlands

2   *The First Relationship: Infant and Mother*, Daniel Stern, Harvard University Press, 1997

3   Separation distress call in the human neonate in the absence of maternal body contact, Christensson, K et al, 1995, Acta Paediatrica, Vol. 84, pp468–473

4   Source: Midwives Information and Resource Service (MIDIRS)

5   Infant crying pattern in the first year – normal community and clinical findings, St James-Roberts I, Halil A, *Journal of Child Psychology and Psychiatry*. Vol. 32, pp951–968, 1991

6   *ibid.*

7   As described in *The First Relationship: Infant and Mother*, Daniel Stern, Harvard University Press, 1997

8   Source: The Association for Post-natal Illness

9   Post-natal Depression, The Association for Post-natal Illness, 1997

10 *ibid.*

11 Can non–psychotic depression be prevented? Perinatal Psychiatry Use and Misuse of Edinburgh Post-natal Depression Scale, Cox J.L, Holden J.M. (Eds): London Gaskell (1994) 1994, Child Abuse Review, 3, pp299–310

CHAPTER THREE

Sleep solutions

1   Separation distress call in the human neonate in the absence of maternal body contact, Christensson, K et al, 1995, Acta Paediatrica, Vol. 84, pp468-473

2   Infant crying pattern in the first year – normal community and clinical findings, St. James-Roberts I, Halil A, Journal of Child Psychology and Psychiatry, 1991, Vol.32, pp951-968

3   The World Health Organisation, Quality of Life Association (WHOQUAL: Development and General Psychometric Properties, Social Science and Medicine, 1998, Vol. 46, pp1569–1585)

CHAPTER FOUR

Feeding and food wars

1 Breastfeeding or Bottle Feeding, Informed Choice for Professionals, MIDIRS (the Midwives Information and Resource Service), 1997

2 Breastfeeding in the United Kingdom in 1995, Office for National Statistics

3 Source: MIDIRS

4 Advice from the Government's Committee on Toxicity of Chemicals in Food, Consumer Products and the Environment (COT), 1998

5 From Chronic and severe eating problems in young children, Jo Douglas, consultant clinical psychologist, Hospital for Sick Children, Great Ormond Street. Health Visitor 1991: Vol. 64. No 10: 334-336

6 Promoting consumption of vegetables; A qualitative exploration study of women's knowledge and attitudes – practice, Stead M, Goodlad N, Glasgow: University of Strathclyde Centre For Social Marketing, June 1996

7 An observational study of mothers with eating disorders and their infants, Stein A, Woolley H, Cooper SD, Fairburn G, Journal of Psychology and Psychiatry 1994, Vol. 35, pp733-748.

8 Children attending the Feeding Clinic, The Children's Hospital, Birmingham

9 Effect of deprivation on weight gain in infancy, Waterston A, Acta Paediatrica, 1994, Vol. 83, pp357-9

10 National Diet and Nutrition Survey: Children Aged 1½–4½ years, Gregory J et al, London, HMSO, 1995

11 Food for the Growing Years, Paediatric Group, British Dietetic Association, 1990

12 Is water out of vogue? A survey of the drinking habits of 2-7 year olds, Petter L P et al, Archives of Disease in Childhood, Southampton University, Vol. 72 (2), pp137-140, February 1995

CHAPTER FIVE

Communication

1 From *Children and Violence*, Report of the Commission on Children and Violence, convened by the Gulbenkian Foundation, Calouste Gulbenkian Foundation, London, 1995

2 Tactics in Social Influence, Mehrabian A, Prentice-Hall, Englewood, Cliffs, New Jersey, 1969

3 The validity and accuracy of a screening test for developmental language delay, Ward S, European Journal of Disorders of Communication, March 1992; An investigation into the effectiveness of an early intervention for language delay in young children, Ward S, accepted for International Journal of Language and Communication Disorders, January 2000

4 Talking About My Generation: a survey of 8–15 year olds growing up in the 1990s, Ghate D and Daniels A, London, NSPCC, 1997

CHAPTER SIX

Dealing with feelings

1   *Children and Violence*, Report of the Commission on Children and Violence, convened by the Gulbenkian Foundation, Calouste Gulbenkian Foundation, 1995

2   The extent of parental punishment in the UK, Newson J, Newson N, Approach 1989; Antisocial boys: A social interactional approach, Patterson G R et al, 1992; Family factors as correlates and predictors of juvenile conduct problems and delinquency, Loeber R, Stouthamer-Loebar M, in Crime and Justice: An Annual Review of Research, Edited by Michael Tonry and Norval Morris, Vol.7, 1986

3   *The Heart of Parenting*, John Gottman with Joan Declaire, Bloomsbury, 1997

4   Process and evaluation of a group intervention for mothers with parenting difficulties, Puckering C et al, Child Abuse Review, 3, 1994, 299-310

5   *Children and Violence*, Report of the Commission on Children and Violence (*op. cit.*)

6   *Self-esteem and Successful Early Learning*, Roberts R, Hodder & Stoughton, 1995; Building intimacy in relationships with young children in nurseries, Elfer P, Early Years, 1996

7   Family Forum, Family Life: The Age of Anxiety, NCH Action For Children, 1997

8   A three-year study of care and learning of children under three in nurseries, Elfer P and Selleck D, funded by the Esmel Fairbairn Charity Trust, spring 1999

CHAPTER SEVEN

Horribly normal

1   *Children and Violence*, Report of the Commission on Children and Violence convened by the Gulbenkian Foundation, Calouste Gulbenkian Foundation, London 1995

2   From Rearing competent children, Diana Baumrind, Chapter 17 in Child Development Today and Tomorrow, Damon W (Ed), New York: Jossey, 1989

3   How toddlers 'do' friendship: a descriptive analysis of naturally occurring friendships in a group child care setting, Whaley KL, Rubenstein TS, Journal of Social and Personal Relationships, 1994, referred to in Communication between babies in their first year, Elinor Goldschmied and Dorothy Selleck, National Children's Bureau

4   *Children and Violence*, Report of the Commission on Children and Violence (*op. cit.*)

CHAPTER EIGHT

Encouraging positive behaviour

1   *Children and Violence*, Report of the Commission on Children and Violence convened by the Gulbenkian Foundation, Calouste Gulbenkian Foundation, London, 1995

2   As in Rearing competent children, Diana Baumrind, Chapter 17 in Child Development Today and Tomorrow, Damon W (Ed), New York: Jossey

CHAPTER NINE

Effective discipline

1   This HMSO publication is the third which summarises and disseminates the results of childcare research, funded by the Department of Health

2   *Beating the Devil out of Them*, Straus M A, Jossey-Bass Inc., San Francisco, 1994

3   Corporal punishment by mothers and child's cognitive development: A longitudinal study paper, Straus MA, Paschall MJ, presented at the 14th World Congress of Sociology, Montreal, Quebec, Canada; Durham NH: Family Research Laboratory, University of New Hampshire

4   *Children and Violence*, Report of the Commission on Children and Violence convened by the Gulbenkian Foundation, Calouste Gulbenkian Foundation, London, 1995

5   Including that summarised in *Children and Violence*, Report of the Commission on Children and Violence (*op. cit.*); Violence – directions from Australia, National Committee on Violence, Australian Institute of Criminology, Canberra, 1990; Summary report of the American Psychological Association Commission on Violence and Youth, 1993

6   Child Protection (1995), Messages from Research, Bullock R et al. Dartington Social Research Unit, HMSO

7   The development of an individual's potential for violence, understanding and preventing violence, Reiss AJ and Roth JA (eds), National Academy Press, Washington DC, 1993

8   A community study of physical violence to children in the home, and associated variables, Marjorie Smith, Thomas Coram Research Unit, London, presented at International Society for the Prevention of Child Abuse and Neglect, Fifth European Conference on Child Abuse and Neglect, Oslo, 1995

9   A community study of physical violence to children in the home (*op. cit.*)

10 Infant care in an urban community, Newson E, Newson J, Allen & Unwin, London, 1963

CHAPTER TEN

Important relationships

1   A community study of physical violence to children in the home, and associated variables, Marjorie Smith, Thomas Coram Research Unit, presented at International Society for the Prevention of Child Abuse and Neglect, Norway, 1995

2   Fathers and Fatherhood in Britain: Findings, Joseph Rowntree Foundation, Social Policy Research 120, July 1997

3   Journal of the Society of Pediatric Nurses, Anderson AM, Vol. 1, no 2, Jul-Sep 1996, pp83-92, MIDIRS Midwifery Digest (Mar 1997) 7:1

4   Parenting in the 1990s, Elsa Ferri and Kate Smith, Social Policy Research, Joseph Rowntree Foundation, October 1996

5   Survey by Mori, commissioned by the NSPCC, published April 1997

6   *Ibid.*

7   Father Figures Fathers in the Families of the 1990s, edited by Peter Moss, Edinburgh HMSO, first published 1995

8   Parenting in the 1990s (*op. cit.*)

9   Fathers and Fatherhood in Britain (*op. cit.*)

10 *Ibid.*

11 Talking About My Generation, a survey of 8–15 year olds growing up in the 1990s, by Deborah Ghate and Andrea Daniles, NSPCC, March 1997

12 Survey by Mori (*op. cit.*)

13 *Children and Violence*, Report of the Commission on Children and Violence convened by the Gulbenkian Foundation, Calouste Gulbenkian Foundation, London 1995

14 Research and policy in early childhood services: time for a new agenda, Mooney A and Munton AG, Thomas Coram Research Unit, Institute of Education, University of London, 1997

15 IDS (Incomes Data Services Ltd), study 630, July 1997

16 Research and policy in early childhood services, Mooney A and Munton AG (*op. cit.*)

17 Parenting in the 1990s (*op. cit.*)

18 *Children and Violence*, Report of the Commission on Children and Violence (*op. cit.*)

CHAPTER ELEVEN

Coping in hard times

1   The Tomorrow's Men/Women at the Millennium projects: Factors associated with high and low self-esteem. A study for the Mental Health Foundation, Katz A, Buchanan A, 1999

2   Child Protection: Messages from Research, Bullock R et al, 1995, HMSO; Dartington Social Research Unit

3   The Tomorrow's Men/Women at the Millennium projects (*op. cit.*), confirming the findings in *The Can-do Girls – A Barometer of Change* by Adrienne Katz, research based on the *Express on Sunday* Girlstalk Survey and further work in association with Ann Buchanan and JoAnn Ten Brinke, University of Oxford

4   Family conflict and slow growth, Montgomery S et al, The Archives of Diseases in Childhood, Vol. 77, No 4, October 1997, 00 326 – 330

5   *Growing Up In Stepfamilies*, Gill Gorell Barnes, Paul Thompson, Gwyn Daniel and Natasha Burchardt, Oxford University Press, 1998

6   *The Snowman*, Raymond Briggs, Puffin Books

7   Sources: National Stepfamily Association, The British Household Panel Survey and Fathers and Fatherhood in Britain: Joseph Rowntree Foundation, Findings, Social Policy Research 120, July 1997

8   *Dinosaurs Divorce: A guide for changing families*, Laurene Krasny Brown and Mark Brow, Little, Brown & Co

9   *Growing Up In Stepfamilies* (*op. cit.*)

10   *Ibid.*

CHAPTER TWELVE

Gender and development

1   *We Know It's Tough To Talk: Boys In Need Of Help*, Mary MacLeod and Christine Barter, ChildLine, April 1996

2   Up to half the space in traditional playgrounds was regularly taken up by as few as a quarter of all pupils (all boys) for football, play analyst Marc Armitage reported to the Children's Oral Culture conference, Sheffield University, April 1998

3   *We Know It's Tough To Talk* (*op. cit.*)

4   From *Children and Violence*, Report of the Commission on Children and Violence convened by the Gulbenkian Foundation, Calouste Gulbenkian Foundation, London 1995

5   Introduction: male violence in perspective, John Archer, in *Male Violence*, ed. John Archer, Routledge, 1994

6   Elizabeth Grugeon, senior lecturer in teacher education at De Montfort University, Bedford, talking to an international conference of Children's Oral Culture at Sheffield University, April 1998

7   *The Can-Do Girls – A Barometer of Change*, Adrienne Katz, October 1997, based on the *Express on Sunday* Girlstalk Survey and further work undertaken at The Department of Applied Social Studies and Research, Oxford University

8   Gender research in educational achievement, Lee B et al, National Foundation for Educational Research, August 1998

9   Source: Department for Education and Employment

10 Trends in reading at 8, Brooks G et al, National Federation for Educational Research in England and Wales, Slough 1997

11 How in the world do students read, Warwick B, Elley WB, IEA Study of Reading Literacy – The International Association for the Evaluation of Educational Achievement, July 1992; Lasting Differences: The High-Scope Preschool Curriculum Comparison Study Through Age 23, Schweinhart LJ, Weikart DP, High-Scope Press, 1997

12 Gender research in educational achievement, National Foundation for Educational Research (*op. cit.*)

13 SATS figures, DfEE: % of 7-year-old pupils achieving level 2 or above, England 1996. In maths and science girls outperformed boys only slightly; in English (teacher assessment) boys 74%, girls 84%

14 GCSE results 1996, DfEE: grades A–C in English, girls 64.4%; boys 46.9%. 1996 AS/A-level pass rates in English, girls 88.5%; boys 86.5%

15 Britain's Early Years Disaster, Mills C, Mills D, Channel 4, November 1997, prepared for the National Task Force on Mathematics. (Formed the basis of Channel 4's Dispatches 'Too Much Too Young', January 1998)

16 *The Can-Do Girls* (*op. cit.*)

17 *Ibid.*

18 Exclusions from LEA primary schools, 1995-1996 academic year: boys 93%, girls 7%, The School Census, DfEE, 1996

19 *Understanding Our Daughters*, Adrienne Katz, Exploring Parenthood, 1998: part of the Women At The Millennium Project

CHAPTER THIRTEEN

Play and learning

1 Child's play: facilitating play on housing estates, Whewa R, Millward A, The Chartered Institute of Housing, June 1997

2 *Children and Violence*, Report of the Commission on Children and Violence, convened by the Gulbenkian Foundation, Calouste Gulbenkian Foundation, 1995

3 US psychologist Prof. Philip Zimbardo, to the British Psychological Society, University College Cardiff, July 1997

4 Recommendation by Peter Avis, director of the British Educational Communications and Technology Agency, following research by Nottingham University psychologist Professor David Wood, May 1998

5 See, for example, research into the effects of television on children on St Helena – project funded by the Economic and Social Research Council and led by Tony Charlton, Professor of Behaviour Studies at Cheltenham and Gloucester College of Higher Education. Also Violence – Directions From

Australia, National Committee on Violence, Australian Institute of Criminology, Canberra, 1990

6   A *Sunday Times* survey of more than 2,250 children, June 1996
7   The *Guardian*, April 27, 1998
8   Children and Film/Video/TV Violence, Glasgow Media Group, 1997
9   *Children and Violence*, Report of the Commission on Children and Violence (*op. cit.*)
10 Recommendations for good practice in the Government's Numeracy Task Force's preliminary report, Numeracy Matters, January 1998

CHAPTER FOURTEEN

Growing independence

1   As detailed in Does friendship moderate the harmful effects of peer victimisation and if so, how? Boulton MJ, Chau C, 1998, submitted for publication
2   The Absence and Presence of Fathers: Accounts from Children's Diaries. O'Brien M, Jones D, Men's Family Relations, Bjornberg U and Collind A-K, Almqvist & Wiksell, Stockholm, 1996
3   Commissioned by *Family Circle* magazine, published January 1988
4   *Why Me?* Children Talking to ChildLine About Bullying, A ChildLine Study written by Mary MacLeod and Sally Morris, ChildLine, 1996
5   The development of an individual's potential for violence, Understanding and preventing violence, Reiss AJ and Roth JA (eds), US National Academy of Sciences, National Academy Press, Washington DC, 1993
6   *Children and Violence*, Report of the Commission on Children and Violence, convened by the Gulbenkian Foundation, Calouste Gulbenkian Foundation, 1995
7   *Why Me?* A ChildLine Study (*op. cit.*)
8   *Why Me?* A ChildLine Study (*op. cit.*)
9   *Children and Violence* (*op. cit.*)
10 As detailed in Peer Mediation Scheme, by Vicki Smith et al, Bristol Mediation, Woodspring Education Resource Centre 1995 (first implemented in Callicroft and Coniston Primary Schools, Patchway, Bristol); and Changing Our School: promoting positive behaviour, Highfield Primary School, Plymouth and the Institute of Education, University of London, 1997
11 Why Me? A ChildLine Study (*op. cit.*)
12 *Ibid.*
13 Child Accident Prevention Trust, June 1998
14 Kidscape, 1993
15 One False Move, Mayer Hillman et al, The Policy Studies Institute, 1991
16 Project Charlie: An Evaluation of A Life Skills Drug Education Programme

for Primary Schools, Prof. Harry McGurk and Dr Jane Hurry, Home Office Drugs Prevention Initiative, January 1995; A Follow-Up Evaluation of Project Charlie, Dr Jane Hurry and Charlie Lloyd, Home Office Drug Prevention Initiative, November 1997

17 *Children and Violence*, Report of the Commission on Children and Violence (*op. cit.*)

Stories to explore with your children

Suggested by Carol Munro, primary headteacher

CO–OPERATION

The Owl and The Woodpecker, Brian Wildsmith (OUP, 1992)
Who Sank The Boat?, Pamela Allen (Puffin Books, 1990)

EMOTIONS

The Velveteen Rabbit, Margery Williams (Roundhouse Publishing, 1998)

RELATIONSHIPS/FRIENDSHIP

The Village of Round and Square Houses, Ann Grifalconi
(Macmillan, 1989)
My Sister Then and Now, Virginia Kroll (Carol Rhoda Books, 1993)

SELF-ESTEEM

Amazing Grace, Mary Hoffman (Frances Lincoln, 1991)
Marcellus, Lorraine Simeon (Black Butterfly Books, 1995)

THE NATURAL WORLD

Out and About, Shirley Hughes (Walker Books, 1988)
Mr Bear and the Bear, Frances Thomas (Red Fox, 1997)

PRIDE/VANITY

The Rainbow Fish, Marcus Pfister (North-South Books, 1995)

BEREAVEMENT

Badger's Parting Gifts, Susan Varley (Picture Lions, 1992)

ASPIRATIONS

Joshua's Masai Mask, Dakari Hru (Lee and Low Books, 1994)

PROMISES
A Promise to the Sun, Tololwa Mollel (Little, Brown, 1992)

LOVE
Dogger, Shirley Hughes (Red Fox, 1993)
Noisy Nora, Rosemary Wells (Doubleday, 1998)

FEAR
The Big Storm, Dave and Julie Saunders (Frances Lincoln, 1994)
Little Beaver and the Echo, Amy MacDonald (Walker Books, 1990)

FRIENDS
My Best Friend, Pat Hutchins (Red Fox, 1995)
The Honey Hunters, Francesca Martin (Walker Books, 1994)

HAPPINESS
From a Child's Heart, Nikki Grimes (Just Us Books, 1994)

BEAUTY
The Whale's Song, Dyan Sheldon and Gary Blythe (Red Fox, 1993)
My Grandpa and the Sea, Katherine Orr (Carol Rhoda Books, 1992)

BEHAVIOUR
The Princess and the Moon, Daisaku Ikeda (OUP, 1991)

SELFISHNESS/SHARING
Mine, Hiawyn Oram (Frances Lincoln, 1992)
John Brown, Rose and the Midnight Cat, Jenny Wagner
(Picture Puffin, 1995)

The Contributors

Corinne Abisgold is an educational psychologist and Project Leader for Early Years Behaviour Curriculum: A Social and Emotional Curriculum for Young Children, Borough of Westminster.

Caroline Abrahams is Head of Public Policy at NCH Action For Children.

Gill Gorell Barnes is an Honorary Senior Clinical Lecturer at the Tavistock Clinic London, a family therapist, researcher and author of: *Family Therapy in Changing Lives*, Macmillan, 1998; with Emilia Dowling (forthcoming) *Working with Families through Separation and Divorce: The Changing Lives of Children*, Macmillan, 1999, and *You're Both Still My Parents*, Prestige Health Productions (Video),1997

Camila Batmanghelidjha is a psychotherapist with extensive experience of taking therapeutic work into communities. She campaigns for improved resources and increased access in child mental health. She founded the charities: The Place To Be and Kids Company.

Paula Bell is a health visitor.

Steve Biddulph is a British-born psychologist and best-selling author who lives in Australia. He visits the UK twice yearly for Parent Network. Further Reading: *The Mother and Baby Book*, Shaaron Biddulph, Leopard Books, 1997; *Raising Boys*, Thorsons UK, September 1998; *More Secrets of Happy Children*, Steve and Shaaron Biddulph, Thorsons UK, March 1999.

Lisa Blakemore-Brown is an independent chartered psychologist, author and Chairwoman of Promoting Parenting Skills, a national group of psychologists committed to the use of an empirical research base for parent programmes.

Dr Michael Boulton is a child psychologist in the Department of Psychology at Keele University. He has carried out extensive research on aggression, bullying and victimisation.

John Bristow is a psychologist working in organisations, a psychotherapist in private practice, and a Parent Network co-ordinator.

Elizabeth Mary Bryan MD FRCP FRCPCH is an Honorary Consultant Paediatrician at Queen Charlotte's and Chelsea Hospital, London, and Director of the Multiple Births Foundation. She was co-founder of the Twins and Multiple Births Association. She is Vice-President of the International Society of Twin Studies. Her books include: *Twins, Triplets and More*, Penguin, 1992; *Twins and Higher Multiple Births: A Guide to their Nature and Nurture*, Edward Arnold, 1992.

José von Bühler, RMN, CPN, Dip. Human Sexuality, BASMT Accred, MSc in Human Sexuality. He is sexual and relationship psychotherapist, Director of von Bühler Associates, working from The Cardinal Clinic, Berkshire.

Domenico Di Ceglie is a consultant child and adolescent psychiatrist at the Tavistock Clinic and Director of the Gender Identity Development Unit,

Portman Clinic. He is Honorary Senior Lecturer, Royal Free Hospital School of Medicine, London, and editor of *A Stranger in My Own Body*, Karnac Books (1998).

Christine Chittick is an NCT ante-natal teacher.

Linda Connell is a counsellor, a trainer in communication and group work skills and a Parent-Infant Facilitator for PIPPIN (see Contacts, p.355).

Anne Cowling is a secondary school teacher working with the Leeds Attendance and Behaviour Project.

Jane Cutler is Head of Music at The Da Capo School of Music, London, 'committed to developing a new approach to music education'.

Barbara Dale is a Parent Network co-ordinator and counsellor

Sarah Darton works as a health visitor and Parent Network co-ordinator.

Hilton Davis is Professor of Child Health Psychology at Guy's, King's and St Roman's Hospitals, The Medical and Dental School and the Lewisham & Guy's Mental Health Trust.

Peter Elfer is Senior Development Officer in the Early Childhood Unit at the National Children's Bureau.

Dr Michele Elliott is the Director of Kidscape children's charity and an author.

Pat Elliot is a psychotherapist, bereavement counsellor and trainer. Further reading: *Coping with Loss – For Parents*, Piccadilly Press, 1997.

Christine Fahey is a Montessori nursery teacher and proprietor.

Dr Robert Fisher is Senior Lecturer in Education and Director of the Centre for Research in Teaching Thinking at Brunel University. His books include: *Teaching Children to Think*, Stanley Thornes, 1995; *Teaching Children to Learn*, Stanley Thornes,

1995; *Stories for Thinking*, Nash Pollock, 1996; *Poems for Thinking*, Nash Pollock, 1997; *Games for Thinking*, Nash Pollock, 1997; *Teaching Thinking*, Cassell, 1998.

Hugh Foot is Professor of Psychology at the University of Strathclyde, specialising in child psychology and social development.

Robin Freeland is a freelance educational psychologist.

Edie Freeman is a homoeopath (LCH) who works from two clinics: The North End Road Practice, 8 Burghley Road, London NW5 1UE and The Viveka Clinic (see below).

Yehudi Gordon is a consultant gynaecologist and obstetrician, specialising in holistic health. He works at the Birth Unit of The Hospital of St John & St Elizabeth, London and at his clinic, Viveka, 27a Queens Terrace, London NW8 6EA.

Vivienne Gross is Clinical Director of The Institute of Family Therapy.

Angela Gruber is a psychotherapist.

Gulbenkian Foundation The foundation gives grants in the UK and Ireland for the Arts, Education and Social Welfare.

Kitty Hagenbach is a psychotherapist.

Carol Ann Hally works as a health visitor and clinical practice teacher.

Dr Gillian Harris is Senior Lecturer in Developmental Psychology at the School of Psychology, University of Birmingham. She is also a clinical psychologist and is Head of The Feeding Clinic at The Children's Hospital, Birmingham.

Eileen Hayes is The Parenting Advisor to the NSPCC, a Trustee of Parenting Education and Support Forum (c/o National Children's Bureau, 8 Wakely Street, London EC1V 7QE) and Chair of its Media and Parenting Group. This forum brings together those concerned with or working in the field of preparation, education and support for parents.

Ann Herreboudt is a midwife and family therapist on the Birth Unit at St John and St Elizabeth's Hospital and at the Viveka Clinic (see above).

Dr Andrew Hill is a psychologist at the Division of Psychiatry and Behavioural Sciences at Leeds University.

Nancy Hobbs is a drugs education consultant with Project Charlie, a drugs prevention programme for primary school children.

Simon James, The Association of Post-natal Illness (see Contacts, p.355)

Noël Janis-Norton is the Director of The New Learning Centre, offering training workshops for pupils, parents and professionals who work with young people and parents.

Adrienne Katz is an author, journalist and research associate (Department of Applied Social Studies, Oxford University). Further reading includes: *You Can Teach Your Child to Read*, Thorsons, 1989; *Can-do Girls – A Barometer of Change*, The Department of Applied Social Studies and Research, Oxford University, October 1997.

Gez Lamb is an osteopath with special emphasis on the 'cranial' approach. He works from 1 Oldbury Place, London, W1M 3AN.

Mary MacLeod is Director of Policy and Research at ChildLine (see Contacts, p.355).

Doro Marden is Chair of Parent Network Executive Committee and a Parent Network co-ordinator.

Bethan Marshall is a lecturer in education at King's College London, specialising in gender and literacy.

Peter Mellor is a counsellor and parent skills trainer.

Clare Mills is a qualified speech and language therapist and co-author (with David Mills) of *Britain's Early Years Disaster*,

Channel 4, 1997, prepared for the National Task Force on Mathematics.

Sue Monk is the Chief Executive of Parents at Work (see Contacts, p.355).

Ann Mooney is a child psychologist and Research Officer at the Thomas Coram Research Unit, Institute of Education, University of London. Recent publications include: Mooney, A and Munton, A.G. (1997) *Choosing Childcare*. Aldershot: Arena. Mooney, A and Munton, A.G. (1997) *Research and Policy in Early Childhood Services: Time for a New Agenda*. London: Institute of Education.

Carol Munro is a primary headteacher and member of Brent SACRE (Standing Advisory Council on Religious Education).

Elizabeth Newson is Emeritus Professor of Developmental Psychology, University of Nottingham, an author and consultant to The Early Years Diagnostic Centre. She has researched and published extensively in child development.

Gavin Nobes is a lecturer and researcher in developmental psychology at the University of East London, specialising in moral development and social influences of pro- and anti-social behaviour.

John Oates is a developmental psychologist in the Centre for Human Development and Learning, Open University. Further reading: *The Foundations of Child Development*, Oates, J (ed), Blackwells, 1994.

Jenny Oberon is a deputy-head teacher presently seconded to the Leeds Attendance and Behaviour Project. This project aims to engage children with education and schooling by working with children, their parents, schools and communities. It is jointly funded by Leeds City Council and DfEE and presently works with 20 primary and six secondary inner city schools to reduce exclusions.

Susie Orbach is a psychotherapist and writer.

Dr Pat Petrie is Senior Research Lecturer at the Thomas Coram Research Unit, Institute of Education, University of London.

Dr Greg Philo is Research Director at the Glasgow University Media Unit.

Judith Philo is a psychotherapist.

Christine Puckering is a clinical psychologist and Senior Research Fellow at the University of Glasgow. She is Co-founder of Mellow Parenting which is an intensive prevention and intervention programme for situations where there is grave concern about parenting. Recent publications: Taking Control: A single Case Study of Mellow Parenting, Puckering C, Evans S, Maddox H, Mills M and Cox AD, Clinical Child Psychology and Psychiatry 1 p539-550, 1996; Bringing about change in parent-child relationships, Mills M and Puckering C, in *The Emotional Needs of Young Children and Families*, J. Trowell and M. Bower (eds), Routledge, 1995.

Professor Kathryn Riley is Director of the Centre of Educational Management, Roehampton Institute, London.

Penelope Robinson is Director of Professional Affairs, The Chartered Society of Physiotherapy.

Dr Dorothy Rowe has worked as a teacher, child psychologist, and clinical psychologist in the NHS. She has researched and written extensively. Her work is concerned with meaning and communication. Her books include: *Depression: The Way Out of Your Prison*, Routledge, 1983, second edition 1996; *Beyond Fear*, HarperCollins, 1987; *The Successful Self*, HarperCollins, 1988; *The Depression Handbook*, HarperCollins, 1990, reissued as *Breaking the Bonds*, 1991; *Time on Our Side*, HarperCollins, 1994; *Dorothy Rowe's Guide to Life*, HarperCollins, 1995.

Dorothy Selleck is a Senior Development Officer in the Early Childhood Unit at the National Children's Bureau.

Marjorie Smith is a psychologist, Deputy Director at the Thomas Coram Unit and Reader in the Psychology of the Family at the Institute of Education. She has been carrying out research on children and families for over twenty years.

Lolly Stirk is a child-birth educator who specialises in pregnancy and post-natal yoga.

Brigid Treacy is a Parent Network co-ordinator.

Professor Colwyn Trevarthen is a biologist specialising in the communication of feelings, purposes, interests and ideas. He is Professor (Emeritus) of Child Psychology and Psychobiology at the University of Edinburgh. Further reading includes: Conversations with a two-month-old, *New Scientist*, 2 May: 230-235, 1974; Playing into Reality: Conversations with the infant communicator, Winnicott Studies, Number 7, Spring, 1993: 67-84. London: Karnac Books Ltd, 1993; The child's need to learn a culture, Children and Society, 9 (1): 5-19 1995.

Nicholas Tucker, formerly an educational psychologist, is now lecturing in Cultural and Community Studies at the University of Sussex.

Peter Walker is a pioneer of baby massage and soft gymnastics for children. His new video *Baby Massage and Movement* is available for £13.99 (p&p inc, UK only) from Little Venice Films, PO Box 8293, London W9 2WZ. Further reading: *Baby Massage*, Piatkus, reprinted 1998.

Brian Waller is a Director of Home-Start (see Contacts, p.355).

Cheryl Walters is Head of Research and Policy at the National Stepfamily Association (see Contacts, p.355)

Louise Walters works as a volunteer with Serene and the Cry-sis Helpline and was

Chair of Serene and Cry-sis from November 1996–November 1998 (see Contacts, p.355).

Dr Sally Ward is a specialist paediatric speech and language therapist. She is also the originator of the Wilstaar Programme (a preventative programme for speech and language disability and accelerated language development in all children).

Stella Ward is a qualified nurse and now works as a Parent Network co-ordinator.

Frances Wheen is a journalist and broadcaster.

Jim Wilson is a psychotherapist. He works as a family therapist with The Family Institute in Cardiff (Banardos) and as a freelance trainer and consultant. Further reading: *Child-Focused Practice*, Karnac, 1998.

Peter Wilson worked for many years as a social worker and psychotherapist, both in the community and residentially with emotionally disturbed young people. He is the Director of Young Minds, the children's mental health charity (see Contacts, p.355).

Gill Wood is an NCT ante-natal teacher.

In writing this book we have spoken to hundreds of parents from all walks of life in a huge variety of settings and situations. Those quoted have been identified in the text by their first name and first initial of their surname. Some parents have requested that their first names be changed.

Contacts

Help with specific problems

Bereavement

Cruse Bereavement Care
  Cruse House
  126 Sheen Road
  Richmond
  Surrey
  TW9 1UR
  Tel: 0181 940 4818 (office)
Offers free help to those affected by bereavement, with opportunities for social support and practical advice.

  Cruse National Bereavement Line: 0181
  332 7227
  Cruse Youth Line: 0181 940 3131

FSID (Foundation for the Study of Infant Deaths)
  14 Halkin Street
  London SW1X 7DP
  Tel: 0171 235 0965 (office)
  Helpline: 0171 235 1721
Provides support to bereaved families and advice to anyone concerned about cot death.

London Bereavement Network
  356 Holloway Road
  London N7 6PA
  Tel: 0171 700 8134
A referral network for bereavement training, counselling and practical help for people in London.

Child Development Support

Child Growth Foundation
  2 Mayfield Avenue
  London W4 1PW
  Tel: 0181 994 7625
For parents who are concerned about the growth of their children. Information and support groups.

Gender Identity Development Unit
  Portman Clinic
  8 Fitzjohns Avenue
  London NW3 5NA
  Tel: 0171 794 8262
Offers a service to children, adolescents and their parents where there are concerns about the gender identity development of the young person; a parent group is available for parents of children who attend the clinic.

Information Service of the Early Years Diagnostic Centre
  272 Longdale Lane
  Ravenshead
  Notts
  NG15 9AH
  Tel: 01623 490 879
For parents of children with communication disorders.

The Speech Language and Hearing Centre
  Christopher Place
  Charlton Street
  London NW1 1JF
  Tel: 0171 383 3834
A new centre for pre-school children with hearing impairment and delay in speech or language

Child Protection/Abuse

Children 1st
  Melville House
  41 Polwarth Terrace
  Edinburgh
  EH11 1NU
  Tel: 0131 337 8539
Scotland's own childcare agency for prevention of
cruelty to children.

The National Society for the Prevention of Cruelty
to Children (NSPCC)
  National Centre
  42 Curtain Road
  London EC2A 3NH
  Helpline: 0800 800 500
The NSPCC is the UK's leading charity
specialising in child protection and the prevention
of cruelty to children. Their Helpline provides
counselling, information and advice to anyone
concerned about a child at risk of abuse.

Parents Anonymous
  Manor Garden Centre
  6-9 Manor Gardens
  London N7 6LA
  Tel: 0171 263 8918
Help to parents who are tempted to abuse their
children and to those who have done so.

Counselling/Advice

The Association for Post-natal Illness
  25 Jerdan Place
  Fulham
  London SW6 1BE
  Tel: 0171 386 0868
Provides information, advice and support for
sufferers of post-natal depression and their
relatives/friends.

British Association for Counselling
  1 Regent Place
  Rugby
  Warwickshire
  CV21 2PJ
  Tel: 01788 550899
Can provide a list of qualified counsellors in your
area.

Centre for Counselling and Psychotherapy
  Beauchamp Lodge
  2 Warwick Crescent
  London W2 6NE
  Tel: 0171 266 3006
Offers individual, couple and child/adolescent
psychotherapy.

ChildLine
  Freepost 1111
  London N1 0BR
  24-hour Helpline: 0800 1111
The 24-hour National Phone Helpline
for children and young people in trouble
or danger. All calls are free and
confidential and children may call
about any problem.

Child Psychotherapy Trust
  Star House
  104-108 Grafton Road
  London NW5 4BD
  Tel: 0171 284 1355
Provides publications on request on a wide range of
subjects concerned with the emotional development
of children.

Samaritans
  Tel: 01753 532713
  National Helpline: 0345 909090
The Samaritans offer confidential,
emotional support to those in crisis and in danger
of taking their own lives.

Young Minds Trust
  2nd Floor
  102-108 Clerkenwell Road
  London EC1M 5SA
  Tel: 0171 336 8445 (Office)
  Helpline: 0800 018 2138
Parents' advice line and information line for those
concerned with the mental health of a child.

National Childminding Association
  8 Masons Hill
  Bromley
  Kent
  BR2 9EY
  Tel: 0181 464 6164 (office)
  Advice line: 0181 466 0200
Help and advice to those looking after other
people's children.

Daycare

The Daycare Trust
  Shoreditch Town Hall Annex
  380 Old Street
  London EC1B 9LT
  Tel: 0171 405 5617
Free advice to parents on childcare issues;
promotes affordable childcare for all.

Help for all the family

The Benefits Agency
  Child Benefit – Central Helpline
  0541 555501
  Central Helpline – Family Credit:
  01253 500050
Your local benefits agency is listed in the
telephone directory under B.

Family Welfare Association
  501-505 Kingsland Road
  London E8 4AU
  Tel: 0171 254 6251
Provides practical and emotional family support
and family centres throughout the south east.

General Osteopathic Council (GOSC)
  Osteopathy House
  176 Tower Bridge Road
  London SE1 3LU
  Tel: 0171 357 6655
Provides a list of registered osteopaths and
information.

Home-Start UK
  2 Salisbury Road
  Leicester
  LE1 7QR
  Tel: 0116 233 9955
Support, friendship and practical advice to families
with children under five in their homes, provided
through local schemes.

Institute of Family Therapy
  24-32 Stephenson Way
  London NW1 2HX
  Tel: 0171 391 9150
Couple and family counselling and mediation.

Kids Company
  Arch 259
  Grosvenor Court
  Grosvenor Terrace
  London SE5 ONP
  Tel: 0171 703 1808
Provides caring adults for children to talk to about

their concerns and can visit them in their schools
or homes.

Kidscape
  2 Grosvenor Gardens
  London SW1W 0DH
  Tel: 0171 730 3300
  Helpline: 0171 730 3300
For parents of children being bullied.

Marriage Counselling Scotland
  Helpline: 0131 558 3334
Counselling help for marriage and family
relationship needs.

Meet-a-Mum Association (MAMA)
  26 Avenue Road
  South Norwood
  London SE25 4DX
  Tel: 0181 771 5595
  Helpline: 0181 768 0123
Provides friendship and support to all mothers and
mothers-to-be, and those suffering from post-natal
depression.

Multiple Births Foundation
  Queen Charlotte's & Chelsea Hospital
  Goldhawk Road
  London W6 0XG
  Tel: 0181 383 3519/20
Provides specialist professional advice and
information to parents of twins and more.

National Association of Citizens Advice Bureaux
(NACAB)
  115-123 Pentonville Road,
  London N1 9LZ
  Tel: 0171 833 2181
The National Association of 1400 local Citizens
Advice Bureaux, which provide information and
advice on subjects such as housing, benefits,
finance, consumer complaints and family matters.

National Family Mediation (NFM)
  9 Tavistock Place
  London WC1H 9SN
  Tel: 0171 383 5993
The national organisation fostering the provision of
independent family mediation services to couples
experiencing separation or divorce whilst focusing
on the children involved.

National Stepfamily Association
  Chapel House
  18 Hatton Place
  London EC1N 8RU
  Tel: 0171 209 2460 (office)
  For Helpline, call PARENTLINE:
  01702 559900
Provides information, books and leaflets to anyone
working in a stepfamily or anyone working with
them.

Stepfamily Scotland
  Helpline: 0131 225 5800

Northern Ireland Family Mediation Service
  76 Dublin Road
  Belfast
  BT2 7HP
  Tel: 01232 322914
Helping parents negotiate the raising of their
children whilst living apart.

Osteopathic Centre For Children
  109 Harley Street
  London W1N 1DG
  Tel: 0171 486 6160
A charity providing fully qualified osteopaths for
children (a donation of £15 is requested for each
treatment).

Parents at Work
  45 Beech Street
  Barbican
  London EC2Y 8AD
  Tel: 0171 628 3565
A charity which supports parents and helps

employers in developing family-friendly policies of concern to working parents.

Relate: National Marriage Guidance
Herbert Grey College
Little Church Street
Rugby
Warwickshire
CV21 3AP
Tel: 01788 573241
Helpline: 0870 601 2121
Counselling help for marriage and family relationship needs in local Relate centres.

Royal London Homeopathic Hospital NHS Trust
60 Great Ormond Street
London WC1N 3HR
Tel: 0171 837 8833
Provides information on services including a children's clinic. All services are free.

Serene (Incorporating CRY-SIS Support Group)
BM CRY-SIS
London WC1N 3XX
Tel: 0171 404 5011
Self-help and support for families with excessively crying, sleepless and demanding children.

Society of Homoeopaths
2 Artizan Road
Northampton
NN1 4HU
Tel: 01604 621400
Provides a register of professional homoeopaths throughout the UK and an information leaflet.

Twins and Multiple Birth Association
Harnott House
309 Chester Road
Little Sutton
South Wirral
L66 1QQ
Tel: 0151 348 0020
Helpline: 01732 868000
Information and support for families with twins, triplets or more.

Women's Aid Federation (England)
PO Box 391
Bristol
BS99 7WS
Tel: 0117 944 4411
National Helpline: 0345 023 468
Offers advice and refuge to women and children threatened by violence.

UK Homeopathic Medical Association
6 Livingstone Road
Gravesend,
Kent
DA12 5DZ
Tel/Fax: 01474 560336
Supplies a list of qualified homoeopaths and an information leaflet.

Help for breastfeeding mothers

La Leche League Great Britain
BM 3424
London WC1N 3XX
Tel: 0171 242 1278
Offers telephone help, publications and support groups run by trained breastfeeding counsellors.

Association of Breastfeeding Mothers
PO Box 207
Bridgwater
Somerset TA6 7YT
Tel: 0171 813 1481
Support for breastfeeding mothers.

Help for single parents

Gingerbread
16-17 Clerkenwell Close
London EC1R 0AN
Tel: 0171 336 8183
Advice line: 0171 336 8184
Runs a network of self-help groups for single parents.

Gingerbread Wales
Tel: 01792 648728

Gingerbread Scotland
Tel: 0141 576 5085

National Council for One-Parent Families
255 Kentish Town Road
London NW5 2LX
Tel: 0171 428 5400
Information service for single parents.

One-Parent Families Scotland
Tel: 0131 556 3899/4563
Scottish organisation for single parents.

Legal help

Children's Legal Centre,
University of Essex
Wivenhoe Park
Colchester
C04 3SQ

Tel: 01206 872466 (office)
Advice line: 01206 873820
Free advice by telephone or letter regarding legal
issues involving children and their interests.

National children's organisations

Barnardos
Tanners Lane
Barkingside
Ilford
Essex
IG6 1QG
Tel: 0181 550 8822
The country's largest children's charity offers a wide
range of supportive projects in the following areas:
disability, education, children needing families, dis-
advantaged communities, disadvantaged young
people and families with young children.

ChildLine (see counselling)

The Children's Society
Edward Rudolph House
69-85 Margery Street
London WC1X OJL
Tel: 0171 837 4299
Independent charity working with children, young
people and their families throughout England and
Wales.

NCH Action for Children
85 Highbury Park
London N5 1UD
Tel: 0171 226 2033
A leading children's charity running projects in the
UK and abroad and campaigning on behalf of
children and their families.

NSPCC (see child abuse/protection)

Parenting education

National Childbirth Trust
  Alexandra House
  Oldham Terrace
  Acton
  London W3 6NH
  Tel: 0181 992 8637
The NCT offers information and support in pregnancy, childbirth and early parenthood and aims to enable every parent to make informed choices.

National Newpin
  Sutherland House
  35 Sutherland Square
  London SE17 3EE
  Tel: 0171 703 6326
Peer support, training, individual counselling, group therapy and family play therapy for parents and children.

Parentline
  Endway House
  The Endway
  Hadleigh
  Essex
  SS7 2AN
  Tel: 01702 554782
  Helpline: 01702 559900
For any parent or helper who is experiencing any kind of difficulty.

Parent Network (Charity)
  Room 2, Winchester House
  Kennington Park
  11 Cranmer Road
  London SW9 6EJ
  Administration: 0171 735 4596
  Parent Enquiry Line: 0171 735 1214
Now the leading national provider of parenting courses, run by specially trained parents in their local area. Several of these courses are now accredited by the Open College Network, and may be available through adult education and further education colleges. Some of the skills described in this book are included in these courses, described by Steve Biddulph as the 'best in the world'.

Parent Network Scotland
  Tel: 0131 555 6780

PIPPIN (Parents in Partnership – Parent Infant Network)
  'Derwood'
  Todds Green,
  Stevenage
  Herts
  SG1 2JE
  Tel: 01438 748478
A national charity providing structured parenting courses for expectant and new parents.

AUSTRALIAN CONTACTS

Breastfeeding

Nursing Mothers' Association of Australia (NMAA)
　　National Headquarters
　　PO Box 4000
　　Glen Iris 3146
　　Tel: (03) 9885 0855

Breastfeeding Information Line: 1902 2416 18

Childcare Information

Child Care Access Hotline: 1800 670 305
Provides information on types of government childcare services available, and offers help in making a choice.

Child Health

Australian Association for the Welfare of
Child Health
　　National Office:
　　PO Box 113
　　Westmead 2145
　　Tel: (02) 9633 1988
　　Freecall: 1800 244 396
This national organisation advocates the emotional and social needs of children and adolescents in hospital/health care. Call the national office for local referral.

Children's services

Lady Gowrie Child Centre:
　　Freecall: 1800 803 825
An information referral service for children aged 0–18 years.

NSW　Contact Inc.
　　　Freecall: 1800 670 305
Will provide a list of support services for parents and carers of young children.

Counselling

Lifeline (24 hours)
　　Freecall: 13 1114
Counselling for all ages.

Kids Help Line (24 hours)
　　Freecall: 1800 55 1800
A counselling and support service for young people.

Multiple births

Australian Multiple Birth Association
　　Tel: (02) 9875 2404
Support for parents, as well as information on the raising and care of multiples.

Natural therapies

The Australian Traditional Medicine Society
　　27 Bank Street
　　Meadowbank
　　Tel: (02) 9809 6800
Call for a free directory of registered practitioners of all natural therapies, such as naturopathy, homeopathy, herbal medicine, remedial massage and reflexology.

Out of school hours care/vacation care

NSW　Network of Community Activities
　　　Old Children's Court
　　　66 Albion Street
　　　Surry Hills 2010
　　　Tel: 9212 3244
This organisation gives comprehensive information and advice on a range of available childcare.

Parenting resources

ACT Parent Support Services
     Tel: (02) 6278 3995
NSW Parentline
     Freecall: 13 2055
Qld Parentline
     Freecall: 1300 301 300
SA   Parent Helpline
     Freecall: 1300 364 100
Vic Parentline
     Freecall: 13 2289
WA   Parenting Line
     Freecall: 1800 654 432

Counselling for parents, as well as information on a range of services available to them.

NSW Karitane
     Parent Help Line (24 hours)
     Tel: (02) 9794 1852
     Freecall: 1800 677 961

     Tresillian Family Care
     Parent Help Line (24 hours)
     Tel: (02) 9787 5255
     Freecall: 1800 637 357

Help with a range of problems, including post-natal depression, and teaching of parenting skills.

Sudden Infant Death Syndrome

SIDS Australia Inc.
     Floor 1/891 Burke Road
     Camberwell 3124
     Tel: (03) 9813 3200

CANADIAN CONTACTS

Bereavement

Bereaved Families of Ontario
     562 Eglinton Avenue East, Suite 401
     Toronto, Ontario M4P 1P1
     Tel: (416) 440 0290

Child protection / counselling

Kids Help Foundation
     National Office
     439 University Avenue, Suite 300
     Toronto, Ontario M5G 1Y8
     Tel: (416) 586 5437

Kids Help Phone
     439 University Avenue, Suite 300
     Toronto, Ontario M5G 1Y8
     Tel: (416) 586 0100
     Kids Help Phone: 1 800 668 6868

Child development support

Childhood and Youth Division
　　Health Promotion and Programs
　　　Branch
　　HEALTH CANADA
　　Postal Locator 1909C2
　　Jeanne Mance Building
　　Ottawa, Ontario K1A 1B4
　　Tel: (613) 952 1220 or (613) 952 5850
Provides further information on federal
programmes and services for children, organized
thematically around such topics as education,
families, health.

Children's Miracle Network
　　837 Princess Street, Suite 302
　　Kingston, Ontario K7L 1G8
　　Tel: (613) 542 7240
The aim of the Children's Miracle
Network is to generate funds and awareness
programmes for the benefit of children served
by its associated hospitals, health centres, and
foundations.

Canadian Institute of Child Health
　　885 Meadowlands Drive, Suite 512
　　Ottawa, Ontario K2C 3N2
　　Tel: (613) 224 4144
Dedicated to improving the health and well-being
of children and youth in Canada.

Help for all the family

Canadian Child Care Federation
　　Tel: (613) 729 5289
　　Hotline: 1 800 858 1412
The overall mission of the Canadian Child Care
Federation is to improve the quality of child care
services for Canadian families.

North American Society of Homoeopaths (NASH)
　　1122 East Pike Street, Suite 1122
　　Seattle, WA 98122
　　Hotline (General and Registration
　　　enquiries): (541) 345 9815
　　Membership enquiries: (206) 720 7000

One-Parent Families Association of Canada
　　1099 Kinsgton Road, #222
　　Pickering, Ontario, L1V 1B5
　　Tel: (905) 831 7098
　　Toll-free tel: 1 877 773 7714
A volunteer association offering a wide variety of
social activities focused on the children in a one-
parent family unit.

Parents of Multiple Births Association of Canada
　　Box 234, Gormley
　　Ontario L0H 1G0
　　Tel: (905) 888 0725

SOUTH AFRICAN CONTACTS

Gauteng

Child and Family Centre
Tel: (011) 486 2890

Child Emergency Service
Toll-free tel: 0800 12 3321
24-hour service for children under 18. Part
of the Department of Welfare.

Child Guidance Clinic
Tel: (011) 484 1734

Child Welfare Society, Johannesburg
Tel: (011) 331 0171

ChildLine, Johannesburg
Toll-free tel: 0800 55555
Tel: (011) 484 0771 or (011) 484 1284

Zamokuhule Child Centre (Zola Clinic)
Tel: (011) 934 9415
Child Abuse Clinic and Family Centre.

Teddy Bear Clinic
Tel: (011) 642 7554
For abused children.

Child Abuse Centre, Alexandra
Tel: (011) 440 1231

Family Life Centre
Tel: (011) 788 4784
Parent counselling.

Child Protection Unit, Johannesburg (CPU)
Tel: (011) 403 3413

Western Cape

Child Welfare Society, Cape Town
Tel: (021) 761 4128
Counselling for children under 12 on all areas
of abuse.

ChildLine, Western Cape
Tel: (021) 461 1114

Child & Family Unit
Tel: (021) 685 4103
Scholastic evaluation and behavioural problems.

Parent Centre
Tel: (021) 61 9142
Counselling groups for parents and children
and behavioural problems.

Rapcan
Tel: (021) 448 9034
Workshops for adults and children on
prevention of abuse.

Red Cross Children's Hospital
Tel: (021) 685 4103

Child Care Information Centre
Tel: (021) 689 1519

Child Protection Unit, Cape Town (CPU)
Tel: (021) 24 6020

Kwa-Zulu Natal

ChildLine
Tel: (031) 303 2222

Child Welfare Society, Durban
Tel: (031) 23 9313 or (031) 309 1508

Child Protection Unit, Durban (CPU)
Tel: (031) 307 7000

Index

Valuable and wide-ranging contributions from parents, professionals and organisations have helped make *Raising Happy Children* so pragmatic and thought-provoking. If you have experiences to share or observations to make, we would like to hear from you. Please write to us % Hodder & Stoughton, 338 Euston Road, London NW1 3BH.